ELVIS
IGNITED

UNIVERSITY PRESS OF FLORIDA

Florida A&M University, Tallahassee
Florida Atlantic University, Boca Raton
Florida Gulf Coast University, Ft. Myers
Florida International University, Miami
Florida State University, Tallahassee
New College of Florida, Sarasota
University of Central Florida, Orlando
University of Florida, Gainesville
University of North Florida, Jacksonville
University of South Florida, Tampa
University of West Florida, Pensacola

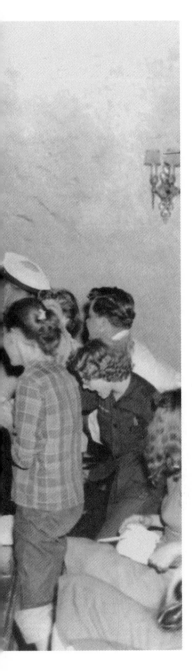

ELVIS IGNITED

THE RISE OF AN ICON IN FLORIDA

Bob Kealing

University Press of Florida

Gainesville · Tallahassee · Tampa · Boca Raton

Pensacola · Orlando · Miami · Jacksonville

Ft. Myers · Sarasota

This book may be available in an electronic edition.

22 21 20 19 18 17   6 5 4 3 2 1

Frontispiece: Elvis at the Polk Theater in Lakeland, August 1956. Photo courtesy of Special
Collections, Lakeland Public Library, Lakeland, Fla.

Library of Congress Control Number: 2016948257
ISBN 978-0-8130-6230-3

The University Press of Florida is the scholarly publishing agency for the State University
System of Florida, comprising Florida A&M University, Florida Atlantic University, Florida
Gulf Coast University, Florida International University, Florida State University, New College
of Florida, University of Central Florida, University of Florida, University of North Florida,
University of South Florida, and University of West Florida.

University Press of Florida
15 Northwest 15th Street
Gainesville, FL 32611-2079
http://upress.ufl.edu

CONTENTS

Introduction

As a young performer, Elvis Presley forged a unique and lasting history with fans in every state in the American South, including Florida. His birthplace in Tupelo, Mississippi, welcomes a hundred thousand pilgrims annually from all over the world. Six times that many dedicated fans visit Graceland, Presley's Memphis home for the last twenty years of his life and an enduring shrine to him many years after his death. Had Presley never made his way to the one man intent on finding unknown voices of any race—Sam Phillips at Sun Records in Memphis (and to the secretary, Marion Keisker, who would not stop talking to Sam about the unknown kid)—none of it would have happened.

The unfortunate truth, though, is that many younger people are familiar only with parodied Presley: cloistered behind the high walls of suffocating fame, well past his prime, and emerging only to fulfill an endless touring schedule, a bloated caricature performing karate chops onstage in a dazzling jumpsuit. His days on the decline evoke his struggle with prescription drugs and weight gain. To view Presley only at this stage is like thinking of America's space missions only for how astronauts returned to earth, discounting each heart-stopping countdown, ignition, and adrenaline-filled, death-defying, jaw-dropping liftoff.

Scores of southerners were fortunate to get to know the other Elvis, up close. The young and hungry Presley; the rising star, bursting onto stages large and small, sexy, controversial, brimming with talent and ambition. The shrieks of young fans at the sight of the young rockabilly god who fell to earth still ring in their ears, as do the time-stands-still memories of hearing his hit songs for the first time.

In one memorable engagement in Lubbock, Texas, Presley performed with then unknown Buddy Holly. Other young stars on the rise like Roy Orbison and Waylon Jennings saw Presley live in Texas. Seeing Presley perform in Waycross, Georgia, was a life-changing experience for nine-year-old Gram Parsons, who went on to pioneer the country-rock genre.

The *Louisiana Hayride* in Shreveport became an important regional broadcast venue where Presley's unique sound gained early acceptance. The more prestigious and formulaic Grand Ole Opry was lukewarm to him after his only appearance there in 1954. As a result, Presley maintained a regular appearance schedule on the *Hayride* into 1956.

In Bono, Arkansas, the early reception for Presley was so rabid that part of the gymnasium floor collapsed. With the passage of time, no doubt, descriptions of events like this have grown more dramatic. Hyperbole has crept in, perhaps. Presley appeared in concert near Muscle Shoals, Alabama, years before it became the most prestigious small-town recording destination anywhere.

Presley's early barnstorming days between 1954 and 1956 focused primarily on Texas, Louisiana, Mississippi, Alabama, Georgia, Tennessee, Arkansas, the Carolinas, and Florida. Local legends abound of Presley concerts in high school gymnasiums, nightclubs, radio stations, even shopping centers—no venue too small. He appeared at watermelon festivals, parades, and live remote broadcasts and received his fair share of boos and taunts for how he looked, dressed, and performed.

By the time Presley was a national sensation in 1957 playing large venues across the United States, having made a big splash on the *Ed Sullivan Show*, he was already splitting time with acting; he was making millions, estranged from his legendary bandmates Bill Black and Scotty Moore, and bypassing the hysteria associated with touring. In 1958 he was drafted into the army and gone. Most of America got only fleeting glimpses of Presley during his most electric and influential period as a live performer. The American South—where Elvis Presley plied his trade, made his name, and fell in love again and again—remains the only exception.

Still, historian Joy Wallace Dickinson points out, some southern places like Florida are often overlooked in discussion of Presley's time in New York, California, or Nashville. In researching this book, I realized that her observation was dead on. Momentous events in Florida especially, tied to the ignition of Presley's career, deserve closer attention and exploration: the iconic images and songs; the controversy; and the roles of one-time Floridians like Tom Parker and Mae Axton, without whom Presley's career would have been far different.

Looking at Presley's early days in Florida from 1955 to 1961, we're reminded how much has changed in American culture and celebrity. If we applied today's standards of propriety, a Jacksonville judge's 1956 threat to throw Presley in jail for obscenity is laughable. But as an unmarried, world-famous twenty-something actor in 1961, his tendency to gravitate toward and romance underage girls would draw much greater scrutiny today.

As the years pass, young Elvis Presley's history in Florida continues to fade like a forgotten back road advertisement. In this time capsule of words, pictures, and pages we savor Presley's enthralling energy prior to his era of world fame, melancholy, B movies, and boredom. At the same time, we recognize and celebrate those prescient enough to see how special Presley was before the rest of the world caught on. Presley's Florida journey begins on a beach.

1955

Hank Snow All-Star Jamboree

Sun Records in Memphis, where Elvis Presley made his earliest recordings.
Photo by author.

1

In Waves

On a warm central Florida day, perched on a beachside motel balcony, twenty-year-old Elvis Presley gazed upon the churning Atlantic Ocean. As the sticky-cool, salted sea air whistled through Presley's dark brown pompadour, only the Atlantic's vastness and the din of crashing waves could begin to compare with the tumult that awaited rock's soon-to-be king. The darkened horizon off Daytona Beach loomed like his limitless potential; mysterious and awe-inspiring.

At this snapshot in time, Elvis was not yet *Elvis*. On May 7, 1955, Presley was just ten months removed from the historic Sun recording sessions back home in Memphis, when visionary recording engineer Sam Phillips brought in Scotty Moore on guitar and his buddy Bill Black on bass to see what kind of talent this raw young singer had. This was his first professional recording session—if you want to call it that. Elvis Presley had never performed in concert.

Nothing much happened in the audition until late that evening, when the trio started messing around with an up-tempo number. Phillips recognized, at the very least, that the sound of it was *different*. Then, as his biographer Peter Guralnick wrote, "The rest of the session went as if suddenly they all were caught up in the same fever dream." The recording they made that night, the rockabilly version of Arthur Crudup's "That's All Right" with an up-tempo version of

Elvis with Mae Axton, hired by Tom Parker to promote Presley's 1955 tours.
Courtesy of Heather Axton.

Bill Monroe's "Blue Moon of Kentucky" recorded soon after as the flipside, was to modern music what splitting the atom was to warfare. Presley had his first regional hit and staunch backer in Phillips, who employed an evangelist's zeal to prove that his gut instinct about this kid was right.

In May 1955 Presley had yet to record the string of breakout national number 1 smashes with RCA Records that ushered in the rock and roll era for good, had a profound impact on American popular culture, and secured Presley's status as a singer and entertainer for the ages.

Nothing more than a working performer with less than a year of experience in a ragtag trio of journeymen musicians, not yet dying his hair jet black, Presley toured under the moniker the "Hillbilly Cat," a hip-swiveling oddity stuck at the bottom of Opry acts on a country package tour. Neither success nor his career path was certain as Presley made his first tour through Florida. Just the thought of him pursuing a career in music was pure audacity. What dirt-poor kid from rural Mississippi via the inner-city projects of working-class Memphis *dared* to aspire to a life of fame and riches as a recording artist or actor?

Most broad-shouldered young southern men of Presley's time and social standing wouldn't have been caught dead singing, dancing, or obsessing about garish pastel-colored clothes and cars. To most boys, stardom only went as far as high school careers lettering in football or basketball, then maybe college. During the staid, adult-dominated era permeated by the wholesome sounds of Mitch Miller and the McGuire Sisters, childhood dreams faded into reality's far recesses; expectations moved on to marriage, children, and a workaday job like Presley had just a year previously; driving a pickup truck for Crown Electric.

Sometimes great artists emerge from the most unlikely circumstances. Presley once said, "Ambition is a dream with a V8 engine." That engine stoked his desire to escape the life he'd known in the projects; often doing without; not getting much notice from girls at

Crooms High School in Memphis, getting teased for daring to dress in original ways and look different. Ambition pushed Presley to pursue his dreams because, truth be told, there was no plan B. His natural talent and ambition, like a souped-up hot rod burning deep in his soul, were his only ticket out of poverty.

Presley's genre-bending voice heralded the dawning of rock and roll and America's youth culture, borrowing from the African American strains of Beale Street in Memphis and church hymns echoing over the cotton fields of Mississippi. Via air waves and hand-held transistor radios, a developing teenage consumer culture devoured a new kind of music aimed only at teens.

Sam Phillips, the non-musician most crucial to developing the soundtrack of this new era, did so with a conscious, colorblind motive; a determination to root out and record talent, black or white, from the poor sides of town and far out in the country. The voices of the ignored that stuck with him growing up on a farm in rural Alabama. He made it his mission to find perfection in the imperfect voices of unknowns like Presley, Howlin' Wolf, and Johnny Cash; he dared them to discover their own essence no matter how long it took. In his efforts to excavate the soul of these hardscrabble but ambitious people, to give them a voice, Phillips was crowned "the man who invented Rock and Roll" by his biographer Peter Guralnick.

In early live shows Presley writhed with a primal, sexual energy soon to draw an avalanche of contempt, criticism, and concern from the civic, religious, and law enforcement establishment. Columnists, reporters, even fellow musicians minimized and mocked Presley and his fans. The kids tuned it out, but adults already concerned about Presley's impact on their kids denounced him. Pastors prayed for him. Presley wasn't just a new teen obsession; to many adults he was downright dangerous. When he burst onto the airwaves with a voice belying his identity as a young Caucasian male, neither the segregated South nor its music could ever again be painted in black or white. Presley became America's first rock and roll star; a teen idol and avatar of cool rebellion whose profound influence on young people is impossible to quantify.

"To say that Elvis Presley has been mythologized into an iconic state of quasi-religious significance is not an exaggeration," wrote British scholar Richard Parfitt. "Elvis belongs to an elite group of one." What person in a developed country anywhere in the world with even a minimal knowledge of history and popular culture has not heard and been moved by Presley's voice? Growing up on the Mesabi Iron Range west of Lake Superior, Bob Dylan reminisced about the soul-stirring experience of hearing Presley for the first time: "I wanted to see the powerful, mystical Elvis that had crash-landed from a burning star onto American soil. The Elvis that was burning with life. That's the Elvis that inspired us to all the possibilities of life."

John Lennon was more succinct: "Before Elvis, there was nothing."

The day of Presley's first-ever Florida performance, a woman leaving her motel room noticed him at the railing. Forty-year-old Mae Axton was promoting the package tour in which Presley, Scotty, and Bill were playing a bit part. To supplement her income, the married Jacksonville schoolteacher and mother of two boys did public relations and writing on the side.

Axton wore a dark bouffant typical of the time, had a warm southern way about her, and showed plenty of gumption to stand up for herself in the male-dominated music promotion business. Like the young showman she was promoting, Mae Axton had big dreams. The fact wasn't lost on Axton that instead of thinking about the bevy of young beauties on the World's Most Famous Beach, Presley was missing his mom and dad.

"Miz Axton, look at the ocean," Presley marveled." "I can't believe that it's so big. I'd give anything in the world to have enough money to bring my mother and daddy down here to see it." Soon enough Presley did just that and far more, moving Vernon and Gladys Presley out of the Memphis projects forever, buying them a big ranch house that even had a swimming pool; an unimaginable luxury in the days before their son embarked on a singing career. Presley's sentiment struck a deep chord. "That just went through my heart," Axton recalled. "All the guys looking for cute little girls, but his priority was doing something for his mother and daddy."

That vignette captures the character of young Presley. Though burning with his own desire to be a star, with a newfound freedom to pursue all the trappings road rules allowed a handsome young and unmarried performer, Presley remained a devoted, religious son; intent on lifting his parents from the poverty to which they had long become accustomed. His respect for adults was never an affectation; as is tradition in the Deep South, he often addressed older people as *sir* or *ma'am*, *Miz* or *Mister*.

The Sunshine State hot-fueled Presley's rise from hillbilly novelty act in 1955 to headlining megastar the following year. Appropriately, his moonshot began just north of the region soon to be known as Florida's Space Coast, where so many daring dreams and seemingly impossible missions would soon take flight. Presley logged thousands of miles, grinding and glad-handing his way through one Florida town after another. Influential and astute disc jockeys like Ward Goodrich in Ocala, who went by the radio name "Nervous Ned Needham," and Brad Lacey in Fort Myers, championed the unknown, talented young singer.

As in Axton's interaction with the young would-be king, to this day an aging legion of fans up and down the peninsula cherish the time they shared with Presley during his rise to stardom. Presley burst into their predictable lives like a Technicolor Romeo and left an indelible impression; they hold onto those memories with fierce devotion. Before Presley became a prisoner of fame he performed for them; talked, danced, and played with them; took them in his arms and kissed them. Those teens of long ago keep close the photographs and memories, in purses and wallets, and even on tee shirts; Presley's autograph is framed alongside family keepsakes. It's as if they need a constant reminder; proof to themselves and others, that the time they shared with pre-iconic Elvis was indeed *real*. He was *real*.

In fifteen months from May 7, 1955, to August 11, 1956, Presley played fifty-nine Florida shows in a dozen cities; sometimes three or four concerts *a day*. In 1956, his most crucial and transformative year, Presley and his underappreciated and underpaid bandmates played forty-one Florida concerts, more than in any other state; more than in Texas, Mississippi, and Tennessee combined. Before any of his historic appearances on the *Ed Sullivan Show*, where most Americans first became aware of him, Presley's barnstorming days in Florida were already over.

While most young people his age matriculated in colleges and universities, Presley honed his talents by way of Florida back roads; his home away from home. From Pensacola to Jacksonville up north, Daytona Beach and West Palm Beach to the east, Fort Myers, Sarasota, St. Pete, and Tampa to the west, and Ocala, Orlando, and Lakeland in the center south to Miami's beaches, in 1955 and '56 Elvis, Scotty, and Bill were *everywhere*.

"I don't think there was a better time and place to be a teenager than in Florida in the 1950s," said former Florida governor and United States senator Bob Graham. "It was such a magical place. Elvis is part of what contributed to that excitement."

By 1961 the most controversial figure in Presley's career, his Svengali-esque manager Tom Parker, transformed the shy kid from Memphis into the biggest star in the world; rich beyond his wildest dreams. But that mountain of cash came at a steep price; Parker maintained a vicelike grip on Presley, controlling his personal life, limiting his career choices, squelching again and again his ambition to tour outside North America and tackle more challenging acting roles. Thanks to his star-maker turned puppeteer, Presley never performed live shows east of the Atlantic Ocean or west of Hawaii; he never played Europe's grand halls, never had a chance to perform before record crowds in Japan and the Far East, to thrill throngs of devoted Aussies. Other than performing just a few shows over the border in Canada, Presley was trapped stateside. The waves he found so awe-inspiring might as well have been prison walls.

Parker, the former Tampa dogcatcher and carnival confidence man kept a deep secret from Presley and the world. To allow Presley access to his fans outside North America would have brought with it the risk of exposing that secret. Ever the chameleon, Parker had the wit, work ethic, and cast-iron will to transform himself; and he had the ego and audacity to wear the honorary title *Colonel* like the decorated military officer he never was.

His true record showed Parker to be a military misfit who saw his share of real prison walls then was drummed out of the service. Despite Parker's overbearing, controlling ways and a penchant to think of his client as a mere commodity, Presley felt he owed his success and undying loyalty to Parker, whom he considered a father figure.

"I knew he wanted to go out and climb new mountains; there were no new mountains to climb—the Colonel squashed everything," said Steve Binder, the producer and director behind Presley's acclaimed 1968 television special. Presley's longtime bodyguard Red West, who wrote a controversial tell-all book and was fired shortly before Presley's death, said of Tom Parker: "The Colonel got him where he was, but he also put him where he is." Nevertheless, during Presley's launch to stardom, Parker was instrumental in getting him there.

In Tampa a local photographer hired by Parker to shoot an early Presley concert snapped a photo that through the decades has become emblematic of the essence of the young, iconic Presley (see chapter 8) and the soul-shouting rock and roll rebellion he represented.

Fortunately, for history's sake, a group of early female Florida journalists eschewed preconceived notions of most of their male counterparts and filed far more detailed and compelling reportage about young Elvis. Had it not been for their ability to see Presley more like their young fans did, and his openness to them, the picture of his barnstorming days in Florida would be far less complete. This journey is also a celebration of their work and legacies.

Axton too, played a role much larger in Presley's career than merely serving as a PR person. In the living room of her unremarkable and forgotten single-story block house just west of downtown Jacksonville, the kind as ubiquitous as palm trees throughout Florida's sun-drenched landscape, Axton and a pair of journeymen musicians made music history, cementing their own place in rock and roll lore, writing and recording for Presley the single that changed everything. Presley's association with Axton resulted from Parker's shrewd assessment in

1955 that his young star needed some PR help in Florida, where Sun's distribution was limited and his music was not yet well known.

After that first show in Daytona Beach, Presley's Jacksonville connections furthered his career and lit the flame of what would become a nationwide controversy over his live performances. In 1956 Presley spirited his young girlfriend along on his most heated and controversial Florida tour. Her bittersweet memories of being in the eye of it all give us an uncommonly intimate account of Presley's response to the tribulations as well as the overwhelming success.

In Miami, after Presley's return from the army in 1960, Frank Sinatra himself, formerly one of rock and roll's most vocal detractors, kicked off the next stage in Presley's career as a matinee crooner. By then it was clear that Presley's rock and roll days were over. In 1961 Presley the twenty-six-year-old actor spent six weeks in Crystal River and the surrounding area filming *Follow That Dream,* leaving an indelible impression on locals like "little" Tommy Petty. This extended residency gave Presley the chance to charm and disarm adults who five years previously had likened the singer and his gyrations to the devil himself.

Presley's co-star in the film, Anne Helm, saw the early stages of his long descent into prescription-drug dependency. It all started as what they both considered a bit of innocent pill popping here and there for nighttime carousing and to prop them up for early morning shoots. Helm's memories of their off-screen relationship in the sleepy Florida back country while making the film remain vivid.

In May 1955 triumphs, adulation, and mountains of cash all awaited, the likes of which no one had ever experienced: more than one hundred top-forty hits, including eighteen number 1 singles in his lifetime; the money to buy and hand out jewelry, cars, and guitars like Santa Claus; the ability to choose any woman he wanted in the crowd. Mothers and their daughters flocked to him.

In this minimally educated man-child, legions would come to feel an enduring and genuine sense of love and devotion. Presley did more than just entertain and seduce fans; his humility and charm led them to believe he was theirs. Elvis Presley *belonged* to them. Long term, who could survive and thrive in such a fishbowl? Who else could understand the price of losing any semblance of privacy? How could anyone, much less an unsophisticated but uber-ambitious country boy, be prepared for such an onslaught?

At that beachside railing on May 7, 1955, Elvis Presley stood alone at ground zero, a tsunami of fame and riches barreling right down on him.

May 7–9

Daytona Beach, Tampa, Fort Myers

At his first-ever Florida concert, Elvis Presley made fifty dollars as a warm-up act for headliner Hank Snow. In newspaper ads, promoters billed the 8:15 p.m. show at the Peabody Auditorium as "The Biggest Jamboree of the Year." Presley along with Scotty and Bill were listed far down the bill as "Special Added Attractions." In some ads, they weren't listed at all.

Snow, nicknamed "the singing ranger," had fourteen straight top-ten hits on the Billboard country charts. At that point Presley, who would go on to sell more than a *billion* records worldwide, had none. The Daytona Beach jamboree boasted a cavalcade of Grand Ole Opry stars, but for Presley that billing was a stretch. In 1954 during his first and only appearance at the Opry, the proving ground and mother church of country music, Presley bombed. Opry bigwigs suggested he consider a return to truck driving.

Even if he was developing a buzz throughout the South for his electric live performances and more successful appearances on the *Louisiana Hayride* radio and TV show, Presley's lack of major hits meant no star billing; for most supporting acts that meant a couple of songs, polite applause, then get off quick and make way for the headliners.

The country performers like Snow dressed in typical Nudie Cohn–inspired Western wear—bright colors and rhinestones—but not the "Hillbilly Cat." Presley hit the stage in a red-sequined dinner jacket contrasting with his white shirt and dark pants. His hair, slicked with a pomade ducktail in back, pompadour in front, gave off a greasy sheen. Dressed in a white dinner jacket and dark pants himself, teen-age usher Holmes Davis, stationed close to the performers, witnessed the early stages of Presley's emergence as a star and the crowd's reaction: "The way he sort of bounced around on stage," Davis recalled. "Even the old people, they were all standing up and clapping and going with him."

Mature country audiences like the people who had given him such a tepid response at the Opry in Nashville less than a year before were starting to see something in this young albeit oddball performer. Contrasting with Snow's ballads like "Hello, Love," Presley performed pulsating rockabilly rhythm and blues, making the most of his short time on stage. Young girls in the audience responded to his sex appeal and boundless energy. Not knowing what to make of him, offstage some of the performers kept their distance from Presley.

"I was there to see *him*," remembered Davis's Mainland High class-mate Doris Tharp-Gurley, "I had heard him on the radio." Gurley grew up in a conservative Volusia County household where the notion of a male performer radiating sex appeal was taboo to her parents. They were convinced their daughter was going to the Peabody to see wholesome entertainers like the Carter Sisters from the first family of country music, known for singles like "Wildwood Flower" and "Keep on the Sunny Side."

Even Gurley, who was forced to watch Presley from a much greater distance than Holmes Davis, had a hard time understanding what she was seeing. It was such a contrast to the other performers. "Everybody there was speechless," Gurley declared, the sense of wonder still evident in her voice. "They'd never seen anything like it."

While Presley bounced and strummed, Bill Black slapped and twirled the stand-up bass, punctuating the music with a hoot or holler. In contrast to his frenetic cohorts, on stage Scotty Moore was a handsome, zenlike presence plucking measured lead guitar licks. A former navy man, Moore managed Presley for a short time and promised Gladys Presley he would take care of her boy. The trio was having fun, barely making ends meet, hungry and ambitious for whatever the road had in store.

As quickly as it started, Presley's part of the show was over. Audience members disagree on whether he played two songs or just one. Most of the trio's early performances included "That's All Right," the song recorded by Sam Phillips that started Presley on his trip to the stratosphere. His revved-up version of "Blue Moon of Kentucky" was another oft-played number. Presley didn't have enough time onstage to create the kind of fan frenzy that many have come to associate with this iconic era. Still, by the middle of Presley's first week in Florida, much more established and sedate country performers got tired of trying to follow him onstage.

After Presley finished performing, there was plenty of concert left. In a move that now seems unimaginable, he slipped out into the audience to watch. Sitting just a few seats away from Davis, all by himself, was the young man who would soon by mobbed by fans everywhere he went. Between acts Davis thought nothing of striking up a conversation: "How do you think things are going?" Davis asked. "Do you think you're gonna make it?" Presley responded with an understated confidence, "Things seem to be goin' pretty good." For Davis it would have been a brief, forgettable conversation from a fleeting night in his youth, had it not been with the future king of rock and roll.

After concerts it was common for Presley to hang around outside the venue, talk with fans, and sign an autograph for anybody who wanted one. With female fans who met his fancy, Presley would sign an autograph and try to get a kiss or a date in return. The lucky girl that night was Mainland High sophomore Marsha Connelly, whose photo with Presley from that evening ended up in the school yearbook. The night before, Presley had taken his own teenage girlfriend Dixie Locke to her junior prom in Memphis.

"He was kind of innocent at the time. He was very quiet. He was a nice guy. I can't say a thing bad about him," Connelly reflected. "He was very mannerly, very much a southern gentleman. It never escalated into anything. There was never a romance. He took my girlfriend and [me] home after the show. He kissed me, and then my mother came out." Doris Gurley wasn't so lucky. She witnessed Presley's performance from a distance, which left her unsatisfied and wanting more. She and her friend hatched a plan to see Presley again and next time get much closer to the object of their schoolgirl crushes.

Thanks to months of touring small southern towns and venues, by the time the trio made it to Florida, Elvis, Scotty, and Bill were already seasoned performers. With one-nighters at places like Porky's Rooftop Club in Newport, Arkansas, the Big Creek High School Gym in Big Creek, Mississippi, and Cook's Hoedown Club in Houston, Texas, no venue was too small; no stretch of overnight miles too long. Thanks to their performances on the *Louisiana Hayride*, originating from the Shreveport Municipal Auditorium, Elvis, Scotty, and Bill were building a regional following.

In outlying areas like Florida, where Sun's distribution could best be described as hit-and-miss, Presley's music had only begun to reach local radio stations. Decades before live-streaming on the internet, radio stations were the crucial lynchpin for performers intent on getting their music to young listeners; there was no other way. Like any other musician-on-the-rise, Presley lived for his brief time in front of audiences, traveling the long miles in between, the thankless grunt work that occupied the lion's share of his time, just to get there.

Their ritual was always the same. After the show the boys loaded their meager instruments into a four-door sedan. In early '55 Presley made enough money to buy his first Cadillac, a '54 model spray-painted pink. Black's bass was strapped to the rack on top. Moore tucked his amplifier in the trunk, padded it with foam rubber, and placed his guitar in the car. His years in the military showed: "I didn't pack the car with reckless abandon and I didn't play guitar with reckless abandon," Moore declared. "I packed and played with purpose."

On Sunday, May 8, the trio was booked for matinee and evening performances at Tampa's Homer Hesterly Armory, an already historic military depot where in 1898 Teddy Roosevelt and his Rough Riders camped on the grounds before heading off to Cuba to fight in the Spanish-American War. Presley played nine shows here over the next fifteen months. In the history of young Elvis in Florida, Tampa's armory is hallowed ground. No other venue in the state hosted Presley more often during his four barnstorming Florida tours encompassing his transition from unknown to megastar.

In 1955 there was no Interstate 4 to provide a fast, straight shot on a divided highway between Daytona Beach and Tampa. The boys set off on US 92 until it converged with US 17; highways that brought travelers through, not around, quaint downtowns in Deland, DeBary, and Sanford. The ghost of young Elvis and his pink Cadillac screams through the humid Florida night on these lesser-traveled byways; largely ghost roads of the 1950s now, they remain evocative of the period.

The Tampa shows proved every bit as electric as Presley's Daytona Beach performance. "I was amazed at the reaction of the crowd," remembered Bill Hipp, just fifteen at the time. "He sang 'That's All Right,' gyrated over the stage with great enthusiasm with his legs whirling around. The girls started standing and screaming. I was flabbergasted at their reaction to Elvis. My Dad, who took me to the concert, was a country music fan, and even more surprised."

One of the evening's headliners, Faron Young—whose hit "Live Fast, Love Hard, Die Young" embodied the youthful rebellion Presley personified on stage—nonetheless tried to calm him down. "I used to tell him not to shake his hips," Young recalled. "I said, 'Don't do that. That's real dirty. You shouldn't do that. He said, 'Well it's goin' over and until it stops, I'm gonna keep doin' it.' He was right and I was wrong. I thought it was a fad. Everybody thought he was gonna be a fad." Some young men in the audience, not too happy that this Johnny-come-lately was getting all the girls' attention, openly mocked Presley.

From small town to small town Presley was winning over the most important voices of the emerging rock and roll era: radio disc jockeys.

Their enthusiasm carried over from town to town, drawing more teens to his live shows, creating stronger and stronger reaction to the newest phenomenon in what was still being called hillbilly music.

On Monday, May 9, Presley visited the studios of concert sponsor WMYR radio in Fort Myers, the southernmost stop on his Florida tour. Disc jockey Brad Lacey, who went on to have a long, distinguished career in southwest Florida radio and television, liked to tell a story of loaning Presley a pair of pants that were too big, prompting Presley to gyrate all the more on stage, just to keep them up.

Whether the story is true or not, fans like Bill Gilmore who saw Presley's performance that night at the City Auditorium in Fort Myers agree: "He did steal the show from all the other performers." The bigger stars forced to follow with their country songs of heartache and lost love had had enough. "I said I don't wanna follow him, 'cause he was tearin' 'em up," Young remembered. "But see, they didn't let him have but maybe 10 minutes and that wasn't enough for 'em." Presley needed an advocate who could get him better billing.

It was just the opening Tom Parker had been looking for.

3

May 10–13

Ocala, Orlando, Jacksonville

Long before Elvis Presley stormed the peninsula, the west coast of Florida was Tom Parker country. A Dutchman and illegal alien whose real name was Andreas van Kuijk, Parker was prematurely bald, loud, and given to chomping on Havana cigars. Often wearing a fedora, he radiated a take-charge, in-your-face attitude that would seem to reflect his nickname, "Colonel" Tom Parker. But like much of Parker's background, this was a ruse, a smokescreen, an honorary title bestowed upon him by a crony in Louisiana, not an actual rank earned through service to country. As was the case in other aspects of Tom Parker's public biography, when the layers were peeled back, reality was far different.

Parker was drummed out of the U.S. Army as a young enlisted man, a drama that played out in Florida long before he started promoting his newest rising star and potential cash cow. Then he started to rebuild his life in the Sunshine State, at first barely surviving in a hand-to-mouth existence as a "carny"—promoting carnival acts and animal shows. Parker would do anything to separate spectators from their money; Tampa police once had to put a stop to a scheme where

Parker buried a pony up to its knees and then charged customers a dime to view "the world's smallest pony."

In 1940 Parker landed employment as a field agent for the Hillsborough County Humane Society. The job provided a steady paycheck and a rent-free second-floor apartment in the Humane Society's surprisingly well-appointed, Spanish-accented headquarters at 3607 North Armenia Avenue in West Tampa.

Parker cared for homeless animals, raising money and the Humane Society's profile in the community; a job he pursued with a carny's sense of showmanship and zeal. One of his most famous moneymaking schemes involved the establishment of Tampa's first pet cemetery on the Humane Society's grounds; a move that proved prescient, considering how commonplace such memorials are now.

Around 1935 Parker married Marie Mott, who had a young son from a previous marriage. Throughout a fifty-year marriage that included frequent lengthy separations, Parker and his wife remained devoted to each other. In the early days Marie helped Parker manage the animals and the shelter's books. Long before he masqueraded as "Colonel" Tom Parker, he told volunteers at the humane society to refer to him as "Doctor." During the holidays Parker reveled in playing the role of Santa Claus for Tampa-area schoolchildren if it meant he could be the center of attention.

Though he had multiple chances to become a United States citizen with little or no penalty, Parker never did so. That decision would have a dramatic effect on Elvis Presley's career. What remained certain about Tom Parker's character was his lust for money and games of chance, his iron will to the point of being a bully, a tin ear for music, a love of cigars, and his indomitable work ethic. Tom Parker was a force of nature.

His first venture in concert promotion came during World War II. As a vehicle to raise money for the Humane Society and the war effort, Parker and two partners rented out the Homer Hesterly Armory, the same venue into which he would see to it that Presley was booked again and again.

Fort Myers Auditorium, 1958. Photo by Johnson, State Archives of Florida, *Florida Memory*, https://www.floridamemory.com/items/show/75517.

Parker may not have known music, but instinctively he knew the Grand Ole Opry stars' appeal to central Florida's working class. In a shrewd move he managed to get a local grocery chain to sell tickets discounted with a newspaper coupon. Fans turned out in large numbers for the show featuring Grand Ole Opry host Roy Acuff and the college-educated actress Minnie Pearl, who played the role of corn pone hostess. After that initial show's success, Parker equated concert promotion with dollar signs; this was the perfect vehicle for his endless ambition and for a carnival man's mastery of manipulation. Parker had found his calling.

Holmes Davis, a teenage usher at the Peabody Auditorium who spoke with Elvis Presley after his first-ever Florida performance. Courtesy of Holmes Davis.

By the time "the kid" Presley came to his attention, Parker had already parlayed concert promotion and artist management into his ticket out of Florida. By 1955 he had moved to Nashville, and he managed country crooner Eddy Arnold until the singer felt Parker was being dishonest and fired him. Despite their parting of the ways, Arnold never lost his respect for Parker's business acumen: "He was a ball of fire, he worked hard, he got up early, and he was a nondrinker," Arnold reflected. "He was good with the record company and he was good with the personal appearances. He was absolutely dedicated to the personality that he represented."

By May 1955 Memphis disc jockey Bob Neal had taken over management of Presley from Scotty Moore. Neal brought in Parker, then an agent for Hank Snow Attractions, because of Parker's ability to get Presley on out-of-state package tours like his initial foray through Florida. It was Parker who enlisted Mae Axton to promote Presley's first Florida tour; that alone turned out to be a monumental development in Presley's rise to stardom. After watching from the shadows Presley's effect on audiences, Parker had designs on taking over the young entertainer's entire career, leaving small-timers like Neal and Moore behind.

Parker put his boundless energy to work as Presley's advance man. That meant getting into town early enough to schmooze with the people promoting the upcoming show. On May 10 Parker asked Jim

Kirk, a legend in Ocala broadcasting and politics who at the time was just starting out as general manager of the town's first country radio station WMOP, to meet him after lunch at a restaurant on the town square.

"He was one of the rarest human beings I have ever met," said the affable Kirk, recalling the forcefulness of Parker's personality. "He assumed everyone thought as he did and if not you were wrong so let's get on with it."

As the two began discussing his new star, Parker checked his watch and told Kirk, "Just sit there. I want you to see him come into town." Kirk wondered how Parker knew precisely when that was going to happen.

In no time, Kirk said, "This pink Cadillac comes down the square, down the street and this young man with slicked back hair is driving, a good lookin' lady beside him and he drives by and he waves." Dumbstruck, Kirk asked Parker how he knew exactly when Presley was going to show up. Parker, basking in the glory of his maneuver, told the inquiring young radio man, "I told him." At times, Elvis Presley was a

The Peabody Auditorium in Daytona Beach, where Elvis Presley performed his first Florida concert. Photo by author.

Above: The author with Jim Kirk at the Southeastern Pavilion in Ocala, where Kirk booked Elvis Presley for his first Florida head-lining performance. Courtesy of Marc Rice and the author.

Left: Jim Kirk, who gave Elvis Presley his first opportunity to headline in Florida. Courtesy of Marc Rice and the author.

puppet on a string to Parker's gamesmanship, but Ocala was another small step toward stardom.

That episode convinced Kirk of the young singer's star power and the authority his promoter wielded: "He choreographed how the kid was coming into town. It tickled me a lot," Kirk said.

Prior to that Parker had been calling Kirk, urging him to abandon the advertised line-up WMOP had put together for that night at the

Southeastern Pavilion, a sprawling open-air venue with grandstand seating for 2,500 and a red clay floor used for rodeos and livestock showings. Parker wanted Presley as the headliner and didn't care if the more established country stars—whom the majority of the crowd had bought tickets to see—performed at all. "I want to center it all on him," Parker insisted. "He can carry the whole show." There were stories of Parker offering the other musicians extra pay if they would step aside and let his young protégé close the show.

"He's not exactly country music," Kirk hesitated, not sold on the idea of an unknown kid closing a show full of established stars like Hank Snow, Faron Young, and Slim Whitman. This was still almost a year before Presley had any of his best-known hits and appearances on national television. Parker would not let up: "I guarantee he won't hurt it, or I'll make up the difference."

In making his decision, Kirk had more to go on than just the bombastic Parker's assurances and gut instincts. WMOP's best-known disc jockey Ward Goodrich, who went by the name Nervous Ned Needham, was also an early fan of Presley and a well-known music promoter.

At barely five feet tall, Needham wore a cowboy hat and bright yellow boots and played all kinds of music: country, gospel, and ethnic. Like Brad Lacey in Fort Myers, Needham played Presley's earliest singles and helped build a buzz with his audience over Presley's high-energy live shows. "This kid Elvis Presley is going somewhere," Needham told his listeners. "He's going to be big time, mark my words." Unlike Parker, Needham had an ear and eye for upcoming talent and a significant background, having seen other stars on the rise.

Needham lived the typical journeyman radio man's life. In 1951, as an all-night country disc jockey in New Orleans, he booked and met another young star about to make history—Hank Williams, whom he described as "a mournful soul." Williams's career trajectory resembled Presley's and came crashing down even sooner. His death nine months shy of his thirtieth birthday was brought on by alcoholism.

"Ned was a marvel at all kinds of music and told me all about Elvis," Kirk recalled. But there was still a significant risk of offending the other performers and the audience, many of whom wanted to see a traditional, wholesome country concert. Though all of the posters promoting that night's show to this day still list Presley far below Hank Snow, Faron Young, and Slim Whitman, Kirk decided to make Presley the night's headliner. He acknowledged that his on-air announcer Ned Needham wasn't the only one nervous that night: "I worried a lot about the show."

It was all set. Elvis Presley would perform his first headlining Florida concert in a back country livestock pen with a flatbed trailer as his stage. If anything went wrong or the crowd got mad and wanted their money back, Jim Kirk would become the focal point of their ire, and he knew it. The stakes were high.

According to Needham, other stars from the Hank Snow jamboree, tired of being upstaged by Presley, weren't all that upset to do one or two songs and exit. It was almost like having the night off and still getting paid. But the audience didn't see it that way. Kirk said some fans, upset at not hearing many of the hit songs they wanted, "were cussing." As the time grew nearer for Presley to perform, one thought kept repeating in Kirk's mind, "What are we building up to? Are they going to buy it or are they going to kill me?"

At 9:30 Presley windmilled onto the stage in that red-sequined jacket with black lapels, white shirt, and black pants, belting out his most famous song to date, "That's All Right." Sensing the gravity of headlining, Scotty Moore and Bill Black juiced up their accompaniment of the frenetic young performer. "He was unbelievable," said Needham, who had seen the best many other big-time music stars had to offer.

Generations later, sitting in the exhibition hall where it all happened, Jim Kirk agreed: "It was quiet for a minute, then all hell broke loose."

"He was jumping up and down like a Mexican jumping bean. He was buzzin'," recalled one of the legion of teenagers in the audience, Nita Billera. Sixteen-year-old Dale Summers had crawled under the fence, his main objective to meet girls. He had neither seen nor heard of Presley: "We were impressed by the wildly gyrating, new young singer who broke three guitar strings during one number and ended up playing a guitar belonging to Hank Snow before it was over." Teen girls started coming out of the stands, preferring to take a seat in front of the stage on that red clay floor. It could have been made of hot coals; nothing would keep them away.

"We just lost control of the crowd," Kirk remembered. Even more startling was how Presley, the mild-mannered kid who drove into town so calmly, could have such a commanding stage presence, such an alter ego. "I was looking at someone who transformed himself when he got on stage with a guitar in hand," Kirk marveled.

Kirk said the other stars who'd taken a back seat to Presley for the night looked on trying to comprehend just what they were seeing. When it was all over Presley remained at his makeshift dressing room in the cattle pens, signing autographs and mixing with the few new fans who sought him out. According to local lore, one schoolgirl who felt sorry for Presley kept going back and asking him to sign the same piece of notebook paper.

Today when we look at vintage film footage of Presley gyrating his way across some early southern stages, we're watching it through blinders, taking in what amounts to a black and white negative of someone who burst into the milieu so full of life, in such vivid *color*. That is the advantage those early fans hold over us all. Years before the Beatles, love-ins, the *Laugh-In* TV show, flower children, social media, and smart phones that bring all that is unknown to within a simple few key strokes, Presley's young audiences witnessed full-on the explosive, immediate impact of his talent when it was all still fresh and new. This was merely the first inkling of Presleymania in Florida.

The 25- to 30-minute performance also made a negative impression on many older people in the audience. Security guard Tom High told his daughter, "The man should be ashamed of himself the way he shakes his hips and moves his body." Others accused Kirk of just trying to make a buck. "The fella who managed the pavilion thought it was the nastiest thing he'd ever seen," said Kirk. "He never did forgive us for bringing something like that in."

The next day Presley was all anybody wanted to talk about in the local high schools. When the night's receipts were counted, it was the most successful show WMOP staged at the pavilion. Kirk's assistant handed Parker his share; the energetic promoter's instincts had paid off. From that night, Kirk said he was forever on Presley's boat. His take on Parker remained equally indelible: "He was the damnedest salesman I've ever seen," Kirk declared. "I thought about him a number of times when we had trouble with the Russians, we should have sent him over."

Kirk, the man to bring the first country music radio station to Ocala, had unwittingly unleashed rock and roll there too, with all its excitement and controversy, in one explosive and memorable performance.

Elvis, Scotty, and Bill moved on to Orlando, the next stop in what had already been a remarkable week in Florida. Compared to some of the long drives between one-night gigs, the eighty miles between Ocala and Orlando meant an easy trip down US 441. With plentiful visual ephemera like the faded glory of vintage motels and lakeside resorts, it is apt to compare the old mother road, also known as the Orange Blossom Trail, to America's far larger bygone byway Route 66, now enjoying a tourism revival. In 1955 both were in their heyday.

Elvis, Scotty, and Bill were scheduled for two evening shows at the Municipal Auditorium in downtown Orlando, known by locals as "Muni-Aud." As an added bonus, having no matinee show meant the boys would have some actual downtime. Presley decided to take a trip out to the Butler chain of lakes in southwest Orange County, where a family of country music enthusiasts had invited artists on the Hank Snow tour out for some relaxation and home cooking.

Today the Butler chain is home to some of the most opulent communities in central Florida. Celebrity athletes, actors, and assorted well-to-do families enjoy picturesque lakeside living in high-priced, gated golf communities. In 1955 the area was considered out in the country; more of a camp with weekend homes you could buy cheaply, accessible strictly by dirt roads.

Local resident Larry Grimes recalled the pink Cadillac he saw in the driveway at 5405 West Lake Butler Drive. "I didn't really know who the guy was," said Grimes. "Just a young musician visiting the folks two doors down." When the young man came over and asked, "Could you teach me how to water-ski?" Grimes was happy to oblige.

For decades Grimes's aunts argued over which one of them drove the speed boat towing the future king of rock and roll. On May 11, 1955, Presley could mix with everyday people and enjoy simple pleasures without worry of being swarmed. One of the most endearing aspects of Presley's earliest days barnstorming Florida was his open accessibility to fans. He had yet to start living within the cloistered walls of fame.

In short order Presley was able to get up on water-skis and circle the cove on Lake Butler. Grimes said, "He seemed to enjoy it, but didn't say a whole lot." After a couple of trips around the lake Presley swam back to shore in a motion Grimes found "awkward." Almost as soon as the young man came over, he thanked Grimes and headed back to the neighboring lake house.

It wasn't until later that Grimes and his family found out who the young musician was. "To me, he was just another hillbilly singer," Grimes said, chuckling at the notion that at one time, Presley really was nobody. Helping him water-ski was nothing more than a neighborly gesture of friendship to a stranger out in the country.

That evening Presley pulled up behind Orlando's Municipal Auditorium. He and the boys were once again relegated to warm-up status, back down from the headlining heights of the previous night in Ocala. With little time until he was due to go on, Presley breezed his way toward the back door when a young girl stopped him. It was Doris Tharp-Gurley, the Daytona Beach teenager who had seen him live from a distance earlier that week. There were no security guards, nor massive tour buses, and no entourage. All Gurley had to do to achieve her dream of meeting Presley was wait near the back door.

The enormous risk she took to achieve her secret dream was deceiving her parents.

Doris Tharp-Gurley wearing tee-shirt of 1955 images with Presley. Courtesy of Doris Tharp-Gurley.

The day before, Gurley and her friend Janet Green fibbed about staying the night at Gurley's sister's house. To catch a ride from Daytona Beach to Orlando, the girls bought Greyhound bus tickets. "Janet and I sat up all night at the bus station," Gurley remembered. Too wired to sleep, they talked about Presley until it was finally time to board. After a long bus ride fraught with worry and excitement, their teenage conspiracy was paying off.

"Could we get a picture with you?" the girls asked him.

"Sure, but you're gonna have to make it quick, I've gotta get inside," Presley told them.

There's one photo of Presley with a girl on either side, holding each at the waist. In pretty dresses, Gurley and Green are the picture of 1950s Florida schoolgirls: beaming, made up, happy to be on the arm of the pseudo prom king. Then, to Gurley's astonishment, Presley took her in his arms and kissed her right on the lips; a moment forever frozen in time, captured on film. And then as quickly as it

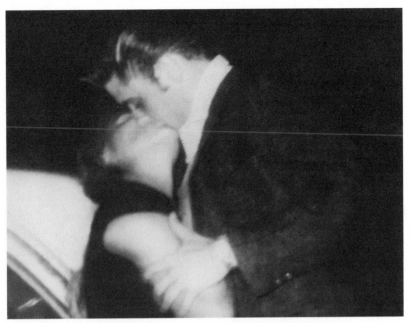

Presley kissing Doris Tharp-Gurley. Courtesy of Doris Tharp-Gurley.

Doris Tharp-Gurley, Elvis Presley, and Janet Green outside Municipal Auditorium in Orlando. Courtesy of Doris Tharp-Gurley.

happened, like an apparition Presley was gone. The star-struck young friends didn't even have tickets to get into the concert.

The long bus ride home meant the two had to breach another rigid parental expectation: they skipped school the next day. "I never had the nerve to tell my parents what happened," Gurley confessed. "They were very strict."

In this vignette we see the youthful rebellion Presley was beginning to inspire. Never before had Gurley dared deceive her parents this way. But that fleeting kiss with him, and the excitement of seeing and hearing Presley perform earlier in the week, had made all the risk worth it. Within months his critics would seize upon this kind of behavior in America's youth to denounce Presley. Hard as it is to imagine now, law enforcement leaders sought help from FBI Director J. Edgar Hoover himself to stem the subversive tide they felt Presley represented.

In the audience at the Municipal Auditorium that night, Florida troubadour-to-be Gamble Rogers, son of celebrated Florida architect James Gamble Rogers, witnessed the power of musical performance in Presley. In his own performances from Florida roadhouses to Carnegie Hall, Rogers adapted a preacher's cadence, spinning yarns of Florida folk life in "Oklawaha County"; he was the Sunshine State's Garrison Keillor. On this night Rogers was eighteen and living in Winter Park.

"To be part of that audience was an astounding thing," Rogers remembered. "It was an experience I will never forget. It was as to be part of a cauldron of raving sycophants. I have never seen such an effusion of emotion. This blue collar audience of country music fans recoiled at first because of his movements and attitude. First they thought he was drunk, then they thought he was daft, but before the first song was over they were caught up in it and swept away."

The *Orlando Sentinel* columnist Jean Yothers was the first Florida journalist to write about the growing Presley phenomenon, in her "On the Town" column: "What really stole the show was this 20-year-old sensation Elvis Presley, a real sex-box as far as the girls are concerned," Yothers observed. "They squealed themselves silly over this fellow in an Orange coat and sideburns who 'sent' them with his unique arrangement of 'Shake, Rattle and Roll.'" After the show Yothers noted how Presley gave each girl seeking an autograph a long, slow look with his sleepy, puppy dog eyes: "They ate it up."

Yothers's colorful description of the concert, echoing Gamble Rogers, illustrated the effect of Presley's music: "What Hillbilly music does to the Hillbilly fan is absolutely phenomenal. It transports him into a wild, emotional and audible state of ecstasy," she noted. "He thunders his appreciation for the country-style music and the nasal twanged singing he loves by whistling shrilly through teeth, pounding the palms together with the whirling momentum of a souped-up paddle wheel, stomping the floor and ejecting yip yip noises like the barks of a hound dog."

In her 1955 column Jean Yothers captured the birth of rock and roll for whites in segregated Orlando. Parents had no problem sending their children to what was *supposed to be* a benign Grand Ole Opry show, but in return Presley delivered something parents did not expect or necessarily approve of; a synthesis of countrified rhythm and blues that artists like Little Richard Penniman were already delivering to African-American audiences throughout the South on the so-called Chitlin' Circuit.

Orlando had its own venue on the circuit, the South Street Casino, about six blocks from the Municipal Auditorium. For Presley's young white fans, it might as well have been on the moon. Vanilla crooner Pat Boone made a laughable attempt to cover Little Richard's 1955 classic "Tutti Frutti." Presley was the first white artist who belted out those songs with credibility, bridging the color gap, and like Johnny Appleseed, spreading nascent rock and roll in all its vibrant, sexual, hip-shaking color to cloistered, impressionable youth worldwide. Less country, more juke joint—that was Elvis Presley's magic and remains his most important legacy.

At the last stop on Elvis, Scotty, and Bill's week-long Florida tour putting the jam in the Hank Snow jamboree, in Jacksonville their friend and local promoter Mae Axton was waiting. On the way out to the band's motel, Presley and Axton spoke of family, home, and his determination to make something of himself.

"His clothes were a little 'freaky' for that age of sweaters and skirts, bobby sox, shirts and slacks and burr haircuts," Axton remembered. "But I liked him immediately. I could sense something rare in this quiet, but extremely polite youngster." In return, Axton was like a mother figure, and since she lived in Jacksonville, she could offer the boys a chance to stop by her house in the suburbs for a home-cooked meal; a rare treat in their world of truckstop burgers and diner flapjacks.

Like the good promoter she was, Axton spread the word to local newspapers, radio stations, and her sons Hoyt and Johnny about Presley's alter ego and the dynamic performer who had made a splash around the Sunshine State during his first week of live shows.

Despite the positive buzz surrounding Presley's act, at least one Jacksonville disc jockey was not impressed. "We felt Elvis was on the wrong show," said Jeannie Williams of WRHC radio. "We were all pure country. He was different. Nobody was real excited to have him on the package deal. His music was not our music . . . I didn't think he was much of a singer."

Some believed the headliner Hank Snow, a diminutive man at just five feet, four inches tall, had a Napoleon complex and the self-doubt that came with it. Though Snow was business partners with Tom Parker, the ecstatic reactions Presley was receiving increased Snow's insecurity. As evidenced by Parker's willingness to make Presley the one and only featured attraction in Ocala earlier that week, Parker and his promoter Mae Axton were all in on Elvis. The performances in Jacksonville left no doubt and provided an exclamation point for Parker in his attempts to bring the young star into his stable permanently.

Ardys Bell and her brother Phil had no professional connections in the music business, no preconceived notions about Presley. A recent graduate in a class of ten from tiny Boca Grande High School, Bell was new to town and living at the local YWCA. "I was just getting

Ardys Bell with Presley after excited fans had torn off his shirt. Courtesy of Ardys Bell.

acquainted with life," Bell recalled. It was her brother's idea to attend the concert at Jacksonville's new baseball stadium, Wolfson Park.

Named after millionaire baseball owner Samuel W. Wolfson, the new stadium had opened just two months previously, providing the largest Florida venue Presley had played to date. The Bell siblings would be part of a crowd some estimated to be as large as twelve thousand. On this night Bell and her brother got their first look at both the dawning of rock and roll and the earliest stage of Presley-mania in Florida. Fittingly, it was Friday the thirteenth that Presley performed in this navy town on the Atlantic.

As usual, he chose outlandish colors for that night's performance: a pink suit and shirt, frilly enough that Axton playfully teased Presley to let her have it as a blouse. At dinner, other female performers on the evening's bill, the Carter Sisters and Skeeter Davis, also commented on Presley's garish shirt revealing his bare chest. Presley was due to close the first half of the night's show; Snow would headline the second half. Just before Presley went on, Pat Miles, the daughter of a local disc jockey, was introduced to him. "He was watching the entertainers, mesmerized. Very shy, polite, and always stood by himself."

All the nerves evaporated as soon as Presley went on to close the first half of the show. After two songs the teenage crowd poured from the stands over the barricades and, as at the Ocala show a few nights earlier, gathered directly in front of the stage. Pat Miles saw it happen right in front of her: "The crowd came over the barricades and rushed the stage," she remembered. "I had never seen this before." Sensing the excitement in his audience, at the end of the set Presley uttered a single sentence that triggered a watershed event: "Thank you ladies and gentlemen and girls, I'll see you back stage."

According to Axton, hundreds of young people emptied from the stands immediately. Though she and Parker had arranged for police security in the players' locker rooms that served as a performer dressing area, someone had left an overhead door open, through which girls came like a tidal wave of teen lust. "It was like a sudden ocean swell," Axton marveled.

In minutes, as the story goes, dozens of teenagers mobbed Presley, tearing off his pink jacket, tie, belt, and frilly pink shirt. "Ripped to pieces," Axton recalled, "and divided among the teenagers as souvenirs." Presley climbed to the top of the showers to make his escape while Jacksonville police attempted to clear the room. In her memoir Axton recalled asking a young student nurse why she was screaming and crying over Presley. In a response famous to Presley fans worldwide she told Axton, "Well, he's just a great big beautiful hunk of forbidden fruit."

It is likely this so-called riot has grown in legend and intensity over the years, but Ardys Bell and her brother Phil witnessed one remarkable aspect of the aftermath. As they walked underneath the grandstands the two happened upon Presley. Wearing no shirt and winded, he was eating ice out of a soft drink box near a remote concession area.

"When we saw him, I walked up and asked permission for us to take pictures," Bell recalled. "I wasn't 'ga ga'—I was talking to him." The resulting image snapped by her brother Phil shows Ardys looking at a bare-chested Presley with a grin on her face. He appears nonplussed. It's such an odd moment; if not for her perspective on the image, you would swear this classic snapshot is a scene from an early Elvis movie; it looks so staged. The only thing comparable to this fan reaction would come nine years later when the Beatles played Jacksonville's Gator Bowl across the parking lot from the baseball stadium.

According to legend and Mae Axton, the Jacksonville fan frenzy left Parker with "dollar marks in his eyes" and an unshakable resolve to gain full managerial control of twenty-year-old Elvis Presley. He also saw to it that news of the commotion made its way into the papers. The opportunist promoter knew he had found his money train and how to exploit the growing phenomenon. This alchemy was crucial to Presley's breakout stardom.

Soon Parker would make it clear to Presley's hard-working road brothers Scotty and Bill that their tickets to ride were located far to the rear of their youthful front man. There would only be one star in Tom Parker's show. His earliest Florida tour had come to an end, but in two scant months Presley was right back in the Sunshine State. His second round of barnstorming in the midst of a sweltering summer, Presley's last as a support act, would prove every bit as eventful as the first.

ANDY AND ELVIS

July 25–27

Fort Myers, Orlando

After his first Florida tour Elvis Presley spent the next two months performing in North Carolina and Virginia. He returned to his crucial launching venue, the *Louisiana Hayride*, where he was still under contract to perform. In June, during a series of concerts across Texas, Presley appeared in Midland with Roy Orbison. In Lubbock Buddy Holly opened for Presley as part of a duo known as Buddy and Bob. Presley played Hope, Arkansas, birthplace of William Jefferson Blythe, who became President Bill Clinton; the boy was eight years old at the time.

"Elvis Presley continues to gather speed over the South," wrote Cecil Holifield, operator of record stores in Midland and Odessa, Texas. "West Texas is his hottest territory to date."

There were difficult times on the road; after the gig in Hope, Presley was driving through Fulton, Arkansas, when the brake lining of his car caught fire. He and a local girl he was taking to his next concert managed to escape. All he could do was stand by the side of the road in despair as flames charred his cherished Cadillac, the first he ever owned. Scotty and Bill drove over to Memphis to retrieve as a temporary replacement the car Presley bought for his parents.

At the dedication of the newly air-conditioned Slavonian Lodge in Biloxi, Mississippi, some of the men found Presley "a little cocky," and chided him for having "pimples all over his face." The promoter who booked Presley at the lodge, Frankie "Yankee" Barhanovich, quipped, "The members were all making fun of me for bringing in this hillbilly."

During this difficult stretch, things got even worse at the enlisted airmen's club on nearby Keesler Air Force Base, home of the 81st Training Wing. Presley was booed and stayed back behind the tiny stage area during intermission. A sergeant at the base concluded: "He'll never make it." During his two-night stand in late June, Presley eventually won them over, even becoming friendly with said airman who proclaimed his career doomed. When he was encouraged to play longer Presley confessed, "I only know seven songs."

During this three-date swing through Mississippi, Presley grabbed the arm of an attractive girl walking past. "Where are you going?" he asked playfully. The encounter marked the beginning of his serious romance with seventeen-year-old June Juanico, an auburn-haired beauty whom a reporter once described as a "blue-eyed girl built on the order of the Mississippi River, long and lots of curves." Besides her beauty, Juanico was no shrinking violet. She had a strong will and did not hesitate to share opinions with her young paramour.

That night the two sat in his car outside Juanico's house. She recalled: "The first thing I said was 'what is your real name?' because I'd never heard of a name like Elvis before. He said 'What do you mean my real name? Elvis Aaron Presley." As her mother kept an eye on them from the house, Juanico answered Presley's questions about her parents' divorce, something unusual at a time when marriage was still considered forever. Presley opened up about his twin brother who died at birth. The two talked until dawn, and over the next year found time to see each other during Presley's rapid ascent to fame, including his most chaotic and controversial Florida tour.

In early July 1955 Bill Haley and the Comets began their historic eight-week chart-topping run with "Rock Around the Clock." In a year bookended by bland number 1 hits like the Chordettes' "Mister Sandman" in January and Tennessee Ernie Ford's standard "Sixteen Tons"

Elvis Presley in Orlando. Courtesy of Travis Norby.

in December, Haley's single became an early rock and roll archetype and another clear signal of where popular music was headed. After a history-making year with Sam Phillips and Sun Studios, on July 11 Presley recorded his last Sun single, eventually his first number 1 on the country charts: "I Forgot to Remember to Forget" with "Mystery Train" on the flipside.

At the end of July his manager Bob Neal announced that Presley would embark on his next Tom Parker package tour through Florida headlined by an up-and-coming comedian, Andy Griffith. Years before Griffith enchanted the nation as Sheriff Andy Taylor of Mayberry, in 1953 his monologue comedy record, 'What It Was, Was Football" sold 800,000 copies, led to an appearance on the *Ed Sullivan Show,* and established Griffith as a comedy star. Ads for the tour listed Presley as an "extra" and proclaimed his appearance "by popular demand." In truth he still occupied the bottom of the bill below Ferlin Huskey, Marty Robbins, and a rockabilly singer and radio host out of Jacksonville, Glenn Reeves.

A year to the day after he recorded the breakthrough single "That's All Right," Presley purchased a new pink Cadillac Fleetwood Series 60 to replace the car that had burned. After some minimal days of downtime in Memphis, and that final Sun recording session, three weeks into July Elvis, Scotty, and Bill packed up the new car and headed off on the thousand-mile drive to sleepy Fort Myers, population 20,000.

During lengthy car trips through the South, the trio liked to keep up the chatter and play practical jokes to pass the time. To calm the adrenaline still pumping from a concert, on lengthy all-night drives Scotty Moore said they liked to tune in to a midnight jazz radio show out of New Orleans, *Moonglow with Martin.*

Wafting through the humid night air along endless two-lane roads or the occasional divided highway came the deep, calming voice of all-night disc jockey Dick Martin: "Hi to you big doc and you too baby doll . . . WWL radio, Loyola University of the south, broadcasting from our studios in the beautiful Roosevelt Hotel in downtown New Orleans." Long before you could plug an iPod into a USB port or choose from an immense selection of offerings on satellite radio, as the night wore on there wasn't much left on the airwaves except solitary voices like Martin's. For that they hold a cherished place in the hearts of those who remember them.

During overnight hours the show's AM radio signal could span as far north as the Black Hills of South Dakota and south to the Florida

ELVIS PRESLEY

Autographed 1955 promotional photograph. Courtesy of Travis Norby.

Everglades. From Duke Ellington to Ella Fitzgerald to Charlie Parker, the comforting strains of late night jazz provided company to long-haul truckers, lulled restless babies to sleep in their cribs, and helped Elvis, Scotty, and Bill freewheel it down the road to the next gig. It was usually Moore or Black behind the wheel. "If you let Elvis drive, no telling where you might end up," Moore laughed. "He didn't have much of a sense of direction, so if he got on a road he pretty much stayed on it. We'd wake up and not know where we were."

In those days there was no shotgun-barrel straight Interstate 75 to take you right down Florida's west coast. A 1955 Florida road map shows US 41, the Tamiami Trail—paved in some places, still dirt in others—winding through Sarasota, Venice, over Charlotte Harbor, through Punta Gorda and into Fort Myers. That was Elvis, Scotty, and Bill's winding route to their second Florida tour in late July that year.

Presley stopped in at WMYR radio on Hanson Street for an on-air interview with his biggest backer in southwest Florida, the local pied piper of rock and roll, disc jockey Brad Lacey, who promoted both of Presley's 1955 appearances there. It was routine for young people who listened to Lacey to stop in at the little station by the railroad tracks and see in person whomever he was interviewing. Other fans like fifteen-year-old Diane Maddox had the radio on all day long at home.

"Mom and Dad won a jitterbug contest the night before I was born," Maddox laughed. She still has the ticket stub from Presley's show on July 25, 1955, starring "Deacon" Andy Griffith. The nickname came from the pseudo preacher Griffith played on his hit parody monologue. He described the football as a "funny lookin' little punkin."

"And I know friends," Griffith expounded in an exaggerated drawl, "that they couldn't eat it because they kicked it the whole evenin' and it never busted." That line always brought howls of laughter from live audiences. Like Minnie Pearl, June Carter Cash, and others who played cornpone southern characters, Griffith was intelligent and highly educated, and he rode his comedy acumen to success on Broadway, in films, and on television.

It was the summer between ninth and tenth grade for Maddox, who attended the small town's combination junior and senior high.

The concert was a break in the summer routine, a change from hanging out at the Snack Drive-in near the Fort Myers police station or having a soda on the beach. "The town was so small you couldn't find much trouble," said Maddox. "If you did, news of it would make it back to your parents before you did."

At that evening's show Presley played a longer set than on the first Florida tour, at least twenty-five minutes. According to Maddox an unusual thing happened: "I don't remember any screaming." Maddox recalls Presley including a couple of gospel numbers along with songs from his usual early repertoire: "That's All Right," and "Blue Moon of Kentucky." After the show some of the boys from school went backstage to help the musicians pack up their equipment. They invited Maddox and her friend to join them: "C'mon, they're playing music back there." The fact that there was no security to stop them, no announcement that "Elvis has left the building," is a reminder of what an innocent and far more accessible time this was for Presley as well as his fans.

Maddox ascended the stairs that led behind the stage at the exhibition hall. In the hustle and bustle of people breaking down the equipment, Elvis, Scotty, and Bill had taken off their ties, loosened up their collars, and begun jamming before loading up and heading back to the Holiday Inn. As Maddox stood there taking it all in, Presley approached: "Come on let's dance."

He took her hand. While others stood around or continued loading up the equipment, fifteen-year-old Diane Maddox fast-danced with Elvis Presley. Because he was not yet a major star, Maddox said she did not find those moments intimidating or all that awe-inspiring. He was still so young and approachable: "He could have been any other kid I hung out with at the beach or the drive-in." It wasn't until she saw Presley on the *Ed Sullivan Show* the next year that she regretted not having had a camera to record her time with him.

Someone backstage handed Maddox a picture of Presley, which she asked him to sign. So that he wouldn't risk damaging the back of the photo with a pen, Presley asked her to get him a pencil. Generations later, his autograph remains vivid: "Love ya, Elvis Presley." The musicians asked their teen helpers to follow them over to the hotel to help unload the instruments. In a conservative small town like Fort Myers, it was out of the question for two respectable fifteen-year-old girls to join a group of men and boys at a motel for any reason.

At a time when air-conditioned public spaces were a rare cause for celebration, in the middle of a Florida summer, arenas without it were almost unbearable. Regardless, on the next two nights after Fort Myers, fans braved a driving rain storm and navigated flooded streets to fill Orlando's sweltering Municipal Auditorium for the Andy Griffith show. Perhaps because of the oppressive heat, Presley played only three songs: a cover of the current number 1 hit in the nation, Bill Haley's "Rock Around the Clock," "Shake Rattle and Roll," and "I've Got a Woman."

The headliner Griffith soldiered on, punctuating his comedy sermon with lots of smiles, crowd eye contact, and hillbilly twang. His beloved football monologue brought laughter in the sweat-soaked auditorium. After the evening show, Orlando newspaper columnist Jean Yothers caught up with Griffith backstage. The enthused responses Presley was generating weighed on the comedian's mind:

"That Presley boy purely fractures the people all to pieces," Griffith commented in a voice you can imagine coming from his most famous character Sheriff Andy Taylor. The observant young writer Yothers noted that Griffith's speaking voice departed from the exaggerated North Carolina drawl fans had come to know in the football record, coming across as the more educated man he was.

At times "Deacon" Andy's double entendres bordered on naughty: "The little mother's club is having a meetin' this week," Griffith announced to the audience. "Any of you women interested in becoming a little mother, may meet with the preacher at 3 p.m." Griffith admitted some misinterpreted his act as sacrilegious. Yothers assured her readers, part of central Florida's churchgoing Bible belt of the mid-50s, "Andy's preacher act is extremely comical."

It is hard to believe that at one point in American culture, someone as quintessentially all-American and wholesome as Andy Griffith had an act some that interpreted as risqué. Soon the same would hold true for Presley but in a far more magnified and reactionary way than for Griffith. Yothers cornered Presley before his set, admiring his blue lace shirt. "I'll give it to you," Presley told her. In her Friday "On the Town" column, Yothers noted that she was genuinely touched by the gesture but added, "I'm still waiting." She was unapologetic for the effusive comments she had made in the newspaper when Presley played Orlando two months previously:

"I fully realize many of you sneer at hillbilly music," she wrote, taking on a confessional tone. Still smitten, Yothers declared Presley "the hottest thing to hit Orlando since the Avalon hotel caught fire." Presley gave Yothers the same "love ya" autograph Diane Maddox collected in Fort Myers. Not yet twenty-one, Presley had become adept at using his sex appeal to court young female fans and reporters.

What bothered the prescient young columnist was Presley's hyper-energetic "house afire" performances: "Now it's none of my business," Yothers wrote, "but I think Elvis is pushing himself too fast. He's wearing himself out giving customers more than their money's worth. I just wanted to say to him, 'Slow down boy . . . your fame won't disappear.'" At that point though, Presley was famous only in the South, and there was no telling where his career might lead, if it lasted at all.

Soon enough, Presley's schedule would become even more grueling at the hands of Tom Parker, who also felt a need to exploit Presley's popularity for as much money as possible, in case the young performer's fame should turn out to be fleeting. That anyone would even consider such a thing seems preposterous in retrospect. But he needed to expand his audience beyond the South, and Parker was just the man to help him do it. Meanwhile, the hint of controversy that Griffith and Presley generated on that tour was nothing compared to the widespread scorn awaiting in 1956.

July 28–29

Jacksonville

When the Andy Griffith tour moved on to Jacksonville, site of Presley's first fan frenzy back in May, Tom Parker was determined to build on that momentum and make Presley's two-night stand the biggest thing ever to hit northeast Florida. Parker called a meeting with Florida tour publicist Mae Axton and a couple of influential radio men in town. One of them, Glenn Reeves, a talented rockabilly musician, also appeared on the bill above Presley as an opening act on the Griffith tour. Like Axton, Reeves wore numerous hats in the local music business as musician, promoter, and radio and television host. Two others, Marshall Rowland from WQIK and Frank Thies, were also part of the Parker summit.

After he told them how he wanted to promote the show, Parker made it clear they would be well compensated for helping make it a success. "Don't worry, work hard and promote this great concert," Parker assured them, "and the Colonel will take care of you." Through his third-person reference we get a glimpse of Parker's own brashness, drive, and ego. Those qualities were vital in growing Presley's success, which Parker was already seeing as inseparable from his own.

Rowland took to the streets blaring news of the show from a loudspeaker on top of his car; so loudly that a policeman threatened to arrest him. Axton took Presley to a local radio studio to record an interview, the only known surviving recorded interview from Presley's 1955 Florida tours.

Axton begins, "You're more of a bebop artist more than anything else aren't you?"

"Well, I never have given myself a name," Presley replies. "But a lot of the disc jockeys call me bopping hillbilly, bebop, I don't know . . ."

In some places the interview is inaccurately dated May 13, from Presley's earliest Florida tour. In the exchange Presley comments on already having toured Florida and even complains about the limited distribution Sun is giving his records. Axton, taking on a motherly tone, reminds Presley that national distribution, like becoming a well-known artist, takes time.

"We mustn't forget Scotty and Bill who do a terrific job backing you up," Axton comments.

"They sure do, I really am lucky to have those two boys. They really are good. Each one of them has a style all his own," Presley reflects.

"What I don't understand is how you keep that leg shaking at just the right tempo," Axton chuckles. Presley, seeming a bit embarrassed, explains, "It just automatically wiggles."

In the days before Elvis, Scotty, and Bill had stage monitors to hear themselves perform, in the din of girls screaming the backing musicians had to rely on watching Presley's arm and leg movements to know where he was in the song. Moore once joked to a reporter, "We were the only band in the world directed by an ass."

Besides the interview, Axton enlisted her whole family in promoting the weekend concerts. Axton's high school–aged sons Johnny and Hoyt (who would go on to a successful acting and songwriting career of his own) put up concert posters all over Jacksonville. Mae also risked the ire of local police, riding in a rented sound truck making sure people knew it wasn't too late to head over to the Dixie Music Shop or McDuff Hardware and buy a ticket for $1.25.

That week Jacksonville was hit with what one writer called "the damnedest freak storm anybody could remember." Trees were down, windows were broken, and record-setting rain deluged the city. Fire trucks had to be called to pump out the basement of the First Baptist Church. Workers formed a bucket brigade to get flood waters out of the Windle Hotel. Nonetheless, the baseball stadium dried out in time for the show to go on.

Each night the gates opened at 7:00 p.m. and the show started at 8:15. By the second night fans had broken through the barricades in a replay of the May fan frenzy. Girls chased Presley across the playing field, through the dugout, and into the player locker room artists were using as a dressing area. "I just stood there laughing," Marty Robbins recalled. "I knew then he was going to be big because people didn't even know who he was, and they acted like this."

Tom Parker made sure the press was made aware of the fan reaction. *Cash Box* magazine reported: "Elvis Presley was recently presented with a new sports coat by Colonel Parker, to replace the one torn apart by fans in Jacksonville, Florida." As Presley's stage time slowly increased, bassist Bill Black often goaded him or made Presley the straight man in onstage antics:

"Roses are red and violets are pink," Bill proclaimed.

"No, roses are red and violets are blue," Presley assured him.

"No, no man. Roses are red and violets are pink."

At that point Black produced a pair of pink panties from his back pocket for the crowd to see. "I know Violet's are pink 'cause I got them right here." Given the era, that kind of joke in front of a Florida country music crowd had to be considered R-rated. It was not the kind of material the ever image-conscious Tom Parker wanted associated with Presley, and no one, *no one*, was going divert the crowd's attention away from his star.

He also had to deal with Presley's current manager Bob Neal, who frustrated Parker by making recording deals without his consent and failed to get him a bigger, better record deal to improve distribution and hasten Presley's march to stardom. Disc jockey Marshall Rowland, who had played each star's records for two weeks leading up to the concerts, wondered how well Parker would take care of them as he'd promised. "I was holding my breath at how much we were going to make," he recalled.

At the Roosevelt Hotel in downtown Jacksonville, Parker assembled his four promoters. "When he got to his room," Rowland said, "Colonel Tom put a rubber band around four rolls of big bills and without hesitation threw them down on the floor." Perhaps for his amusement, each of the four had to scramble to the floor like children to pick up their pay for helping make the concerts a success. Parker did not disappoint, giving them a thousand dollars each, a king's ransom for 1955.

In her memoir Axton heaped praise on Parker for his "inherent sense of rightness about anything he dealt with to make its operation smooth and successful." She told Presley that Parker's guiding hand was all he needed: "I'll write your first million-seller," she told him. "You continue to be you, and Colonel Tom will do the rest." Axton, who was indeed a songwriter, said she was just being facetious about writing a million-selling song for him.

Presley's parents Vernon and Gladys were not as easily won over as Parker's Jacksonville minions. Since Presley was not yet twenty-one, they would have to sign off on any plans Parker had to gain control of their son's career. According to some accounts, Presley's parents attended these Jacksonville concerts, and Gladys particularly was unnerved by all the screaming young girls tearing at his clothes. She needed convincing that Parker was not just some snake oil salesman looking to use her son, rather than protect him, as his first manager Scotty Moore had promised he would.

As the Griffith tour wound toward its last two stops, Daytona and Tampa, Parker called on some of his longtime contacts to help raise Presley's profile. The results were historic.

July 30–31

Daytona Beach, Tampa

On July 30, 1955, seven weeks after Elvis Presley made such a distinct impression on Daytona Beach teens like Doris Gurley and usher Holmes Davis, he was performing once again at the Peabody Auditorium. Although he was still an opening act, still trying to forge a career in the music business, on this second tour of Florida Presley's pay was bumped up to one hundred dollars a night, twice as much as he had earned the first time around. The biggest advantage he had at this moment in time, though, was the former carny and Tampa dogcatcher now working to leverage himself to capitalize on Presley's limitless moneymaking potential.

"I never looked on him as a son," Parker admitted in a telling moment of candor. "But he was the success I always wanted." Presley's legion of devoted fans won't begrudge Parker credit for being instrumental in getting the hard-rocking, hip-shaking youngster to the top. But beyond that, one critic noted, "Parker is nothing short of evil incarnate: the moneyman who took him from Sun, to middle-of-the-road RCA, lightened and softened him until the former bad boy fit seamlessly into a string of mostly faceless and mediocre movies." In the days before musicians could depend on their managers to chart a course for their career success, ultimately Parker saw nothing wrong with Presley making ridiculous films and cutting nothing but vanilla ballads, if they included eye-popping payoffs. His was a ruthless pursuit of cash with no consideration of what it was doing to his client's credibility as an artist.

During this early wooing stage, Parker paid for Mae Axton and her family to fly from Jacksonville to attend the show in Daytona Beach. That meant she could be there to help Parker land the biggest fish yet in his management career. Gladys and Vernon Presley traveled to Daytona Beach to see the ocean that had inspired such a sense of awe in their boy. Parker, still trying to edge out Bob Neal for sole control of Presley, made an obvious show of generosity to ingratiate himself with Presley's mom and dad, already impressed by the oceanside environs.

"Oh how proud they were," Axton wrote, "when Elvis walked on stage with a sharp new outfit the Colonel had gotten for him." The old carny's seduction tactics were working; Parker was slowly winning over Gladys Presley, the most important and trusted person in her son's life. By Daytona Beach, Axton declared, "Elvis was sold on Colonel Tom." Soon, so were his parents.

In Tampa, Parker booked the Griffith tour into the Hesterly Armory where he had staged his first concert in 1941 and started forging his own transition from carny to Humane Society huckster to music promoter. In another show of good will and shrewd public relations, he arranged for the July 31 concert to benefit the local Sertoma club, a volunteer group dedicated to helping those with hearing, speech, and language disorders. In return, Sertoma Club volunteers agreed to take tickets and guard Presley's new Cadillac. "His rise to fame has been phenomenal," noted a Tampa newspaper writer, referring not to Presley but to the young comedian Andy Griffith. "This will be an all hillbilly show."

Parker, now laser-focused on raising Presley's profile and proving to the young singer's family that he could make their son a national star, wanted some new photographs taken to capture his dynamic stage performance. A journeyman photographer who spent years

Homer Hesterly
Armory, Tampa.
Photo by author.

recording Tampa history in still images, William "Red" Robertson of the well-known Robertson and Fresh photography studio, was tapped by Parker for the job. Robertson was an impressive and talented photojournalist with movie star good looks, known to post himself on top of his car if necessary to get just the right shot of the Gasparilla parade or everyday scenes in Ybor City.

The armory was the perfect place to capture Presley in his element, starting to stomp down the gas pedal on his road to fame. The small stage was positioned at one side of the large, open hall, surrounded on all sides by fans. Spectators sat in bleachers above and behind the stage, giving the entire set-up inside the cavernous building such an intimate look that Presley appeared in danger of being swallowed by his enthusiastic spectators, many of whom were still only marginally aware of who the charismatic young singer was.

Scotty and Bill wore dark shirts with white ties. In contrast, Presley sported a bright coat and dark shirt with opened collar. Drawn by the magnetism of what they saw and heard, the young people in Robertson's photographs are crowding the stage in front, leaning over the balcony behind. Presley stands on the balls of his feet, strumming an acoustic guitar with abandon, eyes closed, mouth agape like a burning, soul-shouting preacher speaking in tongues to the assembled masses. And in large part, that's exactly what Presley was doing; leading them into the rock and roll era with the driving, pulsating beat that had been missing from their young lives.

All of them witnessed the performance that produced Red Robertson's archetypical photograph of young Presley; known as the "tonsil photo," this cropped image went on to appear on countless historic concert advertisements (see chapter 8) and his first record album, a chart-topper the following year. It is the defining image of the birth of live rock and roll and an iconic performer, snapped in a central

William "Red" Robertson, the photographer who took the so-called Elvis "tonsil" photo used as cover image for his first album and in myriad advertisements. Courtesy of William "Red" Robertson, Special & Digital Collections, Tampa Library, University of South Florida.

Florida hot box in the dead of summer. That image and concert provided the perfect exclamation point to Presley's final Florida performance of 1955; the last time he would come to the Sunshine State as an added attraction or a warm-up act.

It took years for Robertson to be properly credited as the man who took the world-famous photo. Also largely lost to history is the fact that six years later, Robertson shot and killed a business associate during an argument over money in Tampa. Had his savvy young defense attorney not convinced the jury that Robertson fired at his larger adversary in self-defense, the man now known as the photographer who snapped Presley's world-famous tonsil photo could have faced execution in Florida's electric chair.

Within Presley's small inner circle, his bandmates Moore and Black were already getting in Parker's way. The savvy Moore, especially, looked upon himself as a big brother figure to Presley and encouraged him to stand up to Tom Parker, who was becoming an increasingly polarizing figure. Moore was blunt. He thought Presley was being brainwashed, and when Parker told Presley to do something he didn't like, Moore seized on the opportunity to encourage the young star to be his own man.

"Elvis you have to stand up and speak your mind," Moore told him. "There's nothing wrong with you arguing with him about something." Parker would have none of that kind of talk and, along with locking down total control of Presley, set his sights on marginalizing Moore, who was still intent on keeping the promise he'd made to Gladys Presley to watch out for her son.

As Presley moved on to other southern tour stops, just weeks later a trio of Floridians converged one afternoon to create a song that would be the solid rocket booster in Presley's launch to the top of the national charts. Not only was the song written and initially recorded on the same day in Florida, but one of the writers was tenacious enough to get Presley's increasingly divided attention and have him stop and listen to it.

7

A New Place to Dwell

Mae Axton never forgot that facetious comment she made to Presley about writing his first million-seller. The song that fulfilled her promise was not Axton's idea, but she was crucial to writing it and, more important, having access to Presley so he could hear it. The writing and recording happened at warp speed in a small house situated in a west Jacksonville suburb.

Back then Mae Axton's home at 3239 Dellwood Avenue resembled many others one might pass a thousand times without a longer look: single story, small, and built in 1947 from cinder block to accommodate yet another post–World War Two baby boom family. But what happened within its walls in 1955, weeks after the completion of Presley's second Florida tour, brought him the breakout hit he'd been waiting for.

Just where are timeless songs *supposed* to be written? In this case, one took shape in the living room of working people hit by a bolt of inspiration that came and went in minutes, leaving them a legacy for the ages. Such is the fickle nature of creativity and success; some enjoy it over and over, and for others it comes just once.

That summer Tommy Durden was a young steel guitar player in a working band: Smiling Jack Herring and his Swingbillies. For years Smiling Jack employed some of north Florida's best musicians, rolling down the two-lane blacktop back roads night after night, town to town, playing small clubs, dance halls, and radio stations with a catchy mix of blues, swing, and primitive rock. Sometimes an opening act for stars like the Louvin Brothers and Little Jimmie Dickins, journeyman musician Tommy Durden dreamed of hitting it big both as a songwriter and as a touring musician.

At a stop in Gainesville, home of the University of Florida, Durden started his day as he often did, reading the morning *Miami Herald*. A small item caught his eye; an unidentified, well-dressed man had committed suicide. He left no identification or explanation, just a single vexing clue to his agony, a one-line note that read: "I walk a lonely street."

Durden couldn't get the poor man's proclamation out of his head. "That just struck me as lonely," he remembered, "extremely lonely." It also struck Durden as a good idea for a blues song, but as hard as he tried, the lyrics and melody just weren't coming. He put aside the project temporarily, intending to take it to Mae Axton, whom Durden hoped might be able to help develop the idea.

Later that day the Swingbillies were booked for a radio show appearance in Jacksonville. After the gig Durden showed up with the newspaper at Axton's house on Dellwood Avenue. She told him she'd been so busy writing a magazine story that she'd not yet seen the day's paper.

"There is something in this that distresses me," Durden showed her. Clearly moved by the anonymous man's suicide and his notion of walking a lonely street, Durden told Axton, "It worries me to death."

"Think of the heartbreak he must have left behind him," Axton reflected. "So there ought to be a Heartbreak Hotel at the end of that lonely street."

From the visceral reaction of two people empathetic to a suicide victim's plight sprang the seeds of a rock and roll classic. According to the firsthand recollections of the two people who wrote it, this is how Elvis Presley's "Heartbreak Hotel" was created, in the front room of Mae Axton's home in the Jacksonville suburbs.

Mae Axton's house on Dellwood Avenue in Jacksonville, where she and Tommy Durden wrote "Heartbreak Hotel" and Glenn Reeves recorded the song demo. Courtesy of Mike Robinson.

"She sat down at the piano and I walked around and around," Durden remembered. "And within a half an hour we had it." In another version of the story, Durden claimed the song was written in exactly twenty-two minutes. Whatever the timing, the alchemy of Tommy Durden and Mae Axton one Saturday in the summer of 1955 was responsible for "Heartbreak Hotel." Then they went a step further.

Durden and Axton were so enthused by their new composition that they summoned local radio disc jockey and rockabilly performer Glenn Reeves to Axton's house to record a demo. Fresh from performing several shows with Presley on the Griffith tour, Reeves considered the stark, bluesy song silly and declined a songwriting credit.

"I'll be back in about thirty minutes," Reeves told the songwriting team. "But not to help on a crummy idea like that."

Undeterred, Durden took a crack at recording the initial version of the song, but he and Axton were disappointed with the result. Having worked so closely with Presley in the months previously, she wanted a more edgy, Presley-like demo to present to him. Feeling that Durden's version didn't have the dramatic and halting delivery she was looking for, when Reeves returned Axton pressed him to sing the song into the tape recorder in a style that Presley could relate to. As a favor to Axton, who had helped him land his job at WPDQ, Reeves set aside his disdain for the new tune and took a crack at recording it. While Reeves takes his imitation to the point of mocking Presley, the version Reeves sang that day reflected his own considerable talent and gave Presley a roadmap for how to sing the bluesy number.

Of Reeves's version Tommy Durden said, "Elvis was even breathing in the same places that Glenn did on the dub." Thanks to YouTube we can listen to Reeves's initial recording of "Heartbreak Hotel" laying the foundation for Presley to make music history. Reeves declined partial writing credit on the song, not wanting his name attached to it. He was not alone in his dislike for the stark and unusual number. Even the man revered for his golden ear, Sam Phillips, called the song "a morbid mess."

Many promising songs never see the light of day because they don't end up in the hands of people who can do something with them. That was where Axton's access to Presley proved so crucial. She called Bob Neal in Memphis and sent him a copy of the song, insisting that this would be the single to bring Presley his nationwide breakout. When she didn't get an immediate response, Axton shopped "Heartbreak Hotel" to the well-known country act Doyle and Teddy Wilburn. Given the Wilburn's style, heavy on steel guitar and high harmonies, they told Axton her song wasn't for them.

Later that year Axton saw Neal and Presley in person at a disc jockey convention in Nashville. When Neal told her he hadn't had time to play "Heartbreak Hotel" for the young singer, the strong-willed Axton invited them to her room, where she played them Reeves's version. Presley was hooked: "Hot darn Mae," he said. "Play it again."

After Axton obliged, Presley started singing along and that was that. He decided to record the song, likely as a favor to the woman who had been such a big help to him during both his early Florida tours. In return Axton extended to Presley one-third writing credit, alongside herself and Durden. In short order Presley would have the means to record it and the big-time record label needed to get it distributed nationwide.

The seeds of Presley's criticism of Sun Records' limited distribution in his July interview with Axton were no doubt planted by Tom Parker. In Ocala, radio manager Jim Kirk witnessed Parker's zealous promotion of Presley to the point of obsession. In Daytona Beach and elsewhere, Parker made a point of lavishing gifts on Presley in front of his parents, to assure them he cared about their son as more than a musical commodity.

Once Elvis himself was sold on Parker's ability to take his career to the next level, it was only a matter of time before he was able to convince his parents to sign off on Parker taking over as his manager. By then Presley with his V8-powered ambition was convinced Parker knew the path to big-time fame and fortune.

To seal the deal, Parker's biographer Alana Nash reported, Parker had called in his business partner and country headliner Hank Snow to assure Gladys Presley that he wasn't just some con man. With one contract in his right pocket and another in his left, Parker negotiated a deal with twenty-year-old Elvis Presley and his parents. One contract bound the performer to Hank Snow Enterprises–Jamboree Attractions, under whose auspices Presley had toured Florida.

The other contract, the one the Presleys signed, was strictly between them and Parker as "sole and exclusive Advisor, Personal Representative and Manager in any and all fields of public and private entertainment." Just like that, Snow's business partner cut him out of a deal with the kid who had upstaged him all through Florida; a contract that would have brought him millions had Snow been included. Parker even had the nerve to enlist Snow to make it happen.

Scotty and Bill would fare no better. Presley ended the original verbal financial arrangement he had with his bandmates, dating back to their days as the Blue Moon Boys, when the band split with Presley 50 percent on touring fees and recording revenues. Black supplemented his income by selling Presley photos for a quarter. "I'll have about four or five million of 'em, but if anybody'd like to have just one, why I'll have plenty of 'em," Black promised in a 1955 radio interview.

"Before the show, durin' the intermission, after the show, and fact is I might sell 'em out there all night long." Parker put a stop to that, taking control of concessions, often hocking Presley photos himself.

"At the time I couldn't put my finger on it," Scotty Moore wrote. "But the more Parker talked, the less I trusted him." Under the new deal they accepted, Scotty and Bill would receive $200 a week if the band was working and $100 if not. They were now salaried side men, no more, no less, but once and for all no longer bandmates with Presley. They watched from the sidelines as Parker's wheeling and dealing made everyone more money but them.

For Parker it was all about cash flow and control; the less standing Scotty and Bill had with Presley, the less influence they could exert on the star who was now, for all intents and purposes, their boss. Putting Scotty and Bill on salary left plenty of room for Parker's contractual part of the cut, 25 percent. Scotty and Bill's enthusiasm for a hot new drummer they hired, D. J. Fontana, was tempered with the knowledge that his pay would come from their earnings.

Presley's formalized alliance with Parker spelled the beginning of the end for the two men who had his backbeat during every landmark Sun recording; the men who had shown him the way during his very first club gig in Memphis when Presley was still a truck driver. It was the perfect good-cop bad-cop arrangement: Presley was the star and focal point, who left all the business and dirty work to Parker, who was hell bent on making sure he was the one and only person who had Elvis's ear and loyalty.

"As bad as things were going we didn't dwell on our troubles," recalled Scotty Moore. "We had shows to do and regardless of what was happening with Elvis and his management we were too busy to be distracted for long by Parker's not-so-subtle machinations."

Fontana, a good ol' boy from the Louisiana bayou, did not share the Memphis vibe of Elvis, Scotty, and Bill, but he had an endearing way about him that helped him fit right in. Now the boys had a big drumbeat to embolden their live sound and another man to take the wheel between one-nighters. The road was leading toward a tumultuous year ahead, and despite being marginalized, Scotty and Bill were still on board.

Parker kept the wheels turning on his master plan by starting a rumor that Presley's Sun Records contract was up for sale. Sun's impresario Sam Phillips, the man who was in the process of assembling the Million Dollar Quartet of Presley, Johnny Cash, Carl Perkins, and Jerry Lee Lewis, was not of a mind to part ways with Presley.

He threw out what he thought was an outrageous sum for which Presley's recording services could be had: $35,000. "I thought hey, I'll make 'em an offer that I know they will refuse, and then I'll tell 'em they'd better not spread this poison any more," Phillips said. "I absolutely did not think Tom Parker could raise the $35,000 and that would have been fine. But he raised the money, and damn, I couldn't back out then." Parker's persistence had edged out Hank Snow and Presley's Memphis manager Bob Neal; he had driven a wedge between Presley and his bandmates and had courted the star's parents; now his guile and business savvy spelled the end for Sam Phillips.

After much consternation and back and forth among RCA executives, the company put up the asking price, at that time the largest amount ever paid for a performer, which included a $5,000 bonus for Presley. With that Parker had done what he'd promised and brought what Presley coveted: a major record deal, which set the stage for his explosion onto the national charts and into popular culture.

On November 21, 1955, eleven days after Mae Axton presented "Heartbreak Hotel" to Presley in Nashville, a summit of RCA executives, Sam Phillips, Presley, and his parents gathered at Sun Studios in Memphis to finalize the new recording deal. "I feel Elvis is one of the most talented youngsters today," Phillips told a Memphis newspaper. "And by releasing his contract to RCA-Victor, we will give him the opportunity of entering the largest organization of its kind in the world, so his talents can be given the fullest opportunity."

In an interview early the following year Presley called the jump to RCA "my biggest thrill." He credited Parker with much of his success: "I don't think I'd have ever been very big if it wasn't for him. He's a

Photos and documents on the wall at Sun Records in Memphis commemorating Elvis Presley's move to RCA records. Photo by author.

very smart man." It was that sense of undying loyalty and obligation that ended up metastasizing Parker's influence in his career, binding Presley to him forever.

In an accompanying photograph Gladys Presley gives her son a congratulatory peck on the cheek. Looking on smiling, in a conservative suit and tie and with his hand on Mrs. Presley's shoulder, is the balding, portly man who made it all happen, the one-time Tampa dogcatcher turned kingmaker, Tom Parker.

For all of 1954 Presley reported $916.33 in income as a "semi-skilled" laborer. His wages in 1955 reflected all of Presley's hard work as a regional touring musician, jumping to $25,000. Other estimates have him making twice that much. Thanks largely to Parker's deal making, in 1956 Presley would earn $100,000 just to appear in his first film. Varying reports put his income anywhere from $280,000 into the millions.

Early in '56 Floridians had front-row seats to Presley's moonshot to fame. The "Hillbilly Cat" became "Kid Dynamite," transitioning from ballparks and livestock pens in smaller central Florida towns to ornate theaters in larger cities, cutting a much wider swath through the entire Sunshine State. Presley now had the confidence of knowing there were mountains of cash waiting on his path to stardom, guaranteeing that he would never have to return to the Memphis projects or a workaday life.

"In January 1956, the music of Elvis Presley was loosed upon the earth by one of the world's largest record companies," wrote author William McKeen. "The Elvis revolution had begun."

Presley's very first big-time recording session included the odd song that started with Tommy Durden's morning paper inspiration, was written in Mae Axton's living room, and was recorded there by Glenn Reeves, who wanted absolutely nothing to do with it. For so long, people have fixated on finding the real so-called Heartbreak Hotel where the anonymous man in the song died. It was nothing more than a figment of Mae Axton's imagination. The genuine history, however, involves the little house on Dellwood Avenue in Jacksonville where the song was written and recorded in a single day.

Axton capitalized on the success of "Heartbreak Hotel" to pursue a songwriting and record-producing career. She divorced, moved to Nashville, and founded her own label, eventually becoming a beloved figure in the music business. Her son Hoyt Axton went on to become a successful singer and actor who also wrote a song Presley recorded, "Never Been to Spain." Axton also tried to launch Reeves with other songs, but he never charted as a recording artist, moving on to a decades-long successful career in broadcasting and concert promotion.

Durden never again came close to that level of songwriting success; he was okay with that, outwardly at least: "I have come to the conclusion," said Durden, "that the good Lord only allows one 'Heartbreak Hotel' to the customer."

1956

Headlining

Concert handbill featuring Red Robertson's photo with Presley headlining his first Florida tour. Courtesy of Linda Moscato.

8

February 19–21

Tampa, West Palm Beach, Sarasota

For Presley's third Florida tour, February 19–26, 1956, he was eight months and light years removed from the twenty-year-old unknown who had stood at the railing in Daytona Beach, gawking at the ocean for the first time. During a grueling two-day, seven-show stand to begin this run, Presley returned to familiar territory; the Hesterly Armory in Tampa. Posters heralding his return featured Red Robertson's iconic photo taken in the same building. This time and tour, Tom Parker's playbill left no doubt that Presley was the star: "The most talked about new personality in the last ten years of recording music," the headline screamed. The full-on tsunami of Presleymania was coming, a handful of milestone national television appearances and a string of million-selling records away.

Presley now topped a stellar roster of musicians including the first family of country music, Mother Maybelle and the Carter Sisters. The godfathers of high lonesome harmonies, Charlie and Ira Louvin, headliners in their own right, also warmed up crowds, which grew more fervent for Presley at each stop. In another indication of how Scotty and Bill assumed more subservient roles as the backup band alongside drummer D. J. Fontana, they were now called the Blue Moon Boys and not listed by name.

The year 1956 had gotten off with a bang; the young singer celebrated turning twenty-one back home in Memphis on January 8. Two days later he strode into RCA's Nashville recording studio for the first time to begin his first session there. It had to be a combination of intimidation and satisfaction for Presley; only two years previously he had bombed during his first Nashville appearance at the Grand Ole Opry. From Sam Phillips's tiny Sun studio in Memphis, Presley was now in the big time. Guitar great Chet Atkins and piano master Floyd Cramer were there to fatten the sound alongside his regular bandmates.

These were far more workmanlike and rigid sessions compared to Sun's loose let's-have-a-cheeseburger-then-record-something atmosphere. During that session Presley tore through Tommy Durden and Mae Axton's dark tale of woe, "Heartbreak Hotel," following Glenn Reeves's version and taking it to a new level of rock, blues, and sex appeal.

Parker landed Presley his first national television exposure, booking him for a half dozen appearances on the CBS showcase, *Stage Show*. On concert playbills Parker made sure to add that Presley was now working with the *Stage Show*'s producer, comedy great Jackie Gleason. On January 27, the day before Presley's first nationally televised performance, RCA released "Heartbreak Hotel" as a single.

Live from CBS Studios in New York City, Cleveland disc jockey Bill Randle introduced Presley to his first-ever national television audience. "We think tonight that he's going to make television history for you," Randle correctly predicted. All the months of touring had built up to this moment, and Presley was in total command belting out "Shake, Rattle and Roll."

Presley's early *Stage Show* performances paved the way for his landmark appearances later that year with Milton Berle, Steve Allen, and Ed Sullivan. Presley's contract called for him to receive $1,250 for his initial *Stage Show* performance then bumped up to $1,500 for the final engagements of a successful run.

For all the criticism leveled at Parker for his disastrous business deals in Presley's later years, in these early days his shrewd wheeling and dealing in getting Presley to a major label, on national television, and to the brink of major stardom is undeniable. Neither of Presley's two previous managers, Bob Neal and Scotty Moore, had the contacts, the business acumen, or the nerve to do what Tom Parker had done in such a short time.

Presley was no longer the Hillbilly Cat oddball, the dynamic performer but square peg to country music fans and fellow performers. He was now creating his own brand of music and his own fan base. Presley's elevated status and non-traditional sound caused resentment among some of the stars now warming up for *him*.

Just before the tour reached Florida, the hot-tempered, hard-drinking Ira Louvin confronted Presley. As the young star quietly played one of his favorite gospel songs on a piano backstage, Louvin asked "why do you play that trash" out there? Some versions of the story have Louvin using a racial slur to describe Presley and his music.

"When I'm back here I play what I like," Presley shot back. "When I'm out there I play what they like."

In a 2009 interview Ira's brother Charlie Louvin said the two never came to blows, but it was close. Ira's criticism would prove costly to the brothers from Alabama. The Louvins' gospel tunes were always among Gladys Presley's favorites. "We went by her house and delivered our new album to her personally," Charlie Louvin recalled. Because of Ira's harsh criticism of him, Presley never recorded a Louvin Brothers song, and Charlie felt it was due to that backstage confrontation.

"That cost our catalogue millions," he lamented.

Parker drove the musicians hard. When a promoter oversold the show, Parker scheduled an extra concert without bothering to inform or compensate the performers. Determined not to be pushed around, the volatile Ira Louvin demanded that they be paid. Not about to be taken to task by a petulant musician, Parker canceled the extra concert, leaving hundreds of fans in line disappointed.

When Presley debuted "Heartbreak Hotel" on the February 18 episode of *Stage Show*, band director Tommy Dorsey insisted his orchestra accompany Presley. No matter how hard the young star pushed the tempo and intensity of the song, the orchestra could not or would not keep up. A trumpet solo in the middle was more like Taps for the song itself. Like Presley's first visit to the Opry, his first nationally televised performance of "Heartbreak Hotel" was a flop. Some artists on the current tour, jealous of the young star overshadowing them, delighted in watching Presley's song fizzle on television.

After the show, Presley and the band faced a grueling fifteen-hour drive from New York to Tampa to make the Sunday afternoon matinee show. "All we knew was drive, drive, drive," Moore recalled. Another new face to Presley's touring company was familiar; his old Memphis school chum and protector Red West, brought in to help handle the driving and security. West was among the earliest of Presley's entourage of constant companions; employees who became known as the Memphis Mafia.

In the days before luxurious tour buses where you could stretch out for some decent rest, in February 1956 it was still a bunch of men crammed into a sedan driving all the way down the eastern seaboard without the benefit of super highways. After three shows in Tampa, the band was due for four more the next day across the state in West Palm Beach. Sleep or no sleep, Presley's growing fan base expected the same raucous energy for the seven shows he was due to perform in the next forty eight-hours. With that kind of breakneck schedule, one can understand why some performers were tempted to use artificial stimulants to keep going.

In Tampa, headlining a concert still only meant a twenty-minute performance for Presley, perhaps stretching to a half hour. Despite the so-so rendition of "Heartbreak Hotel" on *Stage Show*, the single was starting to get some airplay. In a matter of days it would begin a climb to the top of the Billboard charts.

Red Robertson's photo of Presley taken at Tampa's Hesterly Armory in July was now the centerpiece of concert advertisements by the Nashville-based Hatch Show Prints. Original versions of the now classic playbills used to advertise Presley's 1956 concerts nationwide are highly collectible and can sell for tens of thousands of dollars.

More than 200 miles across the midsection of Florida, in West Palm Beach, was Presley's first theater venue; some referred to these as palaces. Tom Parker booked his young star and aspiring film actor in them as a way to stoke the fires of interest from West Coast film studio executives. As Parker's biographer pointed out, "Booking him into all of the Paramount-controlled theaters in Florida and up the East Coast, where the singer packed every one he played, the word couldn't help but get back to Paramount's top brass." As Presley's singing career took off that year, for better or worse, so did his acting. By the time he made his first appearance with Ed Sullivan late that summer, Presley was beginning work on his first film, *Love Me Tender*.

The Palms Theater at the corner of Clematis Street and Narcissus Avenue seated fourteen hundred. That meant well over five thousand people watched Presley during the course of two matinee and two evening concerts; the schedule called for shows at 2:00, 5:00, 7:00, and 9:00 p.m.—the first time Presley was called upon to perform four Florida shows in a single day. Given the amount of adrenaline and energy required for his concerts, on the heels of an already long week, that one day in West Palm Beach was grueling even by Presley's standards.

"All the girls were hooting and hollering," remembered Joyce Maloney of Lake Worth, who was nineteen when she and a friend saw Presley perform at the Palms. "He was doing something that no one had ever done before, rocking and rolling and doing all these gyrations."

After his second matinee Presley ducked out of the theater, and on the street he ran into Jim Ponce, who had just completed his day shift as front desk manager at the Pennsylvania Hotel, where the artists were staying. "Where can someone get a beer?" asked Presley, who was never much of a drinker. Ponce told the young singer he was headed down the street to the Marine Bar, a hangout for working-class painters and truck drivers in the tony downtown district of West Palm Beach.

"Can I go with you?" asked Presley.

As the two strode in that direction Presley, fresh from performances in the frigid Carolinas and New York City, said he liked being in West Palm Beach, especially for the warm weather. When the two men arrived at the Marine Bar, the bartender's reception of Presley was icy, demanding proof that the singer really was twenty-one.

"Don't you know who this is, this is Elvis Presley?" Ponce told him. After all, his name was on the Palms' marquee. "I don't care who he is," the unimpressed bartender replied. "He needs a card."

Dejected at being unable to help Presley grab a beer between performances, Ponce walked him back to the hotel. Within moments an abrupt and unhappy Tom Parker appeared. Without saying a word to Ponce or even having the courtesy to acknowledge his presence, Parker demanded to know where Presley had been and ordered him back into the hotel.

To Ponce it was clear that Presley hadn't told anyone where he was going before he tried to step down the block for a cold drink. He still had a pair of evening concerts to perform, and the teetotaling all-business Parker acted like an angry parent. "He came on so heavy," Ponce said of Parker. "Elvis sort of cowed down a little. He acted like he was scared of him."

Generations after what he calls his "two-block walk with Elvis," Jim Ponce remembered how he was able to spend time with Presley, even go into a crowded bar with him, without anyone taking a second look. Though Presley's star was beginning to rise fast, no one stopped him for a picture or autograph. Remarkably, despite performing four shows in one day to five thousand fans, he was still able to walk the street between shows like the blue-collar worker he used to be.

"I'm ninety-seven, no wait, ninety-six, no need to rush things," deadpanned Ponce, who was waiting for his clothes washer to click off. "I guess at the time I was disappointed I didn't get to drink a beer with him," he recalled of that late afternoon walk with Presley. The former hotel man of seventy years had another regret. "I thought my God, I should have saved the sheets he slept on." Many hotel managers did just that, and cut them up and sold them to rabid fans looking for any souvenir of Presley.

The same held true for that no-nonsense bartender who refused the young singer a drink. Some weeks later, when Presley became much better known, the bartender asked Ponce: "When I turned that young man down, was that really Elvis Presley?" Ponce assured him it was and pointed to the elevated piano behind the round bar. "I said, 'he most likely would have been singing for us.'" The stunned bartender was left to ponder what could have been, the afternoon he bounced Elvis Presley from the Marine Bar in West Palm Beach.

Within hours of the evening's last performance, Presley and his road warrior bandmates traversed the heart of south-central Florida once more, around the state's largest inland body of water, Lake Okeechobee, bound for Sarasota and four more shows, 175 miles away. To keep them company in such a desolate part of Florida, all-night disc jockey Jerry Wichner spun top-forty tunes on WINZ-AM out of Miami (pronounced "Myam-uh" by locals). Truth be told, Wichner did much more talking than spinning and quickly became a late night fixture to love struck teens and a legion of other dedicated listeners. Within the first seventy-two hours of his latest Florida tour, Elvis Presley performed eleven shows in three cities on two coasts. Later in the week, more shows were booked to the north, crisscrossing the Florida-Georgia border.

Another grand movie palace awaited Presley's arrival in Sarasota. Located at 61 North Pineapple Avenue, the Mediterranean Revival–style Florida Theater made the transition from silent films to talkies. Vaudeville legends like W. C. Fields and Will Rogers performed when it opened as the Edwards Theater in 1926. On January 31, 1952, Dorothy Lamour, Betty Hutton, and Charlton Heston attended the world premiere of Cecil B. DeMille's *The Greatest Show on Earth*, filmed the year before in Sarasota. Today the theater, with its grand three-story atrium, is home to the Sarasota Opera.

This theater, with its elegant environs, represented the most ornate Florida venue Presley had headlined to date; quite a step up from performing on a flatbed trailer in a livestock pen. A bastion of culture, especially in the winter season, Sarasota had a muted response to Presley. Ads in the *Sarasota Herald* listed show times of 2:15, 4:30, 7:45, and 9:45; tickets were 76 cents for the early shows and a dollar apiece for the evening concerts. Although "Heartbreak Hotel" had been out for weeks, the ads list "I Forgot to Remember to Forget" and "Mystery Train" as singles fans would recognize. There is no indication that Presley's arrival drew as much as a small preview article.

"The biggest commotion Elvis created here," remembered Sarasota County's archivist Mark D. Smith, "was when he broke a string and a young girl was sent dashing down to Roehr's Machine Shop, then on Main Street, for an 'A' string for his guitar." An editorial in the *Sarasota Journal* noted Presley's allegedly less than kind behavior toward a group of female fans backstage. Without giving a hint of specifics about the offenses in question, the editorial was but a glimpse of criticism to come.

"There are naturally an abundance of clean-living, unscandalized homebodies in the entertainment world," the editorial board writer concluded. "But apparently the constant exposure to the temptations that go with 'show business' have exploded any moral sense many of them were trained to in their childhood." The holier-than-thou attitude of editorial writers and columnists of the day, based on innuendo and secondhand information, is appalling.

In an era when all-night fast food places were not yet the norm, Presley and his bandmates caught a lot of late-night meals at truck stops and spent a lot of early mornings slugging down black coffee in local diners. In Sarasota the boys took a liking to a breakfast place on Washington Boulevard, the Waffle Stop, showing up the morning of their appearance at the Florida Theater, then returning once more the day after.

Waitress Edith Barr Dunn watched a group of men pull up and vault out of a convertible pink Cadillac, no doors necessary. Wearing black high-waisted trousers, a white shirt with cuffs rolled at the wrists, and his coiffed jet-black hair, Presley took a seat on a stool at the far end of the counter, followed by his bandmates.

"If you give me good service, I'll give you a good tip," Presley promised the attractive early-thirty-something waitress. He ordered three eggs, three bacon strips, home fried potatoes, and three glasses of milk. "Ma'am," he continued, typical of the way he addressed older people even though in this case the twenty-one-year-old was flirting, "your skirt should be shorter because your gams are too pretty . . . you have a nice smile."

True to his word, Presley left a fifty-cent tip. The second morning he toyed with Barr Dunn again. "If you remember what I ordered yesterday, I'll give you another big tip." After another meal of bacon and eggs, and signing two 8 × 10 photos, Presley and the boys were back in the Cadillac headed northbound on the Tamiami Trail for the night's show just over the state line in Waycross, Georgia.

As time progressed and Presley's star rose, owners of the Waffle Stop made sure everyone knew he had stopped there twice on his march to fame, to eat breakfast and flirt with Barr Dunn, who came to be known as the "Queen of the Waffle Stop." Well into her nineties, people continued to ask what it was like meeting the young Elvis.

To say Barr Dunn was unimpressed with him is an understatement. "I thought he was conceited," she recalled decades after she served the king of rock and roll. "He was just a flirt." As for the photos Presley left behind the second morning he came in, Barr Dunn didn't think much of them: "I stuck 'em on the service station where we kept all the syrups."

Today big signs blaze to people passing by the Waffle Stop, "Elvis Ate Here." Kitschy memorabilia items adorn the walls; an animatronic plastic head of Presley in dark sunglasses greets patrons with funny quips. It's fun, to be sure. But there's also a certain sadness about the place—not because it's old, not because it seems frozen in yesteryear. It's as if the restaurant is an homage to the caricature Presley became, rather than a celebration of the flirtatious and dynamic working musician Presley was at the time he passed through, on the brink of enormous hits and history-making television appearances.

And there's little or no mention of the men who were with him; the two who split the atom with Presley at the birth of rock and roll, Scotty Moore and Bill Black.

Though the Waffle Stop is bigger than it used to be, you can still sit right at the curving breakfast counter where Presley sat decades ago; a quick stop along the ghost road where his Cadillac streaked toward north Florida and another history-making concert to be emblazoned in the mind of a nine-year-old boy destined to make music history himself.

The Florida-Georgia Line, February 22–26

Waycross, Jacksonville, Pensacola

As Presley continued to barnstorm Florida in 1956, both girls and boys were moved in profound ways by seeing him; in some cases akin to a religious experience, or a milepost in time from which there was no going back. "He prowled the stage like a big jungle cat," wrote the late Memphis music legend Jim Dickinson in his memoir. "I talked about the show for months. I described it in detail to friends and family whenever I got a chance, spreading the new religion of the King of Rock and Roll, or as George Klein would say, 'Elvis himselvis.'"

Presley's backing band had a similar effect on the lives of ambitious young would-be musicians. Norbert Putnam, who went on to play bass on numerous Presley recordings, including his 1973 Stax sessions, said of Bill Black: "He was my first bass hero. He was a god to me."

"Scotty Moore was my icon," wrote Keith Richards, recalling the night he heard Moore's stark, echo-heavy licks on "Heartbreak Hotel" via Radio Luxembourg. "I'd have died and gone to Heaven just to play like that. How the hell was that done?"

On February 22, 1956, nine-year-old Gram Connor waited for Elvis Presley and his band to complete the five-hour, 320-mile drive from Sarasota to tiny Waycross, Georgia; one of two dates over the state line during Presley's third Florida tour. As "Heartbreak Hotel" started to get more and more airplay, Presley made the song a dramatic, one-syllable opening to his live shows:

"Weeeeell..."

With that the audience of about five hundred jammed into Waycross City Auditorium shrieked in unison. Sitting close to the front of the stage, fourth grader Gram Connor was fascinated. "He came on and the whole place went bonkers," he recalled, "It all penetrated my mind." The next day the Connor boy started slicking back his hair with Brylcream and wearing bright clothes, more like Presley's stage wardrobe. This scenario played out over and over as young boys across America were moved by Elvis Presley's unique star power; by the raw sexuality in his movements and obvious effect it had on young girls. For boys like Gram Connor, being like Elvis became the roadmap to coolness—and girls.

"From that day on," local Waycross musician and music historian Billy Ray Herrin said, "Gram started learning as much as he could about rock and roll and he began to write songs." He held Saturday morning music parties for the local kids and started performing like Elvis on his front porch. This was no mere ripple effect of seeing Presley; it was as if Elvis cannon-balled right offstage into a tide pool of impressionable kids; latter-day musicians, songwriters, and soon-to-be lifelong devotees.

After the loss of his father, Gram's mother remarried and Gram Connor became Gram Parsons. In 1959, after moving from Waycross to Winter Haven, Florida, Parsons joined a succession of garage bands sprouting up all over the peninsula. Call it the Elvis effect, and as Presley's star grew, that effect became magnified in ways even Presley himself could not have imagined. The line-up Parsons saw that night in Waycross—Presley, Charlie and Ira Louvin, and Mother Maybelle and the Carter Sisters—formed a foundation for the unique

The author with Charlie Louvin in Waycross, Georgia, inside City Auditorium prior to its renovation. Courtesy of Mike Robinson.

genre-bending brand of music Parsons pioneered; he was the first musician to go full-on into synthesizing country and rock music.

In 1968 America's most important band at the time, the Byrds, hired Parsons as a side man and, thanks to his vision, recorded the first full-length country rock record in Nashville. They made history as the first rock and roll band to perform live at the Grand Ole Opry. As with Presley's less-than-stellar outcome there in 1954, the Byrds were so ahead of their time that the audience didn't know what to think and gave them a tepid reception at best.

When Parsons recorded *GP*, his first of two landmark solo records in 1972, as an homage to the man who had inspired him, he hired Presley's backup musicians known as the TCB Band (short for Takin' Care of Business) and an unknown folk singer named Emmylou

Harris. Parsons is considered the avatar of country rock or alt-country and launched Harris's Country Music Hall of Fame career. Though Parsons died at just twenty-six in 1973, his contributions to contemporary music are far-reaching.

The organizer of the annual Gram Parsons Memorial Guitar Pull in Waycross, Georgia, says the spirit of Gram Parsons and young Elvis are intertwined. "To say Gram Parsons was impressed with Elvis Presley would be putting it lightly," event organizer Dave Griffin said. Many musicians who come to Waycross to play the tribute event perform Elvis songs that Parsons covered, "in tribute to two music icons."

In 2009 Charlie Louvin, who opened for Elvis that historic night in 1956, returned to Waycross to headline the memorial concert to Parsons. Though the inside of City Auditorium had fallen into disrepair, and the stage upon which both he and Presley performed was boarded up, Louvin took a seat in front of it and recalled the rise of rock and roll's crown prince. "I always thought Elvis was a fad," Louvin opined, "until I saw women as old as my mother outside the rail fence down on their knees pulling grass out of Presley's yard. I knew then it wasn't a fad. He was huge; big as you could get."

Not wanting to lose the spirit of that historic Presley-to-Parsons musical connection, Waycross city leaders embarked on a $1.5 million renovation of the 15,000-square-foot 1937 auditorium. By 2015 City Auditorium was reborn; the stage where young Elvis performed is once again shiny and wide open for all to use and admire, framed in brown with a white wall backdrop. In the Waycross venue where it happened, the history of young Elvis forging his way through the south to fame and passing the torch to young Gram Connor is well preserved.

In 1956 the pause in a little railroad town just over the Georgia border was another of many one-nighters for Presley and the boys, on a road with no clear destination beyond the next gig, and then the next. As they neared the end of the third Florida tour, the workload was getting to Presley. Since the nationally televised Sunday night performance on February 19 in New York City, his tour had been a blur. Each stop meant multiple headlining shows then back in the car to cover hundreds of miles overnight to make it to the next stop. By the time he had traveled from Waycross back down to Jacksonville, Florida, on Thursday the 23rd, Presley collapsed. The doctor at Baptist Memorial Hospital diagnosed exhaustion and told Presley to get some rest. Upon his release, Presley smiled and said the constant attention from nurses made getting rest a tough order to follow.

The Elvis Presley show went on as scheduled on Friday night. During the two-night Jacksonville stand, Presley performed "Heartbreak Hotel," the song about to vault his career into the stratosphere, live in the town where it had been written and recorded in Mae Axton's front room just six months previously. On Saturday the band embarked on a mind-numbing twelve-hour, eight-hundred-mile road trip from northeast Florida to Shreveport in the northwest corner of Louisiana for the Saturday night *Louisiana Hayride* show.

To up-and-coming musicians, the *Hayride* represented the chance to become known in a way the more heralded and exclusive Opry did not. The *Hayride* did not require performers to be established and have hit records; they could play electrified instruments and be who they were, in contrast to what the Opry folks expected them to be. The *Hayride* nurtured Presley in the formative days of his career, and he remained under contract to perform there until the end of the year. By this time in 1956, the logistics of getting there to fulfill his obligations could be hell.

Live on KWKH-AM from the Shreveport Memorial Municipal Auditorium on the same show where Hank Williams first gained a radio audience in 1949, and where Presley's future guitarist James Burton started playing when he was just fourteen, on February 25, 1956, Presley blasted out "Heartbreak Hotel" as far as the 50,000-watt signal would take him. Shortly after Presley and his band were off the air, they loaded up and headed back east to fulfill one more tour stop in the Sunshine State.

As an example of how Presley was still a megastar-in-waiting, during this entire frenetic week in and around Florida, there was minimal press coverage. Although his big new single was gaining airplay,

"Heartbreak Hotel" did not enter the Billboard charts until the week after the end of his third Florida tour. Presley was still on the brink, grinding out a living and catching fire by word of mouth one broadcast, one disc jockey, one promoter, one concert, one small town at a time. When Tom Parker booked Presley for his first-ever concert in Pensacola, it had to spark bittersweet, even harrowing memories; part of Parker's reinvention meant burying his past in the Florida panhandle town.

10

The Promoter and Deserter

February 26, 1956

Pensacola, a picturesque maritime town on the western reaches of Florida's panhandle, home to the navy's world-famous Blue Angels, has a history rife with storybook tales of sunken ships, deadly hurricanes, and tragic endings. A generation before he booked Elvis Presley to play the town's stately bay front auditorium in 1956, Tom Parker endured the most trying episode of his life here, leaving him broken in many ways. The fact that he bounced back to build such a mythic, successful career based largely on deceit and outright lies is testimony to his resiliency, guile, and work ethic. As a young soldier he brought it all on himself.

In September 1932 U.S. Army Private First Class Parker slipped away from Fort Barrancas, a stark hilltop battery overlooking Pensacola Bay: a serious military transgression. The Army listed him as AWOL and after a week stripped Private Parker of his first-class rank. After a month Parker was classified as a deserter; a criminal who had turned his back on his sacred duty to country. His biographer Alanna Nash speculated that Parker had run off with the Ringling Brothers and Barnum and Bailey circus, which happened to be passing through town at the time Parker left his post.

Bay front Municipal Auditorium, Pensacola. State Archives of Florida, *Florida Memory*, https://www.floridamemory.com/items/show/64409.

It was five more months before he returned to the base, hat in hand, asking for leniency. Twenty-three years to the month before he returned to Pensacola backing the young man well on his way to becoming the country's new rock and roll sensation, Tom Parker was thrown into the guardhouse jail at Fort Barrancas to serve a sixty-day sentence in solitary confinement. For a natural-born schmoozer and future showman brimming with wanderlust and ambition, Tom Parker was left to contemplate his desertion, having landed himself in a personal hell.

When Parker reemerged from the dark, dank miserable place in April 1933, he was an emotional and psychological wreck. Doctors at the base deemed him psychotic and prone to emotional outbursts and transferred him to psychiatric lockdown at Walter Reed Medical Center in Washington, D.C. Staff doctors there concluded it was not just the jail stint that had caused twenty-four-year-old Parker to come unhinged; they diagnosed him with "Emotional instability" and "Psychosis, psychogenic depression."

In 1933 the United States Army officially branded Tom Parker a psychopath.

By August doctors approved Parker's return to society but never again as a soldier. Within two years he had drifted back to Florida. In Tampa, where traveling circus and carnival shows spent warm winters, people of questionable backgrounds could join with few questions asked. This was how the military misfit and illegal alien began to build the Tom Parker persona into a remarkable, larger-than-life American success story.

All those years later, in 1956, the nightmare he had gone through must have been on Parker's mind as he performed advance work for Presley, showing up in Pensacola a day or two early to visit radio station disc jockeys and newspaper offices. He must have flashed back to the harrowing memories of his imprisonment in the military fort carved into the bluff guarding Pensacola Harbor, a fort with cavelike brickwork staircases and claustrophobic low-slung ceilings. Spending week upon week confined in such a frightening place dating back to the late eighteenth century, where paranormal activity is routinely reported, had to make Parker feel lost among the ghosts of doomed soldiers in a modern-day medieval dungeon. It's easy to see how anyone, no matter how strong psychologically, could go mad. After his solitary confinement there, even the low moments of his sometimes hardscrabble promoter's life still had to be far better in comparison.

For weeks and months at a time Parker withstood the grind of life on the road, staying in run-down motels away from his devoted wife Marie, performing the thankless duties that come with building an entertainer's career. Parker's zeal for work so transient can be better understood knowing he came from nothing. His monumental success once the gates of hell reopened at Fort Barrancas was every bit as unlikely as Presley's.

Parker's vocal critics, like Ira Louvin, and those who didn't trust him, like Scotty Moore, would have given anything to know the truth about "Colonel" Tom Parker. Louvin tried and failed to get extra money for artists opening for Presley. This humiliating chapter in

Parker's past would have provided validation of the mistrust Moore and Gladys Presley had felt for Parker ever since he inserted himself into Presley's career and began to isolate the entertainer from anyone deemed a potential adversary or rival in promoting Presley.

To Moore, the straight-laced, no-nonsense guitarist, honorably discharged from the U.S. Navy, this would have been what he needed to get Parker out of the picture like a bad memory. In the ultra-conservative days of Communist paranoia fueled by Wisconsin senator Joseph McCarthy, when critics' scorn of Presley's effect on American youth reached its zenith, Parker's past would have been blood in the water to any number of critics. Had Parker's secrets, his desertion, psychological diagnosis, and illegal alien status gotten out, they would have derailed and doomed the Presley phenomenon before it ever got off the ground. Gladys Presley would never have approved of her boy being associated with someone once labeled a psychopath. Presley's place in American music history—if he achieved one at all—would have been far different had Tom Parker's past been exposed.

Even in an era long before instant online background checks and decades-old military records being just one Freedom of Information Act request away, it is still remarkable that Parker was able to bury it all. By the time Presley's first headlining tour reached the panhandle of Florida, that crisis was but a distant memory for his gruff, hard-charging manager.

Elvis and the boys pulled into Pensacola on February 26, 1956, after the long-haul drive from Shreveport. For each of the day's three concerts at 2:00, 5:00, and 8:00 p.m., adults paid $1.25 and kids 50 cents. A photograph taken that evening showed how sparse the set-up still was: Presley stands center stage wearing a light-colored jacket, Bill Black is on his left on the stand-up bass, Scotty Moore flanks his right, and D. J. Fontana is directly behind with a small drum kit. The auditorium, constructed at the end of a manmade peninsula at 900 South Palafox Street, was only a year old when Presley and his band made their first and only appearances there. It stood for fifty years until a direct hit from Hurricane Ivan in 2004 rendered the building too badly damaged to be saved.

Presley on stage with Scotty Moore, Florida, 1956. Courtesy of Linda Moscato.

The Pensacola concerts marked the end of another historic and intense run in and around Florida for Elvis, Scotty, Bill, and D.J.: nineteen shows in seven days covering three states, driving more than two thousand miles. After run-ins Ira Louvin had with Parker and Presley during the tour, this show also marked the last time the Louvin brothers opened for Presley. The fact that Presley was playing several of these cities for the first time could help explain why the reception for him in places like West Palm Beach, Sarasota, and Pensacola was more muted.

Everything changed in March when Tommy Durden and Mae Axton's song "Heartbreak Hotel," the single Sam Phillips and Glenn Reeves scorned, started its slow march to the top of the charts. By

March 7 Billboard reported it had sold 300,000 copies. By the end of March, "Heartbreak Hotel" broke into the top ten at number 9. On May 5 Presley had his first nationwide number 1 smash, and it remained in that spot until late June. The song's success, followed by highly rated, controversial, and at times humiliating national television appearances that summer opened the floodgates. Only Beatlemania in 1964 would be comparable to the Presley phenomenon of 1956.

"'Heartbreak Hotel' zoomed Elvis' star to the high heavens nationally," wrote Mae Axton, the woman who had practically held Presley's hand through his first Florida tour a year earlier. In March Presley bought his parents a new house on Audubon Street in the Memphis suburbs. Knowing he had taken his parents out of the projects and looming poverty and into a home with its very own swimming pool had to give the young performer immense satisfaction. That same month Presley's first full-length LP was released, featuring Red Robertson's cover shot of Presley taken in Tampa on July 31, 1955.

The last vestiges of Presley's early days ended when his Memphis-based manager Bob Neal quietly stepped out of the picture for good, leaving Tom Parker with the complete control he coveted. Given all he had done to move Presley to a bigger label, a national audience, and a rich man's income, Parker deserved it. Presley's next Florida tour in the stormy, sweltering summer of 1956 reflected everything Parker had done to bring him fame and fortune; by then, Elvis Presley was on fire.

PRESLEYMANIA

August 1956

11

A Tsunami Storms Ashore

August 3–4, Miami

The full-on, white-hot onset of Presleymania began in Florida in August 1956, more than a month *before* Presley's first *Ed Sullivan Show* appearance. In June and July he appeared on national television on Milton Berle's show and the *Steve Allen Show*. Berle made fun of Presley's music, to be sure, but it was Allen who took it to an unnecessary extreme by having Presley dress in formal attire and sing his new hit "Hound Dog" to an actual Bassett Hound.

Presley's good nature throughout a humiliating appearance paid big dividends when his next single, "I Want You, I Need You, I Love You," became another number 1 Billboard smash. His debut album became the first of the rock and roll genre to top the Billboard charts, spending ten weeks at number 1. In the summer of 1956 Elvis Presley was a bona fide national phenomenon.

"Who wasn't aware of Elvis in 1956?" asked Florida's former governor Bob Graham, a freshman at the University of Florida that year. "Just being alive, breathing, walking around, you were familiar with Elvis, he was kind of a pervasive cultural figure."

The timing could not have been better. In 1956 there were 13 million teenagers in America with spending power of $7 billion; a massive legion of young people with the money to go to concerts and buy records and record players as never before. That year Tom Parker arranged for more than fifty licenses of Presley merchandise, eventually raking in an estimated $40 million in retail sales. Some 80 percent of the dolls, charm bracelets, diaries, and miniature pink Cadillacs were marketed to teen girls. Elvis Presley memorabilia was big business.

The rising star spent much of July vacationing in the small Gulf of Mexico resort town of Biloxi, Mississippi, with his girlfriend June Juanico (pronounced "juan-ee-coh"), the beautiful brunette who had caught his eye when he performed at a military base there the year before. As an indication of Presley's growing love, his parents traveled to Biloxi to meet Juanico's divorced mother. Photographs taken during the trip showing a shirtless Presley, his hair mussed, making him look like a typical American youngster of the era. In home movies his parents join the young couple and a group of other friends on an offshore fishing trip.

Presley had an underlying motive for bringing his parents along on his summer vacation. After much cajoling from him and assurances from Gladys Presley that her son was a good boy, June's mother gave permission for her daughter to go on the road with Presley during his upcoming Florida tour, with the caveat that she be accompanied by one of her girlfriends. Knowing this would not go over well with his domineering manager Tom Parker, Presley wanted to try to keep Juanico's presence on the tour a secret. Given the amount of attention Presley was getting in the national press thanks to his breakout hit records and television appearances, that notion was impossible.

"He's already told me about seeing too much of you," Presley told Juanico in a moment of total candor. "He'll shit a brick if he sees you in Florida." Nonetheless, the two went on with their clandestine plan, foolish though it may have been to think they could keep any aspects of his dating life a secret now that Presley was the hottest act in American music.

Throughout the most historic phase of Presley's time in Florida, the brash, intelligent, and observant Juanico was along to provide an intimate account of Presley's life in the eye of a hurricane. He was still years away from finding the girl he would eventually marry, Priscilla Beaulieu, whom he met while serving in the army in Germany, well out of the clutches of Parker, who remained stateside. Had it not been for Parker's overbearing control at this stage of Presley's career, Juanico might have had a chance to be The One.

"I'm the first one to say there would have been no Elvis without Colonel Parker," said producer Steve Binder, who clashed with Parker repeatedly during the making of Presley's 1968 comeback special. He watched Parker's attempts at total control of his client, personally and professionally. "Bully is a good word," said Binder. "They're going to push as hard as they can until someone says no. It was amazing to me the whole hierarchy of show business bowed to his demands."

Presley's fourth Florida tour in fifteen months called for the most grueling and profitable stretch yet, barnstorming the peninsula south to north: seven cities, nine days, twenty-five shows, 63,000 fans, and a gross conservatively estimated at $100,000. It was all big cities and swank theaters, starting with his first-ever live shows in Miami, Florida's closest thing to the big time.

"Miami bustles under a golden sun as warm as a woman's embrace," wrote Jack Kofoed in *Moon Over Miami*. "The sun shines on jockies in multicolored silks booting thoroughbreds down the homestretch at Hialeah; on golfers, water skiers, and vacationers; on high-busted slim-legged girls in postage stamp bathing suits lolling along its beaches." When the moon came up, a constellation of talent shone: Nat King Cole, Jackie Gleason, Ella Fitzgerald, and Sinatra held court in grand rooms like the Fontainebleau's La Ronde on Miami Beach or Pompeii in the Eden Roc.

The cool, debonair Sinatra, who had drawn strong reactions from young girls when he debuted a generation earlier, made no attempt to hide his vitriol for rock and roll and its new crown prince. "His kind of music is deplorable, a rancid smelling aphrodisiac," opined Sinatra of Presley and his music. "It fosters almost totally negative and destructive reactions in young people."

"Sinatra was on the way out and this was a giant threat to him," said Linda Moscato, a South Florida teen at the time Presley came to

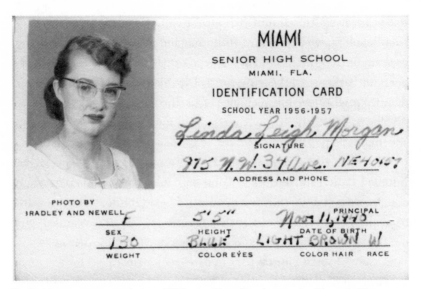

Linda Moscato, pictured circa 1956, saw Elvis Presley at the Olympia Theater. Courtesy of Linda Moscato.

town. Hers was a world of classical music and a staid, regimented life dominated and directed by her parents. That is, until she listened to "Heartbreak Hotel" at a downtown Miami department store. It was a turning point in her life, and Moscato's parents didn't like what they saw or heard.

"Elvis was a breaking out," said Moscato, her voice taking on the vibrancy of that time. "It was like a new world and everything opened up like a flower from a bud, to a full flower. We woke up as people and individuals." Before, there was not a lot to look forward to, but now Presley was coming on like a shimmering streamliner pulling into the Florida East Coast station. When they heard Presley was booked for seven shows at the Olympia Theater, Moscato and her teenage friends were determined to go.

Miami columnist Herb Rau shared the growing contempt adults felt for the new phenomenon. "Every delinquent kid in town—plus many who aren't delinquents but are fascinated by a duck-tailed hairdo playing the guitar and squirming his hips—will be on hand Friday and Saturday."

Florida State Theaters, Rau reported, hired a dozen policemen and even a few firemen to guard Presley during his Miami run, "to prevent the kind of disorders and near riots that characterized Presley's personal appearances elsewhere." Tom Parker, ever cognizant of fanning the flames of controversy, said he turned down an invitation for Presley to stay at the ritzy Fontainebleau, for fear of the damage his adoring fans might cause.

"The Pelvis is due to arrive in Miami Friday morning," Rau sniped, "unless he's arrested again for speeding." What Rau and other columnists could not deny was the money Presley raked in. "We've had the biggest advance sale of tickets for anything we've staged here," Rau quoted the head of Florida State Theaters. Thirty percent of those sales went to adult women.

"Don't expect him for a rehearsal," boasted Parker to theater management. "He just doesn't need a rehearsal. He'll go on stage and kill 'em."

The Olympia Theater, Miami, circa 1926. Photo by W. A. Fishbaugh, State Archives of Florida, *Florida Memory*, https://www.floridamemory.com/items/show/30144.

Elvis Presley on stage at the Olympia Theater. Reprinted by permission of Charles Trainor Jr.

The Olympia provided as ornate a venue as South Florida had to offer. Built in 1926 as a grand silent movie palace in the Vaudeville era, the Olympia featured Moorish architecture and a simulated night sky that provided a dramatic, dreamlike setting. Said to be South Florida's first air-conditioned building, the Olympia provided welcome luxury for Presley's fans who would spend hours in the heat and humidity.

"He'll never last," said Linda Moscato's mother, dismissing the Presley phenomenon. Despite reservations about allowing her daughter to be part of such a raucous atmosphere, she gave her permission for Linda to attend the concert, with one admonition. "Just don't end up in the newspaper," she warned.

On August 3 fans starting lining up outside the Olympia at 4:00 a.m., almost a full twelve hours before Presley's first matinee performance. Black and white photos show young girls looking as though they're headed to church or a special dance: hair done, and some wearing pearls and white gloves. Photo captions also referred to Presley dismissively as "the Pelvis." One girl had cut short her New Orleans vacation to see Presley. There she stood with a tissue-wrapped box containing a stuffed rabbit and money as presents for Presley.

Jim Ponce, the West Palm Beach hotel manager who tried unsuccessfully to buy Presley a beer during his February appearance at the

The crush of fans outside the Olympia Theater. Reprinted by permission of Charles Trainor Jr.

Palms Theater, was also in attendance at the Olympia. Ponce's boss asked, "For one hell of a favor, would you drive my son down to Miami to see Elvis Presley?" If nothing else, Ponce would score some brownie points with the boss and see for himself what all the fuss was about.

Also at the Olympia during Presley's historic run was the studious South Florida teen Bob Graham, who had an inkling of the history he and others were about to witness. "It was an exciting night," he recalled more than two generations later. "People were aware they were going to be entertained by somebody who was special. I don't think we appreciated how iconic he was going to be."

On his manager's orders Presley arrived a day early, navigating his new lavender Lincoln Premiere down US 1. The day of his first show, as usual he hadn't left much time between arriving at the venue and his 3:30 matinee. By the time the doors had opened, the line of teens zigzagged well down the block, cooking in Florida's August sun. Unlike most of Presley's previous Florida shows, all the concerts on this tour were treated like the historic events they became: reporters, photographers, and columnists documented nearly every moment of Presleymania. *Miami News* writer Bella Kelly managed to get into Presley's suite at the Robert Clay Hotel. As he prepared to take a morning nap before a long day of performing before thousands of screaming teens, Presley was asked if he ever really wore blue suede shoes.

"I don't wear 'em cause there's too many people wantin' to stomp all over 'em when I do," Presley declared while reading comics in the morning newspaper. "Except for his gold and brown sideburns," Kelly wrote, "Presley was dressed all in black—like the clerk he sings about in his 'Heartbreak Hotel' record." Presley said these days he preferred black, having "got sick" of the color pink. Nonetheless he performed his first Miami show in a pink jacket.

Backstage a circle of five people chosen by the *Miami Herald*, two adult journalists and three students, the youngest just twelve, were charged with trying to analyze what made the country's rock and roll phenomenon tick. Judging from the way fans were screaming and shrieking, they knew the young king was arriving. Before an exhausting schedule of three concerts that first day, Presley had to face more inquiring minds and more questions right up until show time.

"He knew he was being heckled when he was asked questions of politics, art, current events and classical music," noted one young female interviewer. "He dropped his gaze like a boy in school who hadn't studied and tried to give some answer." That led another student interviewer, Luther Voltz Jr., to conclude, "Golly Presley doesn't know anything about the news. . . . I just thought he was kind of dumb." Presley's knowledge of culture and current events was the last thing on the minds of the throng of teenagers waiting for him to perform.

The Olympia's luxurious environs amped up the anticipation: "Velvet curtains and marble fountains, not really a place you would expect to see Elvis," Linda Moscato remembered. "But it did add an extra element of drama." A half hour after the show was set to begin, fresh from his current events quiz, Presley staggered onto the stage "like a drunken Brando," one reporter noted. Just the sight of Presley in his pink jacket, open-collar shirt, black pants, and white shoes brought a crescendo of roaring adulation from the crowd. Jim Ponce was flabbergasted: "Believe me, I wasn't ready for those kids running up and down the aisles screaming and carrying on. It was quite a revelation to see what was happening."

Juanico stood watching in the wings, also not prepared for the hysteria she was witnessing. Just a year previously when she met Presley at a club show he performed in her hometown, the level of interest had been nothing like this. "I knew the effect he had on me," she recalled. "But seeing so many girls go completely wild was a little frightening." When she retreated to Presley's dressing room, the door was locked. From the sounds inside, it soon became clear that Presley's driver and bodyguard Red West was having sex with one of Presley's titillated fans.

Moscato, in her Sunday-best dress, shoes, and cat's-eye glasses, was in the middle of the screaming crowd right up close to the stage: "It's imprinted on my mind," she said. "The crowd was wild, absolutely wild, everybody was screaming so much you could hardly hear what he was singing." Presley and his bandmates were having a blast; enjoying the rocketship ride to who knew where. Bill Black slapped and twirled his stand-up bass, hooting and hollering back at the crowd. Presley shimmered, jumping, singing, shouting. "His legs were like rubber on stage," said Moscato. Like a "male burlesque star," Presley stood on his toes and shook. Now a seasoned performer, he advanced on the crowd to within a seductive few inches, then withdrew smiling. Within moments of his setting foot on the Olympia's stage, Presley's image would be emblazoned in the minds of concertgoers for the rest of their lives.

For Scotty Moore, the Miami show ended weeks of humiliation and restless waiting to get on the road and make some money. While Presley vacationed in July, per their agreement Parker cut Moore's salary in half, from $200 a week to $100. His ex-wife Mary "had seen me on television and convinced herself that anyone touring with Elvis Presley and appearing on network television certainly had the money to pay his child support." While Presley took time off, deputies came to Moore's Memphis home, arrested the veteran navy man, and booked him into jail on charges of being $240 delinquent on child support.

Once the boys got back on tour and Presley continued his path to becoming the biggest star in the world, Moore struggled to stay above water financially. "I and other band members were not sharing in the wealth," Moore said. To make the monthly child support payments manageable, he had to refinance his guitar and amplifier. The Miami shows were Moore's chance to put all the heartache and embarrassment aside and indulge his passion for the guitar and entertaining.

When the show was over, Moscato and the legion of exhausted and exhilarated young girls weren't about to go home. They hoped to get an autograph from Presley, to touch him, or at least to get one more glimpse of the charismatic young singer. When Presley appeared at the stage door, hundreds of girls broke a police line in hopes of getting to him. "We went outside and the crowd was in a frenzy. They just pushed me down an alley. In those days we wore starched skirts and crinoline and it rained that day and I lost a shoe and all the mud was washed up my leg and the starch was running down it. I went home and my Mom had a hissy fit." To make matters worse, there in the next day's paper was a photograph of Moscato, the girl in the cat's-eye glasses, right up front, going crazy for Elvis.

At this stage in his career Presley still cherished the interaction he had with fans who had helped him get so far so quickly. "Lots of times if I'm in a crowd at the door, and the people who hired us are wanting the crowd to leave," Presley told a reporter in 1956, "it makes me feel real bad because I can't get to all of 'em." But not this time; things were so frenetic, Juanico said, that Presley "held my hand in a death grip" as they ran from the stage door to a waiting car.

The fans managed to tear away parts of his pink jacket and dark pin-striped pants. Black and white photos show Presley sitting in a chair in his underwear, with socks and white shoes on, cutting up his torn stage outfit. He gave a couple of remnants to a young saxophonist whom he'd met on a previous tour in Texarkana, Del Puschert, who was now a local dental school student and had gotten the gig backing Presley in Miami. Since Presley couldn't get to all the fans to sign autographs or take pictures—there were far too many—he'd come up with a novel idea for giving them a way to remember him.

From the safety of his hotel room, Presley started dropping the cut-up remnants of his stage outfit to fans below still holding vigil for him on Southeast Second Avenue. For those who caught and kept them, the ragged strips of fabric falling like gargantuan shards of volcanic ash remained keepsakes. Puschert forgot all about the unusual souvenirs until he found them in a trunk at his mother's home in Hollywood, Florida. Decades later, in Puschert's barber shop in Annapolis, Maryland, the remnants of Presley's pants and jacket are his prized possessions, framed alongside photos of Presley wearing that outfit onstage and of Puschert shaking hands with the young king of rock and roll at the Olympia.

Bob Graham, who went on to become one of Florida's most important and respected statesmen, said Presley's youthful exuberance evokes images of the Miami he called home as a kid; still a relatively quiet, friendly, and laid-back place. "It was hot in Miami, Elvis was hot," Graham remembered. "Miami was a place that was pretty open to out of the mainstream entertainers. Elvis was certainly that."

Newspaper photographer Charles Trainor, a twenty-nine-year-old Korean War veteran, snapped myriad classic images from the Friday shows. Decades after it was shot, a Trainor image graced the cover of a *Rolling Stone* special issue on the greatest singers of all time: Presley as the epitome of cool, on the balls of his feet, guitar slung over his shoulder, wailing into an old-fashioned Shure microphone, with Bill Black and his stand-up bass flanking the star. Once again, an image of Presley in Florida at the end of his early days touring the South came to define what most still regard as the most iconic period of his career.

After his Friday performances, Presley found fan love notes and phone numbers, many scrawled in lipstick, all over his new Lincoln, forcing him to trade it in for a new one the next day. Enterprising reporter Damon Runyon Jr. of the *Miami News Herald* cornered Juanico in the wings during one of the concerts. She told him she was one of Presley's two steady girlfriends. "I don't know if I'm No. 1 or No. 2 in his life—but I'm happy being one or the other," Juanico gushed. "It would be nice if Elvis loved me as much as I love him, but right now he's married to his career and he isn't thinking of marriage. If Elvis doesn't marry it'd be a sin to let something like that go to waste."

Now the secret about Presley's girlfriend was out, and his prediction was spot-on: Parker was furious. Presley had just gotten back to his hotel room and was finally relaxing on the couch when there was a loud knock at the door. "In stormed the Colonel," Juanico remembered. "Elvis jumped up from the sofa and went to his side." Slapping the newspaper with the back of his hand, Parker thundered, "Son we can't have this kind of publicity . . . make damn sure you do something about it." To emphasize his last point, Parker glowered at Presley's young love interest. Juanico saw, even at that stage in Presley's career, Parker's omnipresent influence—and was not a fan. "His relationship with his manager was more like that of a son with his father," Juanico remembered. "I didn't like Colonel Parker, but I respected Elvis's feelings of loyalty."

Runyon had his scoop, and Presley and Parker went into spin control. "I've got about 25 girls I date regular," Presley explained. "She's just one of the girls." That statement had to hurt, considering that Presley had just spent a romantic stretch of his time off with Juanico where the two met in Mississippi. Parker poured salt into her wounds. "They show up—sometimes eight at a time—in the hotel or theater lobby," Parker told reporters. "All claiming they're his steadies."

Runyon dug further, calling Juanico's mother in Biloxi. "When he's in Biloxi, he doesn't go out with any other girl but her," she said of Presley. "He said he can't get married for at least three years and he asked her to wait for him." Though she was only defending her daughter's true standing with the young king of rock and roll, the fact that Juanico's mother confirmed the seriousness of the relationship angered Presley, who yelled at her for the first time: "If only your mother hadn't talked to that damn reporter! Call your mother June, tell her never to talk to anyone else."

His scoop on Juanico aside, Runyon saved his worst words for his review of Presley's two-day stand, referring to Elvis as an "idol of the infantile." Runyon found Presley's stage antics vulgar and his effect on teens unwholesome, unwelcome, and threatening: "His pelvis performance is clearly contrived . . . slack-jawed gibberish, the glassy gape of a hypnotized hillbilly, the unmannered gesture of wiping the nose, the staggering and shaking as if he'd had a bad fit."

Letters to the editor reflected the same holier-than-thou attitude toward Presley's act. "It was apparent the teen agers present had to force themselves to the hysterical peaks which they felt Elvis deserved," wrote eighteen-year-old skeptic Bob Posnak. "There was hysteria, yes, but it was not an honest hysteria."

Columnist Herb Rau ratcheted up the venom for Presley and his young fans to a stunning degree given that many of them were his readers' children: "Elvis can't sing, can't play the guitar and can't dance. Yet two thousand idiots per show yelp every time he opens his mouth, plucks a guitar string or shakes his pelvis like any striptease babe in town." The columnist wasn't done; for the fourteen thousand fans who attended and enjoyed the show, Rau suggested a "gift." In all caps and bold print he wrote: "A SOLID SLAP ACROSS THE MOUTH."

Rau could not see from across the developing generational divide what was at the root of all the hysteria for Presley fans like Linda Moscato and future Florida governor and United States senator Bob Graham. Presley cracked open the door to what awaited in the next decade when these children of the fifties became adults of the sixties: liberation, rebellion, exuberance, finally life on no one's terms but their own. By that time, adults and critics were powerless to try to marginalize rock and roll and youth culture. Elvis Presley was merely riding the first wave.

Well into her seventies, Moscato sat in her central Florida living room surrounded by photos, souvenirs, and memories of Elvis at the Olympia Theater in Miami. "It was a totally unforgettable experience," she reflected. "I'm thrilled to death I was a teen-ager and I got to see him at that time and got to be part of it . . . Elvis happening in Florida."

In Miami there was also a foreshadowing of what was to come when Presley received a script for his first film role, in *The Reno Brothers*. His excitement over what was originally supposed to be a non-singing character role was tempered when the film was later renamed *Love Me Tender* and called for Presley to sing the title number. There, in the midst of Presleymania, was the beginning of Parker's plan to transform Presley from cool and controversial rock and roller into a crooning matinee idol. To be sure, his young star was on board; ready to conquer Hollywood and even bigger paydays.

After the seventh and final Olympia show, a crowd of screaming girls surrounded the Miami taxicab bringing Presley back to the Robert Clay Hotel. Patrolman Al Doncetelli helped clear the mass of youngsters. After the motorcade was finally able to pull away from the theater, Doncetelli hit a strip of gravel at Southeast Second Avenue and Third Street, causing the motorcycle to overturn. Doncetelli went flying off the cycle and had to be transported to Jackson Memorial Hospital with back injuries.

More girls stood outside the hotel for a last look at their idol's departure for the next tour stop. Even late at night, after an exhausting seven shows in the prior forty-eight hours, Presley still had to be surrounded by policemen to get to his new Lincoln parked outside. For the rest of the tour this was the new norm; constant hysteria everywhere Presley went, with very little downtime. For Presley, Juanico, and the rest of the traveling party, a long nighttime drive to Tampa lay ahead, as did big crowds and more critical press.

12

Home Away from Home

August 5, Tampa

Presley and Juanico pulled out of Miami late on the night of August 4, bound for the next tour stop in Tampa. With all the friends and band members, there were now a pair of cars in Presley's touring party. These all-night drives were nothing new, but in 1956, the Tamiami Trail across the heart of the Everglades, teeming with alligators and home of the North American crocodile and Florida panther, was especially desolate. Streaking along the two-lane road under a blanket of stars in the infinite night sky, the group was traversing the middle of nowhere. If they had a breakdown, Presley joked with his girlfriend, they'd be eaten alive by snakes and alligators.

The conversation turned to the long lecture Presley had gotten from Parker about Juanico. Always a prankster, Presley even put an unlit cigar in his mouth and started to imitate him: "She's not good for you son. You can't be linked to any one girl," said Presley in his best Parker bombast. "Don't get any ideas about marriage either. And for God's sake don't get her pregnant." Parker need not have worried on that front; while sexual tension between the two was rising with the South Florida heat and humidity, Juanico insisted they were not having sex.

"And what do you think Elvis, or does it matter?" said a perturbed Juanico, offering to leave the tour right then and there. "Stop the damn car and you won't have to worry about the Colonel or the fans." Presley apologized, insisting he was not worried about his manager or his fans, but June knew better.

Halfway down the Tamiami Trail, still in the middle of the Florida back country, the neon lights of an all-night restaurant beckoned; an oasis for bleary-eyed truckers or an American rock and roll icon hoping to grab a late-night bite. As fame began to envelop him during the day, Presley became increasingly nocturnal. At night he could also spend some time with his girlfriend without the press being able to pick up on it so easily. By that time, as Presley's bodyguard and driver Red West put it, "He was a prisoner of his own career." Perhaps to Presley's disappointment, perhaps to his relief, the restaurant jukebox had none of his records in it, and the waitress had no idea who he was. Looking at the expensive cars in which they drove up, she asked: "What'd you kids do, rob a bank?"

"Yes ma'am," said Presley with a convincing straight face. "But we'd appreciate it if you waited at least an hour before you call the sheriff." The young adults feasted on salad and fried chicken that Presley declared second best in the world, second only to his mother's. He winked at the waitress, who patted his shoulder: "That aint the only thing she did good." After all, the flirty waitress was working for tips, and Presley gave her a good one. Fueled for the rest of the south-to-north drive up Florida's west coast, Presley's tour pulled into Tampa before daylight.

On Sunday, August 5, he returned to the only venue at which he appeared during each of his four 1955–56 Florida tours, Tampa's Homer Hesterly Armory. Unlike the rude treatment he had received from Miami writers, on the west side at least one female bay area journalist took the time to get to know something about Presley in person, and she came away with a far more balanced take. Twenty-year-old *St. Petersburg Times* writer Anne Rowe holed up with Presley in his stifling dressing area before the show. Presley's "reputation," she wrote, "had given this reporter reason 'to proceed with caution' in his presence."

She was quickly disarmed when "the king of rock 'n' roll" picked up a broom and started sweeping out his dressing room.

Missing from Rowe's account is the way Presley turned on a good measure of his public persona to win her over. What starts as a typical interview evolves into another Presley seduction session: he holds Rowe's face in both hands, shows her his tongue, and embraces and kisses her. Then Presley defuses it all with humor; Rowe smiles as Presley turns his back on her.

"One minute he's out on the make," wrote Ger Rijff and Jan Van Gestel in their book *Elvis the Cool King*, "the next he's stepping outside and starts playing with some toddlers."

The young man who had by now appeared repeatedly on national television, and who had several number 1 hits and a number 1 album, nervously swept the dressing room of cigarette butts, then crooned a little "Don't Be Cruel" into the broom handle. He posed for pictures, answered questions, and to reporters like Rowe came across "like a real regular guy" during the hour he spent with them.

Presley picked up his leather-bound guitar and started singing "Don't be Cruel" again, calling it his favorite song because "it has the most meaning." He had another reason to be upbeat; his vocalist friends the Jordanaires were in town to perform and joined him backstage.

As was custom in the singer's harried, circuslike life on the road, Presley now held an impromptu press conference. Snacking on coffee and ice cream, he took questions from a WALT-AM 1110 radio reporter. Initially the WALT station managers tried to avoid playing rock and roll. But spearheaded by the popularity of Presley's music, it changed format and rocketed to number 1 in the ratings as Tampa's first top-forty station.

Unlike some of the mindless questions and pat answers common in most of Presley's early interviews, his answers here had more depth and covered a wider range of issues. He admitted being embarrassed by having had to sing dressed in a tuxedo to an actual hound dog on the *Steve Allen Show*. "All I thought about that suit, was gettin' out of it," he joked. Asked what he would do if his popularity and rock and roll were a passing fad, Presley said: "I'll probably sit back and think about what I once had, with no regrets." It's a statement filled with irony, considering what became of Presley later in his life and career.

He was hopeful his upcoming foray into acting would be a success but promised, "I won't give up singing for acting." In later years that statement proved to be true; but Presley did sing what many early fans felt were inferior songs in bland films. He also cut off his electrifying performances, making tours like this one all the more special to those lucky enough to see him live.

Not fully aware of all the cruel things said about him in Miami, Presley also addressed his critics: "Those people have a job to do just like me. I think when you're in this business you've got to expect that sort of treatment." Presley acknowledged that his music and performances weren't for everyone, but they were clearly a formula for his growing success: "Some people wouldn't pay a nickel to see me. But as long as my records keep selling and these folks keep turning out to hear me sing, I'm happy."

While Presley accommodated the press, local Tampa emcee Frankie Connors warmed up the crowd with a couple of corny Irish ballads. Then the Jordanaires took the stage, followed by a magician named Phil Maraquin. This oddball hodgepodge of warm-up acts had to be interminable for most fans, already worked up for the main attraction. After an hour with Rowe, who was now completely disarmed by the young performer, there was a knock on the door; time for Presley to go on.

Fans shrieked during his still brief twenty-minute headlining concert. "Elvis displayed his terrific showmanship," Rowe recounted. "Now Presley was in his glory. He rocked 'n rolled his way through seven numbers, laughing, winking and wriggling in the well-known Presley manner. While his fans yelled, cried, pulled their hair, held their ears, jumped, clapped and laughed."

The stage consisted of a series of oversized, unstable wooden boxes, the sound system nothing more than a couple of microphones and a pair of fifty-watt amplifiers. At the matinee show there was no spotlight or lighting at all; just Presley out front in a packed auditorium, with Bill Black sweating, hooting, and hollering, Moore coolly pluck-ing out the lead licks, and Fontana keeping the beat. The performance was vintage, raw Presley, almost unimaginable given the Vegas-style glitz and showmanship of his later years.

Though Presley put on in Tampa a mirror-image performance of the same live show he had given in Miami, critical interpretation could not have been more different. Rowe, who went on to have a long and distinguished career at her newspaper, saw that Presley's act, like his mock seduction backstage, was all in good fun. Herb Rau in Miami, in contrast, had encouraged parents to slap the Presleymania right off the faces of their own children. No matter what Presley said to try to explain his motives and put them in perspective, the worst was yet to come. A pair of male writers for the *Tampa Tribune* gave Presley the Miami treatment: "America's only male hootchy-kootch dancer gave 10,000 kids the screaming heebi-jeebies in Tampa," wrote Paul Wilder and Harry Roberts.

They noted that even "ordinary suburban-type housewives" got all caught up in the "pounding, jerking rhythm" of Presley's newest single, "Hound Dog." The writers noted that "the weird pulsating rock and roll song" sold more than a million copies in just two weeks, mak-ing it RCA's fastest selling record of all time. Presley's embarrassing appearance with Steve Allen fueled the song's rise, proving that the joke was not on Presley after all.

The *Tribune* writers compared Presley to a panther that crept across the stage, "with a masculine version of Marilyn Monroe wrig-gle in every jerking step, and blasted his feminine, heart wailing voice into every cranny of the huge armory." Calling Presley's voice femi-nine is ludicrous, and by this point the Wilder and Roberts article has morphed into an editorial. They praised Presley for being patient with reporters' questions, which they called "stupid." Chauvinist and unnecessarily judgmental articles like this one became common in Presley's career. When writers put away their opinions and simply observed what was going on around them, their observations were compelling: "A mad rush of hundreds of mesmerized teenagers became a shouting, pushing, pulling, tugging mess of young human- ity as the gates finally opened to the armory," wrote Wilder and Rob- erts. "At least three persons fainted at two electrifying Rock 'n' Roll performances."

They noted three Chicago housewives who had left their husbands at home to care for a dozen children while the women saw the show and begged for Presley's autograph. Another housewife, Mary Rubio, had her two children with her: three-year-old Terry Lee and two-year- old Michelle Denise. Reporters noted that she was "attractive" and wearing a low-cut black dress "that drew stares wherever she went." But Rubio claimed she was only there because her toddlers listened to Presley on the radio every afternoon. "I can take him or leave him," she nonplussed the reporters.

A dark-haired young man sporting a ducktail haircut was mobbed by girls who mistook him for Presley. Meanwhile Tom Parker seemed to be everywhere at once. He had convinced his friends from the Ser- toma club, forty men who had volunteered their services, to act as bodyguards for both Presley and his newest Lincoln to make sure the girls didn't get to either. One of the volunteers, Dr. West Magnon, helped with ushering duties while his five-year-old twins sat eating peanuts, oblivious to the goings-on around them.

A few girls skinned their knees crawling on the concrete floor to get to the front of the stage with cameras. The flashbulbs bathed Pre- sley in a kind of stop-action strobe light. When each of the two shows was over, those who didn't manage to get an up-close view or photo, didn't get a wink or an autograph from their idol, were crushed. As Wilder and Roberts described it in their review, when "a dozen jump- ing, frenzied teenagers discovered they had missed out on getting a close look at their atomic-powered idol, they left the auditorium weeping, crying real tears."

Policeman Manny DeCastro kept "the negro section" roped off. This is the only mention to date of black fans at any of Elvis Pres- ley's Florida shows; his music was fueled by the unique blending of his appeal as a handsome, magnetic young performer with the magic that came from the unbridled rhythm and blues borrowed from African American songs. Few if any fans in Presley's audience knew that Big Mama Thornton originated "Hound Dog"; perhaps a fair number had heard Little Richard's original version of "Tutti Frutti." The rigid southern divide between black and white was everywhere, including at Presley's concerts and in the words of those covering them.

Wilder and Roberts noted, "Only twelve negroes attended." None was mentioned by name, and there was no description of what they were wearing or if any of them brought children. Apparently the reporters didn't take time to find out Presley's effect on his African American fans. It would have been interesting to know whether any of them was cognizant of how heavily Presley and his act drew on music from black culture. Five years later, in November 1961, Martin Luther King brought to this same venue a stirring call for integration. The history doesn't stop there.

President John F. Kennedy spoke at the Art Deco–inspired armory on Howard Avenue in West Tampa four days before his assassination. The depot has been host to memorable musical performances by Buddy Holly, James Brown, the Doors, even Pink Floyd.

When I stopped there many decades after Presley's historic appearances, the venue most important to Presley history in Florida looked imprisoned; vacant and largely forgotten, it was surrounded by a fence topped with barbed wire. A concrete barrier blocked off the chain-locked front doorway; empty beer cans in small paper bags and a strong stench of urine made it even less appealing to linger there. Peering inside the empty hall, it was easy to visualize the stage and the rising young star when Red Robertson took his world-famous photo in 1955 and where Tom Parker kicked off his own concert promotion career.

Outside, a matching bank of garage doors beyond a "No Trespassing" sign marked where Presley parked his Lincoln in August of '56, showing off the engine to a group of young men, having his picture taken with children, and as always, flirting with as many starstruck girls as he could. All these years later there were plans for what it might look like if renovated, and they rendered it nearly unrecognizable.

Seeing and smelling nothing but neglect, I found the place stood out as one of the few disappointments in this journey of discovery and remembrance.

In May 2015 the building finally received a new lease on life and a new name: the Bryan Glazer Family Jewish Community Center to honor the co-chairman of the Tampa Bay Bucs pro football team, who pledged $4 million to the renovation. Alongside plans for a vibrant new center, the city of Tampa signed a ten-year lease to locate a new city art studio within the 100,000-square-foot confines. As the city of Tampa creates a new opportunity to reacquaint itself with the old armory, and once the dust settles, we can assess how history has been integrated within the renovation. How has the old been recast within the new? Can future generations learn about, walk, and rock with the still-palpable spirit of young Elvis, who made so much history here?

In August 1956 more sold-out shows and controversy awaited the young rock and roll sensation in Lakeland. Once he found out the incendiary things critics like Herb Rau had been saying about him, Presley's patience with the press ran out. In Lakeland he dropped the polite country boy persona and struck back.

13

They're Somebody's Kids

August 6, Lakeland

Lakeland Ledger reporter Elvalee Donaldson perched herself on the back steps of the Polk Theater with a heavy camera, roasting for two hours in the sun just to snap a photo of Elvis Presley's arrival. It was after 3:00 p.m. and his first of three shows was due to start in a half hour. "Finally, Elvis and his entourage drove up in a pink Cadillac. They brushed right by me and into the theater," she recounted. In a later story she said he arrived in a Lincoln.

"Honey, you'll have to come inside if you want to talk to me," Presley said dismissively. Put out and angry, Donaldson did just that.

"I'm a reporter for the *Lakeland Ledger* and I've been waiting two hours for you to show up," the headstrong young reporter announced.

"Oh," Presley said with a frown. "I just thought you were some little girl waiting for me." He apologized repeatedly, explaining that his managers always encouraged him "to hurry inside as fast as I can."

"Go ahead," he said. "Shoot."

Presley paused on the theater staircase and Donaldson snapped a candid photo of him making his way up to a small dressing room. "His girlfriend of the moment, 18-year-old June Juanico, glared at me and ran up the stairs behind Elvis," Donaldson recalled. The *Ledger's*

Reporter Elvalee Donaldson, who covered Presley's Lakeland performances. Courtesy of Pegler Swift.

young reporter had been assigned to write a story every day for seven days in advance of the star's arrival. Her output is some of the most interesting and incisive commentary on Presley's time in Florida.

In one story Donaldson marveled at Presley's car collection: "four Cadillacs, a three-wheeled Messerschmitt sports car, and a motorcycle." She also managed some endearing quotes from Gladys Presley recalling the days when nine-year-old Elvis asked her to let him drive. "We were parked facing a store and Elvis mistook forward for reverse and dropped the clutch. The car shot right up onto the curb and I thought we were going on through the store window," Presley's mother remembered. "But Elvis kept his head and stopped it. He insisted on backing it into the street also."

Mrs. Presley said her son was always picking up things for them while he was out on tour. "His latest is lamps," she confided. "He's bought me so many lamps that I have to put some of them away and take turns using them. If ever there was a boy who cares about his home, it's Elvis."

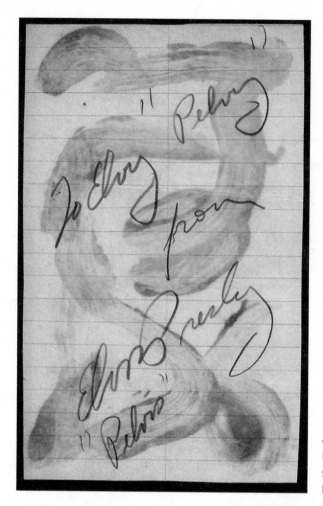

Elvis Presley's autograph to Elvalee Donaldson. Courtesy of Pegler Swift.

In city after city, whether because they were smitten by him or because Presley was more willing to let his guard down, women who covered Elvis on his early Florida tours consistently filed more in-depth, detailed stories about him than did their male counterparts. Thanks to the work of journalists like Jean Yothers in Orlando, Anne Rowe in Tampa, promoter Mae Axton in Jacksonville, and Elvalee Donaldson in Lakeland, a more rounded version of Presley's early years emerges. Some made critical comments, but they were never harsh or obviously condescending.

Donaldson, Yothers, and Rowe had long, significant careers in journalism. Rowe led the transformation of the women's pages at what is now the *Tampa Bay Times*. Previously the ladies' section focused primarily on society, club, and bridal news, and the so-called four fs: fashion, food, family, and furnishings. Rowe spearheaded the transition of women's pages to broader-appeal feature sections; what was revolutionary in the late 1960s is commonplace today in newspapers nationwide.

Elvis Presley just after his arrival at the Polk Theater in Lakeland. Courtesy of Elvalee (Donaldson) Swift via Pegler Swift.

Elvis Presley's dressing room at the Polk Theater. Courtesy of Mike Robinson.

To be sure, even at his young age, Presley was adept at courting and manipulating female reporters. He had to reassure one young woman in Tampa who was shaking as she tried to interview him, putting his arm on her shoulder. Others got dramatic stares and kisses. The way he caressed and came on to them would be out of the question today, or at least roundly criticized, in a professional interview.

Tampa Tribune reporter Paul Wilder, who co-wrote the hyperbole-laced review of Presley's final shows at the Hesterly Armory, caught up with him again backstage at the Polk Theater. Wilder audio-recorded the session for *TV Guide* magazine. In a dry, just-the-facts voice that evokes Jack Webb's Detective Joe Friday from *Dragnet*, Wilder made his feelings apparent by reading to Presley in its entirety what Miami columnist Herb Rau had written.

In retrospect, it's a good thing Wilder went right for the jugular. The usually reserved and quiet Presley was now aware of Rau and angry, more than willing to drop his normal country boy reserve. "He aint nothin' but an idiot or he wouldn't sit up there and write all that stuff," Presley seethed. "He just hates to admit that he's too old to have any more fun." Presley wasn't finished; as Wilder continued his line-by-line dissection of the Rau column with the agitated young singer, Wilder asked, "Do you shake your pelvis like any striptease babe in town?"

"He should know," Presley fired back, speaking of Rau. "I guess that's where he hangs around." Presley saves his most serious contempt for Rau's assessment that all the young fans who'd come to see him in Miami were "idiots."

"I just don't see that he should call those people idiots, because they're somebody's kids," Presley protested. "They're somebody's decent kids, probably raised in a decent home, and he hasn't got any right to call those kids idiots. If they want to pay their money to come out and jump around and scream and yell, it's their business . . . while they're young let them have their fun."

This was still a conservative time in American history, when married television characters weren't allowed to be shown sharing a bed, communist paranoia was everywhere, and Presley's gyrations were generally considered far beyond what was acceptable for public viewing. "My pelvis had nothin' to do with what I do," Presley explained. "I just get kinda rhythm with the music. I jump around to it because I enjoy what I'm doin'. I'm not trying to be vulgar; I'm not trying to sell any sex. I'm not tryin' to look vulgar and nasty." To say he was not trying to sell sex is disingenuous. Presley exploited his sex appeal with overheated young fans and smitten female reporters on every tour stop.

To some in authority, Presley exceeded vulgarity. In his declassified FBI file are letters written by people in law enforcement and the clergy to FBI Director J. Edgar Hoover himself, clearly trying to ingratiate themselves with one of the most powerful men in America and at the same time expressing alarmist worry about the effect Presley was having on America's youth.

"There is also gossip of the Presley fan clubs that degenerate into sex orgies," wrote one pastor from La Crosse, Wisconsin. "I would judge that he may possibly be both a drug addict and a sexual pervert."

From Louisville, Kentucky, Colonel Carl E. Heustis wrote to Hoover of his concern that Presley and Bill Haley and his band the Comets, "rivals for the attention of quote rock and roll fans unquote," were booked on the same date in his jurisdiction. Such simultaneous appearances in other cities had caused riots and "many thousands of dollars in property damage." A man used to receiving speculative, the-sky-is-falling letters, Hoover replied: "The bureau has no specific information regarding these disturbances."

In August 1956 an anonymous postcard mailed from Niagara Falls, New York, and addressed to "Elvis Presley, Memphis Tennessee" threatened: "If you don't stop . . . we're going to kill you." The FBI wrote it off as a "crank" message, but Presley took these threats seriously. Later in his career, after his fame and the unsavory elements it attracted increased exponentially, Presley often worried about being assassinated onstage.

During this final Florida stretch of Presley's early career, another threat loomed just a few more tour stops away: the very real possibility that he could end up in jail.

There were no such threats waiting in Lakeland, just a wave of Presleymania sweeping the town. Luminaries like Babe Ruth, Greta Garbo, and Booker T. Washington had visited Lakeland in prior decades, but nothing compared to the town's anticipation of Presley's three shows at the Polk Theater. The *Lakeland Ledger* dedicated a small army of a half-dozen reporters to examine every aspect of the phenomenon.

Elvalee Donaldson was spot on in deflating the establishment's fears of Presley. "He doesn't drink, he doesn't smoke, and nightclubs bore him. He is devoted to his parents and bought them a $40,000 air-conditioned ranch home," she explained, "with a swimming pool."

Presley liked to hang out at carnival midways and reveled in

Elvis Presley's signature on the wall at the Polk Theater. Courtesy of Mike Robinson.

winning kewpie dolls. When too keyed up at night to sleep, he played old Abbott and Costello movies—on the ceiling. Donaldson labeled Presley "overly polite, extremely self-conscious and aware of the importance of other people." Like those of Orlando columnist Jean Yothers in 1955, Elvalee Donaldson's assessments of Presley are prescient in contrast to some of the other local and national reportage of the day.

"Actually, this guy's just sorta different, you know?" Donaldson opined as if confiding in a friend. "He's unexplainable. In one short year, he shot from nowhere into the hottest spotlight any American entertainer has held in such a short time. The public is examining him from every possible angle. He has no private life. Every bit he used to have is exposed." Donaldson was dead-on again; and this was before Presley made any films, before the first of his *Ed Sullivan Show* appearances.

Three male reporters from the *Ledger* who "covered" Presley's concerts in Lakeland were interviewed for the article "Three Unbiased Males Give Views of Elvis." Bob Swift, the "general assignment man," called Presley "the first male burlesque dancer I've ever seen who didn't have a rhinestone in his navel." City Hall reporter Bob Jarrell said the other acts were "well worth" the price of admission and recommended the show to any parent who accompanies teenage daughters to the theater and whisks them away in the final 15 minutes, when Presley comes on." The rest is similar drivel.

The male-dominated editorial board at the *Ledger* took their predictable shots: "As the tumult rages, most adults look on with attitudes that range from amusement to disgust," the board wrote in an editorial that ran the day of Presley's appearance. "Presley is a fad and an oddity. Within a little while his popularity will begin to wane." The editorial all but apologizes for the amount of coverage dedicated to Presley, "not because he is an important public figure, which he isn't, but because he has managed to create unusual furor and frenzy and thereby upped his income from $40 a week to a million dollars a year."

And, without doubt, he generated a sharp uptick in newspaper sales. To say Presley was not an important public figure at this point reflects the other end of the spectrum when it came to common adult reaction to him: unfounded fears or derision and complete dismissiveness. The editorial board members were so busy pandering to readers that they failed to recognize in their midst a pivotal figure in American culture, representing a turning point in music history from which there was no turning back.

As Presley waited in his small dressing room high above the stage, he scrawled his signature on the wall, circling it for emphasis. Today that faded autograph is still a closely guarded treasure; kept under a clear covering and cut out of the wall after a water leak nearly ruined it. The Polk Theater remains a stately landmark in downtown Lakeland. On the night Presley arrived, seven young male ushers waited outside the theater. One of them sneered at a Presley playbill and remarked: "The thought of him makes me want to go inside and vomit."

After weeks of preview stories, Donaldson finally had the chance to see Presley in action: "He lumbered from behind the curtain . . . hitching up his trousers. Everybody screamed. He leaned back, grinned at the musicians and swayed. Everybody screamed again." As the girls pressed toward the front of the stage, a photo shows Presley leaning forward on one knee, moving tantalizingly close. Lakeland police officer Jimmy Mock Sr. has his back to the crowd, partially bent over, knee up on a low railing, looking none-too-pleased to be the human barrier between the screaming girls and the object of their teen crushes. Staring at Presley, sixteen-year-old usher Clyde Hostetler in a white shirt and bow tie seems oblivious to the maelstrom surrounding him.

While photographer Art Perkins took pictures, Mildred Slayton, who was married and older than most in the crowd, handed him flash bulbs. "It was just absolutely fascinating watching the kids. They tried climbing on the stage and they [the police] kept pushing them back."

Another controversial aspect of Presley's performance was the way he laughed and smiled. Was he laughing with the crowd, or at them? Slayton thought the latter: "He was such an egotist. He kept looking in the wings with such a grin, as if he were saying, 'Look at all these people making asses of themselves.'" Presley told reporters it was fun watching his young fans: "I get tickled at those kids in the front row. And then too I get tickled at my own mistakes. I'm all the time forgetting words."

After the first show, stage manager Lee Gregg had to warn Presley not to be so careless with the microphone, the only one in the theater. "He went out with the mike and he'd let it loose to flop back and forth on the stand," Gregg explained. After a good talking to, he said Presley "behaved himself."

Always standing in the shadows, ready to count up money from the till, Tom Parker complained that fans couldn't hear the singer and demanded a better PA system for the afternoon and evening shows.

Between concerts, June Juanico stepped out to get Presley some water. "Is June just one of your 25 regulars?" Donaldson asked, referring to Presley's attempts to downplay his relationship with June in the press. He looked disgusted, but it was Presley himself feeding that kind of information to reporters, along with Parker. "She means more to me than any other girl ever has," said Presley in a show of candor. "But I haven't known her very long."

Presley, who complained that he slept only three to four hours a night, looked worn out. And who wouldn't be, when the downtime between shows included a continuing dialogue with the press? Donaldson took issue with Presley's explanation that his gyrations were all simply part of feeling the music.

"Surely Elvis," Donaldson probed. "You don't honestly believe that all those motions simply are part of feeling the songs?"

Presley broke into a smile and admitted, "Well, part of it is put on you might say." Score another one for the enterprising young reporter. The most incisive, interesting, and controversial comments from and about Elvis Presley during his Florida tours came in association with his August 6 stop at the Polk Theater in Lakeland. Presley told Donaldson his favorite song was his new single, "Don't Be Cruel." He said he loved his fans and despite all their screaming and hysterics, it didn't make him nervous. He recounted throwing his trousers out of the hotel window in Miami to fans down below. "I don't know if they tore them apart or not," said Presley. "When I left, they were still fighting over them."

Finally, after all the preview stories, interviews, and staking out the young king of rock and roll, Donaldson summed up what it was like to experience Presleymania in Lakeland. "It's hard to make a clear cut statement about the 21 year-old singer," she concluded. "On stage he is obscene, ridiculous and sullen, yet he gets $50,000 a week because of his on stage appearances. Off stage he appears polite and good-natured, only too eager to tell the truth about the way he acts and feels."

In the end, the burlesque dancer analogy was apt. Give them a wink and a nod, a few gyrations. Tease them, get them all worked up, yet show them very little. Take their money and move on to the next town. It was all out of the former carny confidence man Tom Parker's playbook. At the same time, Presley's undeniable talent and one-of-a-kind voice were making an indelible and historic mark on the Billboard charts; the ultimate endurance test separating legends from lessers.

Again it was Donaldson doing all the memorable reporting in Lakeland. She noted that Presley's records had already grossed $6,000,000, not bad for a kid "who never took a guitar lesson and cannot read music." In two weeks leading up to the Lakeland shows, his remake of "Hound Dog" sold 900,000 copies, "to set a new all-time high." Those undeniably remarkable sales figures rarely found their way into the trite musings of small town reporters, big city columnists, or apologetic editorial boards.

Besides the photo of him on the stairs, Donaldson had another special memory of her time with Presley, an autograph which he inscribed: "To Elvy, from Elvis the Pelvis." That night, Parker left town to do more advance work for the tour. Presley and Juanico were assured of having no late night surprise visits from him in their hotel room. After witnessing the extraordinary response from young female fans at a trio of Florida tour stops, Juanico was feeling insecure.

"What's it like to be loved by so many girls?" she asked him.

Presley tried to put into words the feeling of being onstage during all the electrifying hysteria. "It's almost like making love," he explained. "But it's even stronger than that."

In her memoir Juanico said her feelings of insecurity were more justified than ever with that statement: "Not only did he have his choice of girls, he was making love to all of them at the same time."

That night, the two kissed passionately and slept in the same bed. If there was any time for Presley to forget about Tom Parker's admonition not to get too close to his Mississippi flame, it was August 6, 1956, alone with her in a Lakeland hotel room. At what Juanico described as the "point of no return," Presley came to a dead stop. "We can't do this baby, the time is not right," he told Juanico, who was clearly ready to consummate her love for Presley. "I was tingling all over," she wrote.

Within fifteen minutes the exhausted singer had fallen asleep. Juanico's virginity was intact, and even in his absence, Tom Parker's hold on the young king of rock and roll was never more in evidence. Lakeland represented a turning point; the gloves were now off between the press and Presley. With his mushrooming popularity came more and more scrutiny about his effect on fans, some of whom were already lining up in St. Petersburg within hours of his last Lakeland show.

14

A Real Test

August 7, St. Petersburg

"Today's the Day!" screamed the first sentence of the *St. Petersburg Times*'s article on Presley's three-concert appearance, his first in Tampa Bay's southern city.

Reporter Anne Rowe wrote of the recent tug-of-war between leading national television hosts Steve Allen and Ed Sullivan over which of them would be the next to book Presley. Initially, Sullivan had no desire to bring to his widely popular variety show the controversial, oft-criticized rock and roller. Sullivan changed his mind after Presley's ridiculous tuxedoed appearance in early July singing to a hound dog on Allen's program propelled Allen to a Sunday night ratings victory. Wheeler dealer Tom Parker engineered a blockbuster three-show pact for Presley to appear on the Sullivan show later that year for $50,000—equal to about $400,000 today.

In contrast, Presley's bandmates were left out of the lucrative payday. Scotty Moore received $78 for the same three performances. Through these types of deals, Parker reinforced his "you're expendable" message to Presley's guitarist, the man largely responsible for the signature sound of his biggest hits to date. As Presley grew rich and more isolated from the bandmates he once considered equals, who could blame them for resenting being left off the money train? It was human nature and exactly how Parker wanted it. Presley and Parker were the haves and Scotty, Bill, and D. J. Fontana were the have-nots.

"I look back now and realize it was all about the music, never about the money," Moore reflected. "It had to be or we would've quit."

In St. Petersburg, reaction to Presley's tame appearance on the Allen show foreshadowed more of what was to come. "Dressing him up in a designer suit and figuratively tying his legs together on a recent Steve Allen production," said Rowe in her preview article, "has brought tears from many teen-agers who mourn the loss of the 'old Elvis.'"

Such was not the case on the current Florida tour. Articles about Presley's raunchy, naughty-with-a-smile performances left parents worried about exposing their children to such a spectacle. A concerned mother told people at the Florida Theater box office she would consider allowing her daughter to attend the show, but only if she could be assured Presley would behave.

Outside the Florida Theater at 4:15 a.m., die-hard Elvis fans Clare Carter and Donna Bemis claimed the pole position for general admission to the afternoon concert. Setting up shop at the corner of First Avenue South and Fifth Street, the girls brought along newspapers, Cokes, and their Elvis Presley fan book. A half hour later Nila Shea and Anne Muncy were disappointed to see they could not complete their quest: "We were first in line to see him in Tampa and Lakeland but this time we missed out," the two explained, sitting outside the theater in the early morning darkness.

The blond-haired teenage chums already had bus tickets to catch Presley's performance the following day in Orlando. Rowe anointed the pair "Champion Presley pursuers in point of mileage." The giant theater marquee announced: "In Person Elvis Presley." A big sign over the front door read: "COOL air conditioned."

Behind the theater fans jammed into every crevice of open space along the brick-surfaced back alley to await the king's arrival; lining a small stairway below the "Simpson's Good Food" awning, packing

Reporter Anne Rowe with Elvis Presley, 1956. Reprinted by permission of Bob Moreland, *Tampa Bay Times*.

any fire escape that might offer a better view, or just trying to find a small spot to sit or stand among discarded food boxes and standing water.

As people made their way to work on Tuesday morning in downtown St. Petersburg, the crowd outside the theater continued to swell. Around 11:30 the humid summer skies opened up, drenching the young fans. Determined not to lose their place in line, some showed their resolve by chanting, "We want Elvis!" Policemen finally took pity, opening up the doors to the Florida Theater early, letting fans scamper to the best seats they could claim. Some passed the time playing tape recordings of their favorite Presley tunes.

In his dressing room with local radio personality Bob Hoffer, Presley asked him: "Is that your wife over in the corner?"

"That is my wife Joanne yes," Hoffer replies.

"Woo!" Presley hoots, bringing audible laughter from his bandmates.

"Now Joanne will be the envy of everybody at the party tonight," says Hoffer, going along with the joke. "She has been wooed at by Elvis Presley. Thank you Elvis I agree with ya."

Hoffer quizzed Presley about his height, whether he played any sports, and how much sleep he got, working so hard. "We do three, four shows a day sometimes," Presley said, sounding weary. "None of us gets much rest at all. Maybe four, five hours a night."

During the Tampa show, Presley confirmed, fans took the gas cap and cigarette lighter from his new Lincoln but not the hood ornament plated in white gold at a cost of $350. In a relaxed southern accent, Presley denied knowing anything about a possible movie pairing with Jerry Lewis or a feud in the press with crooner Pat Boone. "Pat Boone is one of the nicest guys I ever met," declared Presley, not taking the bait.

Presley always made time for interviewers and questions, no matter how inane or repetitious they were. Hoffer brought up negative fan reaction to the Steve Allen appearance. Presley acknowledged getting letters from a lot of people who didn't like it, but he recognized the PR value of poking a little fun at himself. In the interview's most incisive moment Presley reflected: "I believe that I won a lot of new friends by doing that."

During interviews, in recording studios, or in public Presley at times punctuated his answers with *ma'am* and *sir* for reasons other than respect. "Non-Southerners don't understand that when a Southerner says 'yes sir' and 'no sir' it's not always a sign of politeness,"

Scotty Moore explained. "Coming from a Southerner those words sometimes mean, 'I don't like you much—keep your distance.'"

Before the show, an audio excerpt from Paul Wilder's interview was played for all the fans to hear: "I never was a lady killer in high school. I had my share of dates, but that's all." Wilder chronicled how the formerly shy kid from Memphis had the entire state of Florida buzzing. "There is nothing in Florida entertainment history to compare him with," he observed in a *Tampa Tribune* article. "The startling impact of Presley's sway over Florida's teen-agers—and many adults too—is something unique in the state's social, economic, and entertainment life."

Now it was the Suncoast's turn. After another group of run-of-the-mill warm-up acts, the sleep-deprived crowd who had waited for hours in the rain finally got what they were waiting for. "He hit St. Petersburg with the effect of a small H-bomb," declared Anne Rowe, "sending fans into mass hysteria." When Presley appeared on stage in his Kelly green sport coat and dark pants, girls pulled at their hair and shrieked; boys stared in awe.

The green sport coat was June Juanico's favorite. Despite her discomfort with all the fans shrieking for the man she loved, she could understand the attraction. "He was the most beautiful creature I had ever seen," she said. "I too felt the urge not only to touch him, but to grab bits and pieces of him."

Then, in the middle of his modest seven-song set, came a major technical glitch: Presley's microphone cut out. Lakeland's stage manager, who had chided him the previous night for being too rough with the equipment, would surely have said *I told you so.* As Presley went on with the show, his frantic waving was at stagehands to get the problem fixed. When that issue was solved, another cropped up. Like a short leash, the microphone cord was too short. "I can't stand still when I sing," he told the still shrieking audience.

Unlike the small African American audience at Presley's Tampa concert, across Tampa Bay in St. Petersburg, no integration was allowed. As the *Times* correspondent Jerry Blizin noted: "Had he been travelling with black entertainers, as [Bill] Haley did, he wouldn't have found a venue in Saint Petersburg." Black entertainers were confined to their own venue, the Manhattan Casino on 22nd Street South. The barriers of segregation didn't fall until the early 1960s. "Integrated music just didn't happen in a resort town eager to avoid anything that might drive away family-style tourism," said Blizin.

After one show, police stopped fourteen girls climbing the fire escape to get to Presley. Another left the theater in anguish when the show was over. "I can't stand it, I can't stand it!" she wailed. According to most reports, the audiences of 6,500 who saw Presley in St. Petersburg did not get out of control. But the intermittent periods of heavy downpours, sweltering sun, and sensory overload inside caused some fans to faint.

"I hope we never have anything like this again," declared exasperated Fire Marshal John Gidley. The city newspaper's editorial board took notice of the service its police force provided against the throng of charged-up teenagers:

"These men have faced the toughest criminals, risked their lives in fast automobiles, chased burglars across roofs, directed parades and demonstrations—but until yesterday they didn't know what a fellow gets into when he becomes a policeman," the board opined. "Thousands of screaming, yelling, laughing, pushing, shoving, hysterical teenagers—mostly girls—gave the policemen a real test. Now that it's over, we'll pit the St. Petersburg police against all odds."

The Florida Theater in St. Petersburg was the only grand palace Presley played during his momentous fourth Florida tour that was later demolished. On October 1, 1967, a bank bought the theater for $225,000 and sold it off in parts like an old car. In 1968 the wrecking ball crashed into the marquee that once carried Presley's name so vividly. Timeless images of young fans packed in front and down the sidewalk faded, giving way to a parking lot.

With the tour now past its halfway point, Presley and company were expected in Orlando. The last time he had performed there, a year previously, Presley had opened for Andy Griffith. With a string of number 1 hits and a number 1–selling album in his wake, Presley was now the supernova headliner.

15

Just for You

August 8, Orlando

At the next tour stop in Orlando another soon-to-be icon of the 1950s toiled away in anonymity. During downtime, writer Jack Kerouac and his nephew Paul raced bicycles through College Park to the local department store to pick up the latest Elvis Presley record. Kerouac described the boy's affinity for Presley: "He takes his banjo, closes his eyes, and imitates Elvis to a T."

Some would later aptly describe Kerouac as a literary Elvis. Besides their good looks, both men pushed the societal bounds of post–World War II America. Kerouac went to his sister's house at 1219 Yates Street in Orlando to make the final edits to his 1957 novel *On the Road*, seen by many as the first rock and roll book of the so-called Beat Generation. Kerouac's florid description of a transient lifestyle, casual sex, and drug experimentation was far ahead of its time and brought critical scorn.

Young people devoured the book's message: refusing to accept a perceived ideal of children and marriage, a comfortable home in suburbs going up all over America, providing more ethos to the nation's developing youth culture and generational divide. Presley and Kerouac appealed to the same restless energy; the desire to explore outside the boundaries of stringent 1950s societal norms, to pursue the notion of true youthful freedom, to blaze along America's highways to the sounds of rock and roll and all-night jazz.

Rock and roll's version of *The Wild One*, Elvis Presley, his band, his backup singers the Jordanaires, June Juanico, and driver–security man Red West caravanned along US 92 out of St. Petersburg, turning north on the famous Orange Blossom Trail, past the gleaming new Tupperware Home Parties headquarters where trailblazing female sales maven Brownie Wise was breaking through management glass ceilings.

"We had a certain little game we would play to break the boredom," West recalled. "We'd drive along the countryside, we'd be going over a bridge. We had this little thing where somebody was talking about something really important, you'd tap them on the head, they were supposed to like change the channel, go to completely something different."

As they passed over the bridge, whoever was tapped on the head knew what was expected: "Take his shoes off and throw them out the window into the river!" exclaimed West. "Things like that, stupid little things just to break the monotony." That kind of fun was what Bill Black lived for. Red West called him "one of the craziest guys I ever met."

After finishing the ninety-three-mile journey to Orlando's Municipal Auditorium at 401 West Livingston Street, the touring party stashed their cars out of sight and headed into the auditorium barely a half hour before the first show was set to start. By Wednesday, the middle of Elvis Presley's most historic and demanding Florida tour, the band had already performed more than a dozen headlining shows for 35,000 fans. In Orlando, two more concerts and 6,500 youngsters awaited, as did Florida's first journalist to recognize the coming Presley phenomenon the year before, Jean Yothers.

"How long do you think you'll stay on top in show biz?" Yothers asked.

In a relaxed southern drawl Presley replied, "I wish I knew ma'am, people change a lot."

As hard as it is to imagine now, even at this early zenith in his career, Presley and those around him were still not convinced about his staying power. "He knows he won't be on top forever," added Bill Black backstage. "He's going into movies and maybe save some money to fall back on." In the early days Presley was known for buying lavish gifts for friends and family, but they rarely filtered down to bandmates. "He can spend and spend," Black said of Presley, "and not spend at all."

Writer George Miller described Presley's dramatic entrance in Orlando: "Elvis, in a bright red sport coat, its collar turned up, and white shirt open to his belt buckle, paced out of the dressing room door and into the wings where he hitched his pants, spread his legs like a child walking astride a broomstick, and hobble-swaggered on stage to a screaming ovation and a million exploding flash bulbs."

In the front row ecstatic fan Pat Hix said she liked Presley's "style of singing and his flashy clothes" best. Others had a different take on Presley's wardrobe and what it meant. "My mother was there. She kept saying, 'That guy's gonna make it. He's gonna be big,'" remembered Sanford resident Randi Russi, whose father also attended the concert. "My Dad thought he was gay because he wore silver and pink."

Moore scoffed at any notion Presley was homosexual or bisexual. From time to time, Presley liked to break away and have his own dates during modest downtime. Most of the time, Presley's bandmates were close by and witnessed his habits, including sexual dalliances. In his memoir *Scotty and Elvis Aboard the Mystery Train*, Moore recalled what he believed to be the night Presley lost his virginity. While on a 1954 *Louisiana Hayride* tour, the bandmates waited in the lobby while Presley used their only hotel room to have sex with a girl he'd met.

Suddenly, Presley came down to the lobby with her and exclaimed, "The rubber busted, what do I do now?" Black made a smartass comment; Moore was dumbfounded. Finally Presley took the girl to a local hospital for an emergency douche. When he told the older men what he'd done, both were surprised hospitals did that sort of thing. "Elvis was certainly an original thinker," Moore mused.

During the brief half-hour intermission between the Orlando shows, Presley tinkered on a beat-up piano backstage while five girls hovered, a blond, three brunettes, and another described as "half and half." As Presley picked out a blues tune on the piano, writer George Miller noted the singer's apparent exhaustion, though some of it could have been for dramatic effect to hold the attention of all the girls surrounding him.

"His large eyes almost closed under a shroud of tumbling hair," Miller observed. "One time Elvis slumped over the keyboard exhausted. Half and Half gently messaged his neck." Then Presley arose and starting pounding on some drums backstage, drawing the attention of a new house of fans waiting for the second show. "Half and Half" was likely Juanico. In a rebellious moment, she'd had a blond streak added to her brunette hair at the previous stop in St. Pete. Presley was not enamored with the new look.

"We Want Elvie, We Want Elvie," the crowd chanted.

"He's really wound up tonight," concluded the girl now known as Half and Half. As his band took the stage, Presley walked back into the smoke filled, high-ceilinged dressing room. Noting that Presley wasn't ready, Red West told the boys onstage to begin without him. "Play one," West instructed. When Presley was finally ready to amble out onstage to the familiar shrieks and flash bulbs, he blinked and stared, and pulled at his shirt, once again open to the waist: "Ladies and gentlemen," Presley broke into a smile and a giggle. "Yea, I want to tell you, I'm gonna tell you . . . I HEAR YA KNOCKIN'."

After his now-standard opening number "Heartbreak Hotel," Presley's first million-seller, he hopped around like a june bug to Little Richard's "Long Tall Sally," bringing the crowd into a frenzy all over again. Four policemen kept girls from rushing the stage while Presley removed his coat and belted out his new single, "Hound Dog." Jean Yothers gauged crowd reaction: "A delighted squeal erupted from the house that could have blown the top from Vesuvius."

Like Elvalee Donaldson in Lakeland and Anne Rowe in Tampa and St. Petersburg, Jean Yothers took the time to speak with and observe Presley, finding him to be a "real nice kid." Yothers treasured a photo of Presley giving her a peck on the cheek. "I egged him on," she confessed in an interview years later.

Juanico remembered that one of her all-time favorite moments with Presley came during the Orlando stop. Away from the bevy of other girls, Presley took Juanico's hand backstage and led her to the upright piano. "I've been working on something new, just for you, baby," he said with a grin on his face. With that, Presley started playing and singing "Unchained Melody," an all-time sentimental fan favorite due to the song's soulful, intimate lyrics, Presley's dramatic interpretation of them, and because it was reportedly the last song Presley ever sang the night before his death.

Oh my love, my darling, I've hungered for your touch. A long, lonely time.

"He sang beautifully, looking at me after every tentative chord change," recalled Juanico. "That special afternoon, with just the two of us at the piano, was one of the treasured times in our relationship, and it would stay in my mind forever." Within the din of screaming girls and controversy that dogged Presley during this phase of his career, it's easy to overlook the depth of his talent. Through a plaintive song like "Unchained Melody" Presley's voice, adaptable to so many genres, transported his girlfriend to the depths of his soul.

After seeing the Presley show in Orlando, three young buddies who worked for the local phone company in Deland pointed their car north on Highway 17-92 to head back to their rooming house in Volusia County. In the warm and humid August night the trio passed lakeside motels and restaurants on the road that led tourists to Big Tree Park in Longwood, where the three-thousand-year-old bald cypress known as "the Senator" towered in all its majestic glory.

Cresting a hill where 17-92 becomes French Avenue in Sanford, the boys noticed a brightly colored Lincoln that had pulled into a darkened service station not far from the Farmer's Market. "The service station was closed but the Coke machine was lit up," remembered Roy Brand, one of the three young men who'd seen the show that night and came to realize the star attraction was right in front of them: "My God that's Elvis," he exclaimed to his buddies.

The boys pulled in alongside the two Lincolns from Presley's traveling party. They scrambled over to the machine to buy Presley a contoured bottle of Coke for a nickel, went over to his car, and greeted him. Always one to have time for his fans, Presley started talking with the boys and engaging in the so-called distance game. Up until the 1960s, print on the bottom of Coke bottles included where they came from. In one version of the game, players compared whose bottle was manufactured closest to a player's hometown or to where they were at that moment.

"What do you boys do?" Presley asked.

When they told him they worked for the phone company, Presley decided to stick around a little longer and engage in what Brand called "a little good ol' boy talk." Juanico got into the other car with Red West and the rest of the entourage and headed on to the next stop in Daytona Beach. Presley told Brand and his friends he'd gotten as a gift a phone with a spring cord. Presley said in a near whisper, the phone company didn't know he was using the fancy ten-dollar device. But there was a problem; the phone line was scratchy and Presley couldn't figure out why.

Brand explained that it had to be a party line phone on a private line connection. At that time, people using party lines could expect their conversations to be heard by any one of a number of families using that same line. Brand explained the simple way to manipulate the green and yellow wires to remove the interference. "That's great, that's great," Presley exclaimed, now all alone in the central Florida night with three young men he'd just met. The significance of this random late night meeting was not lost on Roy Brand: "So here he is, already a multi-millionaire and he's screwing the phone company out of ten dollars or ten dollars and fifty cents."

In August of '56 Presley was yet to become a millionaire, but his income for that year alone came to just under $300,000. Brand, like Presley, had grown up dirt poor and concluded after many years of thinking about it that some parts of being so destitute never leave you. When Presley withdrew from the world in later years, Brand saw his situation as similar to that of the world-renowned but famously reclusive billionaire Howard Hughes. Both men ended up prisoners of their own fame and fortune.

But not on this night in Sanford; even as the tumult of fame and controversy swirled around him on his current Florida tour, Presley could stop for a Coke and some idle chitchat about party line phones with three guys he'd never met before and feel secure enough to be left all alone with them. "He was free," Brand declared.

After his late night bull session, Presley bade the trio farewell and took off for Daytona Beach, where inner strife between band members was about to reach a boiling point.

16

Boiling Over

August 9, Daytona Beach

In Daytona Beach Presley and his bandmates could have been forgiven if they brought along a little hubris. Only fifteen months previously, he had stood at the railing of his beachside motel staring at the Atlantic Ocean for the first time, tour promoter Mae Axton practically holding his hand. At Presley's first Florida concert, few in the audience knew what to make of him, fellow musicians kept their distance, and his performance consisted of a quick song or two. But no longer.

Now, the hillbilly oddity was the unquestioned king of rock and roll. Thanks to endless touring, and Tom Parker's fearless deal making, Presley was on a major record label, where he had produced multiple million-selling singles and a platinum album; he had made numerous successful national television appearances with the Dorsey Brothers, Milton Berle, and Steve Allen; and he had moved his family out of poverty in the Memphis projects to their own sprawling ranch home with a swimming pool. Not bad for a young man who had been making forty dollars a week just two years before.

The next chapter in Presley's rise to fame lay just a few short weeks ahead. After he finished the last few dates on this tour, Presley was headed to Hollywood to begin shooting his first feature film. Then he was slated to make his run of appearances on the *Ed Sullivan Show*, the nation's most talked-about variety program. In his storied career, 1956 was the year that made it all possible for Elvis Presley.

There was no hero's welcome awaiting Presley when his tour arrived back at the World's Most Famous Beach; far from it. "Everyone in the show was on edge," Scotty Moore recalled. For whatever reason, the group didn't stay in Orlando, preferring to make the late night drive over to the beach. After Presley stayed behind in Sanford, the rest of the tour members went on ahead. "It was one of those go-dawful all-night rides and everyone was ill and in a bad mood," said Moore.

It couldn't have been worse timing for a lapse in Parker's advance work. Mae Axton wasn't along this time either to make sure things ran smoothly. Late into the night the touring party bounced from beachside motel to motel, none of which had reservations or rooms for them. It was no time for Bill Black to make some sort of wisecrack, but that was what he always did.

"All I remember is that it had something to do with the motel," said Moore. "We went to blows and had a fistfight right there in the parking lot."

Black was a lot bigger than Moore, but as a former navy man, Moore knew how to protect himself. "It was a pretty good fight," recalled Neal Matthews of the Jordanaires. "It didn't last very long. Scotty was a pretty good fighter."

After everything Bill Black and Scotty Moore had done to provide the foundation for Elvis Presley's ascent in contemporary music, both were sick and tired, with no motel room in the middle of an arduous tour; Parker left them all stranded like hobos. Now they were duking it out in the middle of the night.

Ironically, June Juanico found out, the hotel they thought they had booked was jammed with numerous guests in town specifically to see Presley's shows. "We drove for miles down the beach, seeing the 'no vacancy' signs," Juanico remembered. After all the drama and hysteria she'd witnessed to this point in the tour, Juanico suggested

Vintage Copacabana Motel postcard. From author's personal collection.

she spend some time relaxing at the beach and skipping Presley's two Daytona Beach concerts. With Parker watching his young star like an overbearing den mother, Presley agreed that a little distance was a good idea.

"The colonel's been on my ass about you again," Presley told her. "So I'll see you in Jacksonville."

After hours of searching and fighting, the entourage finally found a place to stay. Locals Chuck and Jane Hansen, owners of the beachside Copacabana Motel at 1201 South Atlantic Avenue, welcomed them. By early the next morning, fans started getting word that the young star was staying in room eleven. After some decent sleep, when Presley emerged and walked over to La Casita motel and restaurant next door, plenty of attractive girls and curious young men started to congregate. The miserable all-night ride was giving way to a relaxing morning on the ocean.

In a series of photos taken outside the Copacabana, Presley appears very much at ease with fame and fans, signing autographs and—thanks to his distance from Juanico—flirting with the girls.

Like scenes from photographer Robert Frank's landmark 1950s book *The Americans*, Presley looks like any other young ducktailed guy enjoying the surf, sun, and sights on a warm August day.

For a few precious hours Presley walked the motel's expansive grass courtyard; even taking time to have a seat near the Copacabana's oceanside pool, with its high retaining wall on one end, the only thing separating it from cars cruising by on the sand and from the ocean's pounding surf in the distance. A black and white photo captures Presley, relaxed and with shirt unbuttoned, reading the morning paper with a new young lady friend at his side—one of several he flirted with while Juanico was elsewhere. The innocent man-child who had started his Florida journey here in 1955 was now a world-weary performer on his biggest, most lucrative tour to date.

Presley flirting with fan outside Copacabana Motel, Daytona Beach, August 1956. Courtesy of scottymoore.net.

"We had a nice picture of Elvis signed from him to 'the Hansens' hanging on the motel office wall for many years," recalled their granddaughter Joy Keener-Borresen. "But it was stolen when I was a child." After three hurricanes pounded it in 2004, the Copacabana Motel was demolished.

Presley's appearances have become a part of Daytona Beach lore alongside Fireball Roberts blazing down the hard sand track prior to the construction of Daytona International Speedway; gangster John Dillinger firing his tommy gun in the air to ring in 1934 beachside; Jackie Robinson playing the first integrated spring training baseball game in the stadium that now bears his name; local teens Duane and Gregg Allman honing their chops at Club Martinique along the boardwalk; and Sinatra performing at the Ocean Center in 1994, his final year of touring. In 1999 a large section of the Daytona Beach pier was torn off during Hurricane Floyd and shown on *NBC Nightly News* with Tom Brokaw, floating into the Gulf Stream with light posts still erect.

During his two shows at the Peabody Auditorium, Presley brought the loudest shrieks from the audience when darting from one end of the stage to the other singing his current hit, "Hound Dog." When he dove on his knees toward the audience, coming down part of the stage steps, it brought the house down. Marsha Connelly, who spent time with Presley during his early Daytona Beach appearances, described the madness: "I remember sitting by a woman who at the time I thought was old; she was probably late 20s or early 30s, and she was going nuts. It was phenomenal."

Another fan, Trish Robbins, had a hard time understanding the level to which she was caught up in Presleymania. "We cried so hard, we tore up a hanky in thirds and each piece was soaked with tears," she recalled. "I never really understood why we reacted like we did. But you just couldn't help it."

After the show girls lay flat on their stomachs outside the stage door to pass pieces of paper underneath for an autograph. Others trampled through the bushes outside Presley's dressing room:

"Touch me, touch me Elvis," pleaded one young girl.

"I would if I could," said Presley standing at the closed window and screen.

"Goodbye, I gotta go now," said Presley as he returned to an interviewer. "I love 'em all, without 'em I'd be lost."

"Is there some special girl somewhere?" a reporter asked. "No," Presley replied, not willing to acknowledge June Juanico, his worst-kept secret on the Florida tour. "There's no special girl anywhere."

"Well hang on, Elvis is signing one of his pictures right now," reported radio personality Ed Ripley, trying to interview the distracted star. "It's pretty busy here in the dressing room this evening, and we've got movie cameras, autographs and everything else going on around here. We've even got some people out here knockin' on the windows."

If you only read Ripley's interview, there's little new information revealed. What makes the interview memorable is the audio recording of it, distinctive in its clarity and intimacy. Ripley puts the microphone before a Deland schoolgirl named Peggy, who is in the process of going down an obviously prepared list of questions for Presley, while the din of girls now banging on the windows chanting "we want Elvis" is remarkably clear.

"Uh, do you like the girls going wild over you?" Peggy asks in a southern drawl. "It's what keeps me in business," says Presley, echoing the sentiments of Tom Parker. "I have another one but I don't know if I should ask it or not," Peggy confesses. "Um are you a dope fiend?"

"Ya," says Presley without skipping a beat, drawing laughs from other men backstage. Given all that Presley had been through that week, including widespread criticism from Florida columnists and reporters up and down the peninsula, his sense of humor remained intact. Ripley chimes in admiring Presley's black sapphire horseshoe-shaped ring, and you can hear Peggy remark, "That's neat." Presley comments about the gold records he'll be getting for his "new" records "I Want You, I Need You, I Love You" and "Hound Dog/Don't Be Cruel."

As Ripley inquires about when Presley's next record may come out a loud crash breaks up the conversation, causing one girl to scream. Undaunted, the intrepid radio man reports, "Uh, someone just broke a window here in Elvis's dressing room."

Not at all shocked and chuckling about the madness enveloping him, Presley tells the interviewer his next release will likely be "a couple months yet."

For a man who is just twenty-one himself, Presley is honest, candid, and funny. He doesn't talk down to the schoolgirl interviewing him, and he remains fun-loving even though his dressing room provides no respite from all the questions, cameras, and fans. His nature in this interview evokes the humorous way the Beatles handled all the suffocating attention when they broke big in America. As with the Beatles, Presley's personality was key to his appeal and staying power. It wasn't put on.

"Actually, the Tennessee Troubadour doesn't have a bad voice," assessed Daytona Beach writer Dotti Einhorn, "When his fans will let you listen to it." She noted that Presley's stage dive during "Hound Dog" didn't prompt any of his fans to try to kiss him or tear his clothes off. "There were three cops at each stairway who scared them off," she reported.

Max Norris of the *Daytona Morning News* reviewed Presley's appearance with the same dismissiveness as other male journalists in the course of the Florida tour. "Elvis Presley, whose tortured moans have found a vast audience in a tin-eared nation, slept here Wednesday night," read the opening line of Norris's article, another example of a reporter who had made up his mind and seemingly penned the lines before Presley ever set foot in town. Norris did track down Presley's most devoted Florida tour followers, Anne Muncy and Nilla Shea, who declared Elvis "a nice boy." Norris spoke to other girls who had camped outside Presley's door at the Copacabana Motel and claimed to have hidden in his Miami hotel closet.

Marsha Connelly managed to get close enough to Presley for him to recognize her. "Everybody was getting his autograph and when I came up he said, 'Marsha!' You should have seen the looks on the faces of the other girls when he left with me," she recalled. On a photo he wrote, "I still love ya, Marsha," and included his address and phone number. For a while she allowed herself to believe there might be a chance at romance with the young king of rock and roll, but by then, girls were throwing themselves at him night in and night out.

As was custom on two previous tours, Jacksonville was the last stop on Presley's final Florida tour during his rise to fame. A headline-grabbing judge was waiting to make sure there were no repeats of earlier fan riots—rumored or real. Reactionary preachers were spinning tales of gloom and doom over Presley's unseemly shows. Journalists from the country's leading periodical, *Life* magazine, were in town to document all the drama. The gauntlet was thrown down: clean up your act or go to jail.

A remarkable two-night stand and a six pack of shows lay ahead in the town where fans had rioted over Presley for the first time, setting in stone Tom Parker's ambition to manage Presley, and where his first million-selling single was written and recorded for the first time. More defining moments of Presley's early era awaited, northbound on US 1.

17

The Morals of Minors

August 10–11, Jacksonville

An exhibit called "American Cool" at the National Portrait Gallery in Washington, D.C., many years after Elvis Presley's death included a 1956 photograph of him performing in the South. Fans reach for him as if they're grasping for a rope to keep from drowning; his magnetism was like an irresistible, gravitational pull. In an article on the exhibit writer Ann Greer assessed the uniqueness of Presley's impact in that period: "Elvis had the ability to be playful and seductive at the same time, bringing out the primal side of those around him. It made his concerts almost like revivals but with a twist. The dark-clad man with a commanding manner seems . . . a bit devilish."

That phenomenon was never more in evidence than in Bob Moreland's photo series of Presley's interview with Tampa reporter Anne Rowe. His hands-on seductions of female journalists like Rowe could rightly be viewed as inappropriate and, in a religious context, downright sinful. But as quickly as he came on like a sex machine, Presley switched gears and made a joke or defused the tension with playfulness. This nuanced understanding of the duality of Presley's appeal, given the context of time, was nowhere to be found among civic and religious leaders at his final 1956 Florida tour stop in Jacksonville.

Their perceptions of Presley were far more black and white; the evil and the good.

At Trinity Baptist Church the Reverend Robert Gray held a Bible in his left hand and a concert poster of Elvis Presley in his right. With short black hair, suit, tie and glasses, the preacher resembled Buddy Holly as he stood at the church pulpit. This God-fearing preacher proclaimed his mission was to save Elvis Presley's soul. In advance of Presley's performances Gray held a prayer service in hopes of sparing the controversial performer a trip to the bowels of hell. He instructed teenagers at the service to bow their heads and pray for Presley's redemption. Reverend Gray proclaimed Presley had "achieved a new low in spiritual degeneracy. If he were offered his salvation tonight, he would probably say 'No Thanks.'" A reporter and photographer for *Life* magazine were there to capture the preacher drawing a spiritual line in the sand.

Never mind that Gray's claim was ridiculous, and he had never bothered to find out about Presley's abiding faith in God, or he ignored it. As Presley's FBI file indicated, this kind of misinformed adult reaction to his growing popularity was becoming the norm. Pompous newspapermen all over Florida had helped build on the mistaken notion. Supposedly responsible authority figures were basing their fear on rumored riots and fictional property damage, alleged moral degeneracy that anyone who did the least amount of fact-checking on Presley—or who bothered to take the time and plentiful opportunity to talk to him—soon found out did not exist. Preachers, police, and politicians of the day had ulterior motives: publicity or simply trying to reassure parents who saw their control of children eroding.

Behind the scenes, Tom Parker was chuckling all the way to the bank.

A full-page photograph in *Life* magazine showed Reverend Gray's followers, many of them children, with eyes closed, bowing in prayer. Some of the teens shown in the photograph must have been conflicted; Presley was now a cultural phenomenon, the talk of the town. Tickets to his six shows were selling out quickly. Boys were getting ducktail haircuts to look like Presley and learning his dance moves.

Droves of girls entered a contest to have a dinner date with him. And yet the preacher was trying to convince them Elvis Presley would burn in hell without prayers of the faithful to save his soul.

The buck stopped in Jacksonville by way of Juvenile Court judge Marion Gooding. Upon hearing the tales of woe from civic leaders and reading about Presley in the papers, Gooding filled out warrants on Presley to be served if he repeated his suggestive thrusting moves again in Jacksonville. The charge: impairing the morals of minors. Gooding labeled Presley's act "an obscene burlesque dance" and invited the entertainer to his chambers before the show, "to put him straight." Presley refused.

This took the criticism of influential columnists like Herb Rau to a new and disturbing level; now an authority figure with the ability to stop the show entirely made it clear that he was willing to do just that. The relatively benign and tired criticism of Presley's performances, comparing him to an exotic dancer, had morphed into institutionalized fear of the damaging effect of his concerts. Presley was not about to fire back in the press at Judge Gooding as he had at Herb Rau. Tom Parker, who had seen the inside of a jail cell, was nowhere on this one.

Scotty Moore saw the judge's posturing as pure public relations. "Gooding used the threat as if it were a platform in a political campaign," Moore groused. "He treated Elvis like a terrorist who had invaded the homeland."

Many decades later, former Florida governor Bob Graham, who had seen Presley just a few stops before Jacksonville, said the performance he witnessed was not offensive. "I would say he was certainly provocative," Graham recalled. "I would not use the word obscene." For Graham there was a broader societal context to consider; parents drawing upon the cultural mores of the Depression and World War Two were getting their initial taste of the new America Presley and other cultural figures of the time were ushering in: the hippie movement of the 1960s, civil rights activism, resistance to the Vietnam War, the women's movement, and rock and roll.

"He was kind of the leading edge of the social reforms that were to follow," said Graham, who dealt with more than his share of societal turmoil in Florida. As governor he reinstated the death penalty in 1979, despite harsh criticism for doing so. In August 1956 most Elvis fans could not have cared less about the danger he represented to their parents. As usual, it was good for business. For the 3:30 show on Friday, August 10, a long line of youngsters waited outside the Florida Theater in downtown Jacksonville. "The fans were screaming and hollering for blocks," wrote newspaperman Ron Wolfe. "A total of 13,200 fans got to see the hottest act ever to play Jacksonville."

One of those attending Presley's first show, stern faced and sitting all the way in the back, was Judge Gooding. He told the newspaper: "That was my belief that the vast majority of Jacksonville youngsters didn't believe in Mr. Presley's type of performance." Six sellout shows suggested just the opposite.

Among the young fans in the audience was Ardys Bell, who had run into Presley moments after he'd had some of his clothes torn off in Jacksonville in May 1955. She could feel tension inside the Florida Theater and understood what was at stake: "I knew when we went to that concert he had been told, if he did anything beyond what the judge told him he could do, Judge Gooding would walk him across the street," Bell said, referring to the jail, which was just steps from the theater. Bell ignored what adults were saying about Presley. "Our parents thought he was going to hell in a hand basket," she recalled. "I think Elvis was a very religious young man."

Knowing the eyes of Jacksonville's morality police were upon him, Presley stood mostly still and delivered his show to 2,200 screaming fans. He had been told before the concert to keep things clean and that was what he did. In return, his fans were robbed of the opportunity to see the most dynamic live performer in contemporary music at his most entertaining. In between shows Gooding met with Presley to secure a photo of himself laying down the law to the nation's most famous young singer. "I don't know what I'm doing wrong," Presley told reporters. "I know my mother approves of what I'm doing."

Presley was adept at turning on the dumbed-down part of his personality to counter his controversial side. By this time he was well aware of why adults found his performances objectionable. It was bringing in big dollars and record sales; Presley and Parker had no intention of changing the formula.

If that wasn't enough trouble, a representative from the American Guild of Variety Artists was in Jacksonville to demand that Presley join the union (at a cost of three hundred dollars), or he threatened to stop other performers from appearing. Presley resented the pressure tactics but in the end consented to join. Parker took care of the cost, which also included a performance bond and insurance.

That night Presley started to thrust his hips and caught himself. "Wait a minute, I can't do this," he told the audience. "They won't let me do this here." Standing virtually frozen, Presley wiggled his pinkie finger instead, bringing howls of laughter. "Everybody got the biggest charge out of that," said Gooding's daughter Marilyn, who was also in the audience. In another playful jab at the judge Presley dedicated "Hound Dog" to Gooding as he continued to wiggle his pinkie finger.

In time Gooding became a Presley fan and suggested the reactionary attitudes of those around him were to blame for the warrants and threats of arrest. "They had me convinced no teen-aged girl was safe around Presley," a contrite Gooding recalled years later. Privately, Presley was just as steamed at the judge as he was at Miami columnist Herb Rau. According to June Juanico, at the end of Presley's sixth and last performance that Saturday night, he looked in the judge's direction and, instead of his customary thank you, muttered into the microphone, "Fuck you very much."

After Presley's return to his dressing room, a stunned Juanico asked him if she had heard what he said correctly. "You heard correctly," he assured her. Had Presley's parents or Tom Parker been aware of what he said, they would have been outraged. Had Gooding heard, Presley would surely have ended his Florida tour behind bars.

Presley was proud to have had the last laugh on Gooding and his morality police: "I showed them sons of bitches, call me vulgar. You don't think I'm vulgar do you baby?" When he wiggled his pinkie,

Presley told his girlfriend, it drew the loudest shrieks from the crowd he'd heard, Miami included. Gladys Presley told her son never to go back to Jacksonville; whether fans were chasing him, exhaustion was overtaking him, or a judge was threatening to throw him in jail, trouble always seemed to find him there.

After performing fifty-nine live shows in the Sunshine State over sixteen months, after seeing his star rise like a streaking rocket launched from Cape Canaveral, after Mae Axton and Tommy Durden wrote his first million-seller in Jacksonville and Red Robertson took the world-famous "tonsil photo" of Presley in Tampa, after setting the state on fire over the first week of August 1956 and being threatened with incarceration, the last sentence Elvis Presley uttered to a Florida audience during this historic period started with "fuck you."

1960–1961

18

Presley and Sinatra TV Special

March 1960, Miami

To show how much things had changed since Elvis Presley was the controversial pseudo burlesque dancer who flirted with obscenity arrest in Florida, four years later Frank Sinatra, who often bad-mouthed Presley during his rock and roll years, planned a television special to welcome him back from the army. The bizarre and unlikely pairing was due to film in Miami over three days in late March 1960. The show would mark Presley's first Florida performance since his last Jacksonville concert in August 1956. In four years Presley's life and career had undergone a dramatic transformation.

By the latter part of 1957 Presley ended his touring days to concentrate on his more lucrative film career. For the members of Presley's backing band who'd been with him since day one, Scotty Moore and Bill Black, no touring meant no chance to make more than two hundred dollars a week in salary; about the same money members of Presley's back-slapping entourage of yes-men known as the "Memphis Mafia" made. "Except members of his entourage also received free automobiles and expensive gifts," Moore wrote in his memoir. "Elvis never once purchased cars for Bill or me. It just seems so crazy."

In September 1957, while Presley was in Hollywood shooting a movie, back in Memphis his frustrated bandmates finally turned in letters of resignation. Presley fumed about Moore and Black being disloyal, while the ever-conniving Parker made no attempt to play peacemaker. "Tom Parker had us right where he wanted us," Moore wrote.

To make ends meet, Bill Black took a job at a Memphis appliance store. He told the local newspaper he was "embarrassed." Moore told reporters Elvis had always promised that as his income rose, so would theirs. Nothing could have been further from the truth. In response to Moore's request for a fifty-dollar raise, a pittance given the money Presley was raking in, on September 18, 1957, Presley's father, Vernon, who was now working for his son, wrote Scotty and Bill perfunctory letters to notify them their services were no longer needed.

After a short cooling-off period, Scotty and Bill agreed to accompany Presley as independent contractors for another month of dates in Texas, California, and Hawaii. The last concert the original trio performed during this remarkable era came at the Conroy Bowl in Hawaii on November 11, 1957.

Moore had held on to the notion that Presley would come to his senses and recognize Parker for what he really was. They didn't want to quit Elvis; both men still held on to hope Presley would think about things, come to realize all that Scotty and Bill had meant to him, and bump them up to a decent living wage.

As usual Parker prevailed and, by alienating Scotty and Bill, cut out a sizable chunk of Presley's rock and roll soul. From the distant Sun Records days and all those timeless recordings by the three who altered the course of modern music history, the darkening twilight gave way to night. Parker's plan to soften Presley's image did not include rock and roll or high profile roles for Scotty and Bill. The departure of these two quintessential musicians sounded the death knell for Presley's soul-shouting rebellion; the jailhouse rocker was gone.

Never was the hand of Tom Parker more evident than in the repeatedly cruel and dismissive way he marginalized Presley's musical brothers-in-arms from the early days. Every time they tried to figure out a promotion or idea to augment their earnings, if it had to do with Elvis, Parker slammed the door; no one was going to horn in on his specialty of profiting off all things Presley. When it came to any form of hucksterism or merchandising to generate more money from his client-cum-commodity, Tom Parker was shameless. Hocking Elvis Presley photos and wearing an Elvis straw hat festooned with Elvis buttons appealed to Parker's carny nature. He never had a care in the world about the effect it had on Presley's credibility as an artist.

D. J. Fontana was in a different position; he had been brought on as a salaried side man from the beginning. Starting out, Presley, Scotty, and Bill made a verbal pact to be equal partners. Moore and Black were told they would share in the royalties of Presley's recordings on which they played key roles. That never happened. By the middle of 1957 Presley was rich, while his bandmates struggled on. Tom Parker was the hatchet man, but Presley was well aware of what was happening and did nothing to stop it. The same would hold true for the generally lousy career choices Parker made for Presley during the coming decade.

Parker's plan for Presley's future was to make him more palatable to all those adults who still held mistrust and resentment for him. In the end it was all about money; Parker didn't want to alienate anyone who could contribute to Presley's box office draw. Freewheeling singles like "Jailhouse Rock" gave way to "Stuck on You," among other ballads. Moore was mystified: "It was like Elvis had been kidnapped and taken off to a side show of a circus." Make that a carnival. Television producer Steve Binder knew the trench warfare that accompanied a battle of wills with Tom Parker. When things got really heated, Binder said the former carny had a kind of death stare that convinced him Parker was trying to hypnotize him.

By far the most traumatizing event during this transition period of Presley's life came on August 14, 1958, when his first love, the person Presley was closest to in the world, forty-six-year-old Gladys Presley, died of a heart attack brought on by acute hepatitis.

It's impossible to overstate the impact on Presley of losing such an important friend, confidante, and champion. Gladys was the person Presley could depend on most for unconditional love, honest advice, and understanding.

The emotional ties between Presley and his father, Vernon, were nowhere near as close as the unmovable bond Presley had with his mother, his anchor, and she for her only surviving child. As another member of Presley's growing roster of employees, Vernon was not about to question who was the boss. Adding more tension in the father-son relationship, by 1960 Vernon was on the verge of remarrying. His fiancée Dee Stanley had three young boys of her own from a previous marriage. Presley came to love his younger half-brothers.

In 1957 Presley's longtime girlfriend June Juanico, who accompanied him on his final Florida tour, got tired of waiting around and reading reports of her former paramour in Hollywood with one starlet after another. On a train ride home from Hollywood to Memphis, Juanico got on board in New Orleans only long enough to let him know she was engaged to another man. That meant another close emotional bond from Presley's touring days was severed.

From 1958 to 1960 Presley traveled to Germany, not to perform but to serve a required two-year stint in the U.S. Army. While serving overseas Presley met and was immediately smitten with an officer's daughter, fourteen-year-old Priscilla Beaulieu. During his two years in the army Presley's relationship with the dark-haired young beauty deepened to the point where he was pushing Priscilla's father to let her live with him back home at Graceland after his discharge. This time Tom Parker was stateside and in no position to throw cold water on Presley's budding romance. Eventually Presley got his way.

A dark legacy from the military was the beginning of Presley's descent down the rabbit hole of using and abusing prescription drugs. As a way to stay awake during long, monotonous hours on maneuvers, a sergeant introduced Presley to amphetamines. He started popping pills and washing them down with coffee. "He was so full of energy he never had to slow down," wrote his biographer Peter

Guralnick. "They all took them, if only to keep up with Presley, who was practically evangelical about their benefits."

Soon Presley was buying amphetamines in large supply, telling friends it was a safe way to keep weight down and energy boundless. He knew, however, that it would not be safe to be caught with them coming back home to the United States. When it was time to return, the honorably discharged Presley did something decidedly dishonorable; he put his young assistant and sometime lover Elisabeth Stefaniak in charge of smuggling a half-gallon jar of amphetamines in her luggage.

Had this selfish request of a trusted assistant been discovered, it would have left Stefaniak little choice but to take all the blame and consequences. More than once during interviews about his time in the army, Presley gave the slightest hint of what he'd done, remarking: "I made it just like everybody . . . I mean I tried to play it straight just like everybody else."

During Presley's absence overseas, rock and roll faded from popular culture due to a series of dramatic developments. In February 1959 the prolific young songwriter Buddy Holly, who once shared a 1955 concert bill with Presley, died in an Iowa plane crash. Jerry Lee Lewis was ostracized for marrying his thirteen-year-old cousin, and another early pillar of rock and roll, Chuck Berry, was arrested for transporting a fourteen-year-old girl across state lines for alleged immoral purposes.

For his part, Tom Parker developed a love of locking horns with Hollywood big shots like producer Hal Wallace to make the best money possible for himself and Presley. Being a Hollywood power broker was the realization of a dream Parker had hatched way back during his days at Tampa's Humane Society, when he provided animal actors and kowtowed to filmmakers working in the area. Presley's films were formulaic and churned out quickly, providing solid box office receipts and a princely leading man income for Presley. In return he paid a steep price by losing the artistic fulfillment, adrenaline rush, and unconditional love he received while performing live.

After Presley's return from the army, previous rivals who had held the most mistrust for Tom Parker—Gladys Presley, Scotty Moore, and June Juanico—were no longer in the picture. It was during the 1960s that many fans believe Tom Parker turned from star maker to slave driver and Presley from the epitome of rock and roll rebellion to the indentured actor-crooner content to cloister himself in the highly lucrative world of mediocre films, forgettable songs, and his new preoccupation with pharmaceuticals.

After his less-than-amicable parting of the ways with Scotty and Bill in 1957, upon his return to the United States in March 1960 Presley tried to reconcile with them by inviting the boys to be part of the Sinatra special. As was typical of their on-again off-again professional relationship with Presley, Moore and drummer D. J. Fontana accepted. Bill Black had moved on, citing commitments with his new and successful jazz group, the Bill Black Combo. The bass-slapping good-time Charlie who had provided so much rhythm on the Sun recordings and the comic relief on Presley's early concert tours would never work with him again. Black died of a brain tumor in 1965 at age thirty-nine.

After some recording in Nashville, Presley, Moore, Fontana and the entourage boarded a train bound for Miami. The trip was supposed to be secret, but Parker was never one to ignore an obvious chance for some free and easy publicity. He notified small town newspapers to watch for Presley's train. Even at 2:00 a.m. girls lined the tracks to watch the Presley train roll by. When Elvis and Scotty crossed back into Florida together for the first time since 1956, ironically their first stop was the impressive and stately train terminal in Jacksonville, the town from which Gladys Presley had told her son to stay away.

Like inventor Thomas Edison, and President Franklin D. Roosevelt before him, returning hero Presley took time to appear on the back platform of the train at the Jacksonville terminal. On the train ride, Moore recalled, some of the ice was melting between his old bandmates and Presley. "Everybody would just get in his car and be kibitzing," Moore recalled. When it got to be two or three in the morning, Moore said Presley offered him and Fontana "a couple of little white pills and said, 'Here, these'll keep you awake. It's what they use in the army, driving tanks."

Presley made it clear he was nervous at the thought of his first television appearance in two years coming beside the biggest singer–movie star in show business, Frank Sinatra. "I'm not exactly worried," Presley told an interviewer. "But I'm not sure of myself either." Presley said he hoped to take on more serious roles as an actor. Thanks to Parker's paranoia about doing anything to damage the former rock and roller's more wholesome image, he forbade Presley from accepting anything serious or the least bit controversial, one of Presley's bitterest and most lingering disappointments.

"It was all about power, that's why I was so in shock, people were so in awe of Colonel Parker," said Steve Binder, who refused to acquiesce to some of the ridiculous ideas Parker had; formulaic clichés Binder knew instinctively would ruin the comeback special he produced. "What I saw was a con man the first time I met him."

For his part, Sinatra never took back the awful things he had said about Presley and rock and roll. By this time it didn't matter. Presley was looking and sounding far more like a Sinatra clone than the young rock and roll sex machine that blew through Florida like Hurricane Donna. "The kid's been away two years," Sinatra said before the taping in Miami. "I get the feeling he really believes in what he's doing." Not exactly a ringing endorsement.

In Hollywood, Florida, five thousand fans waited at the station for Presley's train to pass through. He promised disc jockey Jerry Wichner he would step out of his car to say a few words. Some pranksters seized on the opportunity to pelt the train with eggs and tomatoes; that was enough to convince Presley to skip the greeting before his final destination. As a make-good gesture, Hollywood's Mayor William Zinkil later sent an envoy down to Miami to present Presley with a key to the city.

If Presley harbored any unease about fans forgetting him, those thoughts were assuaged upon his arrival at Miami's East Coast Railway station on March 22, 1960. In the shadow of the Dade County Courthouse, fans packed the downtown station. "You'd never know

Elvis Presley had been away," the *Miami Herald* reported. "Thousands of screaming, weeping teen-agers mobbed the downtown Miami FEC station to welcome back the singer-turned-sergeant-turned civilian."

No longer sporting his trademark sideburns, the newspaper noted, Presley looked more Sinatra-esque in a fedora when he checked in at Fontainebleau Hotel on Collins Avenue in Miami Beach. The special was to be shot in the hotel's grand ballroom and aired on ABC weeks later. This was the same hotel where Parker had said he was too afraid to book Presley back at the start of his August 1956 tour for fear his young devotees would trash the place. Despite the fans who greeted Presley at the train station, by March 1960 many of those from his barnstorming years had already moved on.

"I loved him for the early years," remembered Linda Moscato, who was among the screaming crowds at the Olympia Theater in 1956. "By the 1960s he was off my radar, I'd lost track of him." Doris Tharp-Gurley, who skipped school to ride the bus and meet Elvis in Orlando in 1955, recognized that his films were "a cookie cutter thing" to make money. "Some of them were just silly," she said. "I thought he did an okay job of acting." Presley's longtime Jacksonville fan Ardys Bell was more blunt about the Elvis films: "I didn't like 'em. I thought if he was going to act he could have done well in other kinds of movies. Not those silly things."

Parker made sure there was no mention of Scotty Moore and D. J. Fontana in advertisements, no hint of the controversial persona that had drawn so many teens to Presley in the first place. As for Presley's reunion with his old bandmates, Parker squelched any notion of that too, ordering that they be excluded from any social activities. They were to be kept far down the food chain when it came to access to Presley.

Artistically speaking, the cost of Parker transforming Presley for maximum profit and mass consumption was years of cultural irrelevance; the bland Elvis's career slumped. In contrast, after the Beatles stopped touring, they were revered for their continued musical evolution into more complex themes and instrumentation. The same could not be said for Presley. His late '60s renaissance came only when producers like Steve Binder stood up to Parker or when Presley himself circumvented Parker's suffocating influence. Ultimately it was Presley's own willingness to record more socially relevant songs in the late 1960s that resurrected his dormant mainstream popularity.

That fact was not lost on Scotty Moore: "It was fun going to Miami but musically it was a far cry from the good old days when our music was raw and bristling with energy." The last time Presley had appeared on television wearing a tuxedo, Steve Allen had him singing to a real hound dog. This time Presley wore one and looked like a junior member of Sinatra's rat pack, except for one big consideration: Parker secured Presley a pay day of half the show's $250,000 budget—more than Sinatra, more than Sammy Davis Jr. and other established stars also on the bill.

As Moore moved toward the hotel elevator, another crucial figure in Presley's early career, Mae Axton, was also getting on. After the friends exchanged hellos the elevator door opened and a girl in a cap and short matching skirt asked: 'What floor please?'" When the door opened to the floor of Presley's suite, the group found out why the uniformed girl was running a self-operating elevator; she darted in front of a guard and very nearly succeeded in getting into Presley's room.

"It was just one of the many ruses I've seen people use to try to get close enough to touch Elvis," Axton recalled. Compared to the rioting girls Axton saw in 1955 climbing through a window and ripping at Presley's clothes back in the old Jacksonville baseball stadium, this incident was far more benign.

From her time dealing with Presley the greenhorn performer, Axton could tell when he was nervous. Watching his rehearsal in the Fontainebleau's grand ballroom, she was keenly aware that Presley was wound up tight for his return to network television after such a long absence. "I must give a lot of credit here to Sammy Davis Jr., because Elvis was under pressure even more than a little nervous," said Axton. "Sammy took over, entertained the crowd a bit, with his arm on Elvis's shoulder, until Elvis relaxed."

Given his close friendship with Axton, Presley confided in her that he was insecure about the way his hair was piled high on his head with curls to which he was not accustomed. Those close to him knew how particular Presley was about his hair. "I reassured him that he was home—he was Elvis—he hadn't changed, and no flaw in the nation's idol would be seen," recalled Axton, his champion, promoter, and songwriting partner, thanks to Axton giving Presley a one-third songwriting credit for "Heartbreak Hotel."

When taping commenced, Presley made a brief appearance early on in his army uniform. His musical numbers started with abbreviated versions of "Fame and Fortune" and "Stuck on You," slotted forty minutes into the hour-long special. Then the two tuxedoed American icons Frank Sinatra and Elvis Presley shared the stage, with Sinatra singing Presley's ballad "Love Me Tender" and Presley looking awkward snapping his fingers while performing Sinatra's "Witchcraft."

For better or worse, this was the new Elvis his fans would have to endure until his aforementioned comeback special eight long and momentous years later. From 1960 to 1968 Presley poured his most vulnerable and enduring vocal performances into the only work for which he was recognized with Grammy awards, his gospel records. Those who write off Presley's career during this time forget to consider his soul-stirring renditions of songs like "Known Only to Him."

When the Sinatra special aired on May 12, 1960, ratings were stellar, but many reviewers were not kind. "Two years in the Army did more for Elvis Presley than relieve him of his sideburns. His name mellowed with absence, and some people cast a friendlier eye on the new image," wrote a reviewer in *Time* magazine. "Last week ABC's Frank Sinatra Timex Show spent more than a quarter of a million dollars to welcome Elvis home and performed a highly useful service: It reminded the forgetful just how dreadful Elvis really is."

The reviewer compared the unusually curly hair-do Presley fretted over to "a Vaseline halo," called his voice "an ordinary whine, on the point of becoming vinegar," and pronounced the show itself "pretentious and dull." On that last point, judging from surviving clips, the reviewer gives a fair assessment. Like it or not, this was the speed, tempo, and look of much of Presley's 1960s output as dictated by Tom Parker.

Due to the lack of challenging acting roles and loss of the electrified, emotionally charged give-and-take that Presley had enjoyed with his live audiences, it's no wonder he sought refuge in drugs. Tom Parker's consistently lousy career choices and his star client's willingness to acquiesce had the effect of marginalizing Presley and his career.

Despite securing a king's ransom for Presley's appearance with Sinatra, after all the hoopla Parker engineered on the train ride to Miami, the skinflint promoter made Presley and his entourage ride a greyhound bus back to Memphis.

Presley would be back in Florida for a six-week movie-making stint the following year.

19

Follow That Dream

July–August 1961

Since Florida fans could not hope to see Elvis Presley live in concert in 1961, news that he would spend six weeks in the Sunshine State making his ninth film, *Follow That Dream,* was the next best thing. A variety of film locations in Ocala, Silver Springs, Yankeetown, and Inverness provided Presley a Florida homecoming. Making this film afforded him a chance to shed some of the pretense of Hollywood, to emerge from his increasingly cloistered life to some extent, and to walk among his legion of still-devoted fans.

Based on Florida author Richard Powell's 1959 *New York Times* bestselling novel *Pioneer Go Home*, the film focuses on the true story of a group of fishermen who claimed squatters' rights to a tract of land under a new bridge between Fort Myers and Pine Island. The fill dirt used to build the bridge created a stretch of property not seen on existing maps. They eventually prevailed in their claims.

For Tom Parker there was something personal about having Presley in a film about someone coming to Florida, starting with nothing and thriving, just as he had after his release from military incarceration. "I believe that there is as much gold in Florida—of course not in the literal sense—as in the California Gold Rush," Parker said in a prescient moment in 1959. "Many friends I know and have known for 25 or 30 years came to Florida with very little money. Some of them were broke. Most of them are very rich men today."

Twenty years before Presley came to Florida to make the movie, Parker was down and out; he was newly released from the psych ward when he caught on with carnivals and the Hillsborough County Humane Society. Within ten years he had broken into show business management and booking. By 1961 he was a legend-in-the-making and a feared negotiator who had Hollywood big shots agreeing to pay his only client the kind of money reserved for its biggest stars. By one estimate Parker himself was making $300,000 a year.

Tom Parker lived the Florida dream of seeking and earning a better life; how he did so remains a topic of debate among Presley's fans. Still, the film's premise was no hillbilly joke to Tom Parker: "I think that this is a great story that has never been told," said Parker. "Many people who came here for a vacation, or were simply passing through, stayed to become the real pioneers of Florida."

Toby Kwimper, Presley's character in the film, is a strong, good-looking, simple southern kid; an innocent whose brawn often makes up for his lack of brains; a less exaggerated version of the Jethro Bodine character played by Max Baer Jr. in the popular TV show the *Beverly Hillbillies*. In the film, Kwimper's father, played by venerable character actor Arthur O'Connell, makes his family squatters on a picturesque stretch of beach after taking a wrong turn along a newly built highway. Once some disagreeable government men get Pop Kwimper's dander up, they claim squatters' rights, then use their resourcefulness to make a living in a sandy, palm-treed paradise.

Anne Helm, a twenty-two-year-old Canadian model and actress, played Toby Kwimper's adopted little sister, an orphan named Holly Jones. Helm's character is babysitter and caretaker to a tow-headed pair of twin boys, Eddy and Teddy, played by Gavin and Robin Coon—often seen in the film but barely heard. To no one's surprise, an off-screen romance developed between Presley and his leading lady. On

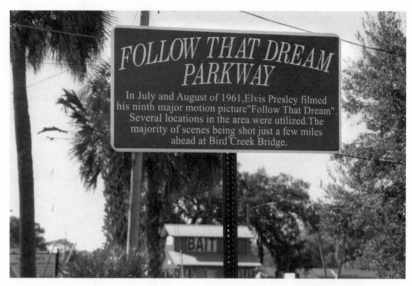

Follow That Dream Parkway, Inglis, Florida. Courtesy of Mike Robinson.

screen, there are enough run-ins with government officials and dangerous, over-dressed gangsters to give Presley plenty of opportunity to act, sing, and karate chop his way out of trouble.

Gambling was illegal in Florida, so some real-life gangsters were enlisted to bring in the dice tables and other equipment needed for Presley's scenes with underworld bad guys. "Maybe they'll have a screen credit," Hollywood columnist Erskine Johnson suggested: "Gambling equipment courtesy of the Mafia." The film went through several name changes before the producers settled on *Follow That Dream*. Even though some consider the film another forgettable Elvis vehicle, the fact that he looks the part and plays a down-to-earth character truer to the young man he was when he first toured Florida explains its enduring appeal to Florida fans. This time he wouldn't be wearing a tux and trying to mimic Sinatra on national television.

Images of the ghastly heat and weather problems the crew endured in July and August 1961 during the making of *Follow That Dream* fall away when you see Presley on screen; still young, still in full possession of his superstar voice and looks. Never mind the plot—just having Elvis Presley in a variety of old Florida locations like the historic courthouse at Inverness makes the film an unforgettable slice of Florida lore; an idealized view of the Sunshine State prior to superhighways and sprawl, and of Presley before his slow, agonizing decline.

Production plans called for Presley to film scenes inside an Ocala bank and to do interiors in the Crystal River High School gymnasium. The majority of the outdoor scenes were to be shot along a scenic stretch of State Road 40 in both Inglis and Yankeetown, before wrapping up inside the courthouse in Inverness. Tom Parker struck a deal for Presley to be paid $600,000 plus 50 percent of the film's box office profits. Thanks to Parker, Presley had become one of Hollywood's highest paid actors; a far cry from his days barnstorming Florida, putting in all those grueling miles crammed into a sedan, hoping to catch late-night truck-stop fried chicken.

Shooting started the first week of July 1961.

20

Crystal River

When Anne Helm read for the role of Holly, the enormity of what could happen if the audition went well was lost on her. Never mind that far more established actresses like Connie Stephens and Tuesday Weld were rumored to be up for the role—there was something about the character that Helm found easy to relate to and occupy. "I remember when I tested for the part, I was able to transport myself into the role of Holly; that doesn't always happen," Helm said. "I remember enjoying the test scene a lot and I really wasn't all that nervous."

Producers leaned strongly toward Weld—some early publicity even suggested she had indeed won the role. In the end they decided she could not be "southern enough." Ironically, Helm was a Canadian-born dancer, actress, and former New York model; not exactly out of the backwoods herself. When word came that she had gotten the role and would star on-screen opposite Elvis Presley, Helm knew it would mean spending a lot of time with him. But grasping the enormity of his fame would come later. In the short term, it was time to celebrate. "When I found out I did get the role I was really surprised and thrilled," Helm recalled. "I went out and bought myself a brand new T-Bird."

Presley and his regular group of bodyguard buddies, the Memphis Mafia, came to town in a caravan pulling Presley's boat. For the first time his teenage cousin Billy Smith was also accompanying Presley to a location shoot. Bodyguard Red West had just gotten married and planned to spend a working honeymoon as Presley's stunt double. In a rented bus Presley and his entourage traversed the pristine waterways and fishing hamlets dotting the outer reaches of Florida's Big Bend region, south across the Suwannee River, headed for Crystal River. On Thursday July 6 Tom Parker and a security contingent met up with them on State Road 19, escorting the convoy toward Presley's home for the next six weeks: the governor's suite at the Port Paradise Hotel.

"Boy this is really a beautiful place," Presley said, adding a whistle for emphasis. After inspecting the grounds, he declared, "This is better than I had in Hawaii." Before to coming to Florida, the last film Presley had shot on location was the still unreleased *Blue Hawaii.* Some 4,600 miles away, situated in the heart of Florida's Nature Coast, Crystal River borders King's Bay, a spring-fed wintertime paradise to scores of manatees migrating inland when the Gulf of Mexico cools. Even in the hottest stretches of summer, the springs flow at or near a constant, refreshing 72 degrees.

"Presley's villa at Port Paradise is barricaded like a prison compound," the *Suncoast Sentinel* reported. "A fence surrounds it, and the entrance gate is locked. Guards are on duty 24 hours a day." The head of security, Deputy Sheriff Louis Pielow, was in charge of deciding who would get close to Presley during his stay and who would not.

Two days before filming was to commence, Helm flew to Florida and with little fanfare checked into a smaller room at the Port Paradise. She busied herself with preparations for her hair, makeup, and wardrobe. After a long day she and her hairstylist caught a bite to eat at a local restaurant. "Somebody's over there looking at you," said Helm's dinner companion. Over in a far corner, in the middle of his entourage, Elvis Presley was setting eyes on his new co-star in person for the first time.

"You know he's checking you out," the stylist whispered.

"I couldn't really see him, he was sort of hidden away," Helm remembered. "I got pretty flustered and I didn't really meet him at that time."

Later that evening Presley sent a message through a production manager requesting an opportunity to meet with Helm privately. When she agreed, Helm received a knock on the door of her room. "There he was with a flower in his hand," Helm remembered. "I just kind of melted." The twenty-six-year-old leading man differed from the impression Helm had gotten watching him on television. "I didn't know what to expect because I'd seen Elvis as a teenager on the *Ed Sullivan Show*, and I thought he was a little strange."

Having been raised by a manic-depressive mother and having had to help support her family from a young age, Helm wasn't the typical carefree teen of the 1950s; she started modeling at age fourteen. There wasn't a lot of time for the fun other kids her age were having, and she was never caught up in Presleymania. Now the controversial rock and roller of the 1950s, whom Ed Sullivan had had cameramen shoot only from the waist up, in no way resembled the far more refined man who'd come by to introduce himself properly.

"He was so sweet and humble and he asked for a glass of water," Helm recalled. "We sat down and began to talk and that was the beginning of our relationship."

The Port Paradise gave Presley a place to park his new twenty-foot Chris-Craft Coronado power boat with easy access to skiing and fishing. The notion that he could enjoy old Florida recreation like any other tourist was pure fantasy; even in this remote part of the state, word of his arrival electrified fans, many of whom were determined to interact with him in person. But being on the water did give Presley the ability to relax and enjoy some separation from ever-present autograph seekers.

Like Presley, Helm was the embodiment of many parts of her character: beautiful, innocent, and down-home. She also felt at home in Florida, having lived and worked previously in Miami Beach. Presley was smitten with her immediately. Besides the card games in which Helm participated, there wasn't a lot to do in Crystal River at night. During the first few days on location, now that the two were acquainted, Presley asked Helm if she'd like to go for a drive. Generations later, this remains one of her favorite memories of him.

The two rode in a white hardtop Cadillac limo down State Road 40, an isolated stretch of two-lane highway dotted by trees adorned with Spanish moss. The dark Florida back country sky beamed with constellations of stars, and cooling breezes brought whispers of romance. "There was something very surreal about it. I thought: *I can't believe I'm sitting in this huge car in a wooded area with Elvis Presley*," Helm said with an air of disbelief. "Then a song of his came on the radio and I thought: *This is just beyond anything I could ever imagine.*" Helm said she liked to think the song was "Loving You" but wasn't sure and didn't think to keep a diary.

On-screen the two were like brother and sister, but off-screen was a different story. In the isolated reaches of Crystal River, a strong attraction was building between two Hollywood stars who might as well have been stranded together on a desert island. Helm became "one of the guys" closest to Elvis week in and week out, seeing better than most what his life was like; the good and the bad. "He was caged by his fame," Helm said. In a fenced-off compound surrounded by twenty-four-hour guards, even in a spring-fed paradise this was never more true.

In the newspapers Parker and his right-hand man Tom Diskin made sure to capitalize on Presley's budding romance with Helm. Within days word had filtered back to Louella Parsons, one of the era's highest-profile Hollywood gossip columnists: "Elvis has been dating leading lady Anne Helm in high style," she reported. "He put one of his cars, a plush white Cadillac, at her disposal. . . . Also he's a great boy with the flowers."

Early on, photos show Presley looking relaxed, standing outside his villa holding an impromptu autograph session with fans. Often they included young children, adults, and seniors—evidence that his persona of five years before, as the rock and roll bad boy who brought controversy to Florida, was long gone.

When filming began in early July, many locals would have the chance to appear as extras, getting paid ten to twenty dollars a day to work, talk, eat, and hang out with Presley. Others were asked to perform odd jobs in and around the set. Local police officers and security men by the dozens earned three dollars an hour making sure fans didn't get too close to Presley. "Don't worry," Parker assured them. "If fans come through and get close to Elvis, he can handle it."

Still others lucky enough to work their regular jobs where some of the scenes were filmed had front-row seats to watch Presley ply his new trade as an actor.

21

Weall House, Inglis, and Commercial Bank and Trust, Ocala

A *Tampa Tribune* reporter was allowed to observe the goings-on in Inglis, where the earliest scenes for *Follow That Dream* were filmed. He noted how professional Presley was during the tedious process of adjusting lights, moving cameras into place, and testing equipment: "Finally someone yelled 'Quiet everybody!' and somebody else yelled 'Take One,' and the first scene of Elvis Presley's new movie was under way." In early location photos shot at the Weall House in Inglis, Presley and Helm have an obvious rapport. One photo caption posed the possibility of an off-screen romance: "Elvis' interest in leading lady Anne Helm appears more than professional."

This deleted scene, the first one shot in Florida, featured character actor Dub Taylor, who would go on to play the farmer who hides under his truck as lawmen make it judgment day for Warren Beatty and Faye Dunaway in *Bonnie and Clyde*. From Inglis, location shooting moved into downtown Ocala.

In the bookkeeping department at the Commercial Bank and Trust at 203 East Silver Springs Boulevard in Ocala, bank teller Betty Larson heard the unmistakable voice of bank president James Richardson, taking a guest on a tour.

"I've got somebody you have to meet," said Richardson as he introduced Presley to the surprised and awestruck young teller. Larson was aware that her place of employment was going to be another early filming location and that Presley would be getting a walk-through before cameras rolled, but still, to see up close the rock star she idolized in the 1950s was stunning.

"It was very hard to believe—everybody knew I was crazy about him," said Larson, who bought a new pink outfit and the highest high heels she'd ever worn, just in case something like this happened. "They started to leave and he grabbed and kissed me right on the lips," Larson remembered. "All the bookkeepers shouted." Clearly they were in on the surprise, as was Presley, who was always ready for a little fun.

During the course of several days Presley spent time in Richardson's office talking finance, impressing the bank president with his interest in business. "The Colonel made him a star," Richardson declared. "But Elvis was no dummy." Richardson did not charge the film crew a location fee for using his bank. The avalanche of positive press attention was worth it.

Members of Ocala's theater community jumped at the chance to interact with Presley. While he was new to town, Michael Hall joined the Marion Players. After Hall directed a couple of one-act plays, the president of their group received a casting call from Hollywood. Would any of the local theater group members be interested in making a little money as extras in a film starring Elvis Presley?

"I got my name on the applicants list just about as fast as I could," Hall said. With his range of experience in theater, Hall got a call back and was offered the chance to work with Presley in front of and behind the camera. So did another Marion Player, Jim Huber, whose mother, Mary Kay, also worked at the bank.

A friend from the Marion Players asked George "Red" Langdon if he would like to sign up to work on the Elvis Presley movie. "I thought he was pulling my leg," said Langdon decades later. At eighty-one he still kept a photo of Presley and himself in his wallet. Because of their comparable size, Langdon would do stand-in work for Presley and a little bit of everything else he was asked. Often he was simply there to help the film's big star pass the time in between takes.

Langdon estimated that more than five hundred people signed up to be extras. Some of those who weren't chosen planned to show up early on Saturday, July 15, to watch the stages of Ocala filming, the first scene being the arrival of Presley's character driving up to the bank in an old Model A Ford. Louise Sherouse, the young wife who thought she had missed her one and only chance to see Presley up close and in person at Ocala's Southeastern Pavilion in 1955, was thrilled to learn she would get another chance. "I was blessed my Dad was a security officer and could get us into the bank," Sherouse said.

Her father, Tom High, was among the adults who condemned Presley for his vulgar movements after the Ocala concert and expressed similar disdain watching him on the *Ed Sullivan Show*. For High, a job was still a job, even if it meant having to stand guard over Presley in person. For Sherouse, Betty Langdon, and other diehard Elvis fans not lucky enough to be extras, getting inside the bank became the ultimate backstage pass. The crew planned to film multiple scenes over the course of the weekend. When cameras weren't rolling, in that controlled environment with Tom Parker perched in a corner like a cigar-chomping gargoyle, Presley could walk and talk casually with fans, not having to worry about being swarmed.

"We arrived at the bank at 8 o'clock Saturday morning in dark suits, blue shirts, plain ties, summer hats and black shoes," said Hall, who was supposed to look like a typical Florida businessman on a summer day. "But if you've ever seen a typical Floridian in the summer you know he wears about as little clothing as possible. We nearly died of the heat in those suits!"

Police in full uniform blocked off traffic on Silver Springs Boulevard, a busy artery running into and through downtown Ocala. Filmmakers announced that Presley was running late; all anyone associated with the film could do was wait. Out in the crowd of hundreds of bystanders was a blond-headed eleven-year-old boy from Gainesville whose family had come down to meet Elvis.

22

A Fella Who Wiggled

"I was eleven years old and I remember this *vividly*," began rock and roll superstar Tom Petty during an interview with author Paul Zollo. For more than a year of Saturdays, Zollo met with Petty for a book entitled *Conversations with Tom Petty*. The superstar talked about his own path to fame and riches, all his lifetime triumphs and tragedies. "I could feel so clearly the sorrow and the joy," said Zollo. "Certain chapters were very sorrowful, and others the opposite. Like when he spoke about the Wilburys, he lit up. It was the same with Elvis. . . . It changed him forever."

Unlike Buddy Holly, Waylon Jennings, Gram Parsons, and Roy Orbison (Tom Petty's bandmate in the '80s super group the Traveling Wilburys), Petty never saw Elvis live in concert during his early tours of the South. Still, Petty's life-altering encounter with him in 1961 remains a testament to Presley's magnetism, charisma, and influence.

Due to his father's volatility, Petty suffered a fearful, physically abusive childhood. Meeting Presley provided young Tom a roadmap, albeit a rocky one, out of workaday Gainesville, Florida. In great detail Petty recounted the morning his life started to change. It began with him sitting in a pile of pine straw under a giant tree, wondering what the day had in store. "My Aunt pulls in the drive and says, 'Tommy, would you like to go and see Elvis Presley?'"

Petty said he thought he might like to go. A week later the family piled into the car to make the forty-mile trek from their home in Gainesville to Ocala, where Presley was filming *Follow That Dream*. "I've always thought that was a cosmic title," Petty recounted. In the days leading up to the shoot, Petty tried to remind himself exactly who Presley was. Prior to search engines and smartphones, there wasn't much information on Presley; just film footage of his rock and roll days. "He was known to me as a fella who wiggled," Petty recalled. "And I did a little impression with a broom of wiggling like Elvis."

That quote evokes memories of nine-year-old Gram Parsons doing an Elvis impersonation on the front porch of his home in Waycross, Georgia, on Saturday mornings. After seeing Presley at Waycross City Auditorium in 1956, Parsons' life was similarly altered; set permanently on a course for music stardom.

Petty's uncle, Earl Jernigan, was the only northerner in their decidedly southern family. Petty's father was also named Earl. Tommy's grandmother, being the suspicious woman she was, thought the name "Earl" was bad luck. Refusing to say that name, she addressed Petty's father as "Petty" and his uncle became "Jernigan." In 1961 Jernigan had gotten a job as prop master on the Presley film. The weekend they shot scenes inside the bank on Silver Springs Boulevard, Petty's aunt and uncle brought along eleven-year-old Tommy and several cousins.

Unlike the lucky ones allowed to remain inside the bank while Presley filmed, Petty and his family had to stay outside in the parking lot. "There was a huge crowd when we got there," Petty remembered. "We were driven through the crowd and around back into the film set." That morning, the film crew was setting up a simple shot; Elvis and Anne Helm were to drive up Silver Springs Boulevard in their old convertible Model A and pull up outside the bank. Anne Helm's character gets out of the car to look for a parking meter with time still on it. Both would appear in their down-home dungarees looking like the squatters they played in the film.

Before cameras rolled, anticipation built for Presley's arrival. At around 10:30 on Saturday morning, July 15, a line of white cars pulled up, sending a jolt of adrenaline through members of the crowd, who roared in response. Petty's account is riveting: "And then suddenly I go, 'That's Elvis.' He stepped out as radiant as an angel. He seemed to glow and walk above the ground. It was like *nothing* I had ever seen in my life."

From about fifty yards away he walked straight toward Petty and his family; the sunlight seemed to cast his dyed black hair a shade of blue. And before the shocked young boy knew what was happening, there was Elvis, close enough to touch. "These are my nieces and nephews, Elvis," said Petty's uncle. Presley smiled and nodded, likely saying something to the children, who were too awestruck to respond. He disappeared into his dressing room trailer. Excited girls pressed against the chain-link fence gripping album covers and pictures of Presley in hopes of getting them signed.

When Presley reemerged in costume to begin the day's work, girls rushed the barricades to get his autograph. Just the process of getting onto the set to film a simple scene took much longer than it should have because Presley continued to oblige fans. He'd made a lifelong devotee in little Tommy Petty. Zollo could see it in the way Petty recounted the experience: "It was like a religious feeling, seeing a vision," Zollo said. "Elvis was shining like Jesus."

Petty wasn't the only youngster moved at the site of Elvis Presley on the streets of Ocala. That Saturday morning a fourteen-year-old African American janitor named Jeremiah Wesley was just finishing his shift cleaning the Florida Theater. Blacks had their own entrance to the theater and were required to sit in the balcony. Wesley caught sight of Presley in costume. "He had on a pair of jeans and a jean shirt," Wesley recalled, not knowing at first Presley was even filming a movie in the teen's hometown. Imagine catching sight of Elvis Presley walking on the streets of your town, not knowing he was going to be there. It must have seemed like an apparition.

Growing up on Magnolia Street in Ocala's Sugar Hill neighborhood, Wesley said he'd heard some of Presley's early standards like "Jailhouse Rock." The fact that this kind of rhythm and blues–influenced rock and roll came from a white artist made no difference. "I just enjoyed the music and color didn't matter," Wesley said. Intrigued by the goings-on, he stuck around to watch Presley that weekend.

In between scenes, Presley continued to mingle with fans and practiced karate, breaking boards, three in quick succession, with short, sharp chops. What guy could possibly be cooler as seen through the eyes of a spellbound fifth-grade boy, or a fourteen-year-old movie house janitor? "That is one hell of a job to have, that is a great gig— Elvis Presley," Petty concluded. "I caught the fever that day and never got rid of it."

Uncle Earl Jernigan, who for decades worked on movie sets and shot films of University of Florida football practices and other Gainesville-area events, managed to get a few candid photos of Presley on the movie set. But only a few, thanks to Tom Parker who admonished him to put the camera away. "Ya'll will sell them to Life Magazine," Parker barked, ever conscious of the Presley brand he exploited for monetary gain at every turn.

From that day, the one and only day he visited the set of *Follow That Dream,* Petty found out all he could about Presley. He sent away for a Presley handbook; he collected rock and roll records. His father worried as Tommy never went outside, preferring to cloister himself in the house playing records all day. "I just *loved* the music," Petty gushed. "I played it *endlessly.*" He took guitar lessons in Gainesville from another young rock superstar-to-be, future Eagle Don Felder.

Petty was right. The film's title was cosmic and apt for the effect it had on him. After that day in a bank parking lot, meeting Elvis Presley became his epiphany, and Tom Petty followed *his* dream all the way to the Rock and Roll Hall of Fame. That story, in slightly differing versions, has become beloved in Florida lore: the confluence of an American icon and little Tommy Petty.

Presley, the Beatles, and BB King, who played Florida at the height of their careers as live acts, had an immeasurable effect in the Sunshine State; thanks to their influence, a stellar roster of soon-to-be stars picked up guitars, wrote songs, and embarked on their own careers: Petty, Gram Parsons, Gregg and Duane Allman, Stephen

Stills, Don Felder, and Bernie and Tom Leadon. They and many other important artists matriculated in Florida youth centers, fraternity houses, and small town juke joints.

"A little abused child took refuge in Rock and Roll," Petty told *Rolling Stone*. After his wife Evelyn died in 1980, Earl Jernigan could only sit by and watch as the convenience and inexpensiveness of videotape destroyed his once-thriving Gainesville film business: Jernigan's Motion Picture and Video Service. In 1992 he sat in his store among the unused processors, spools, and projectors that once hummed. "I have stuff here that I can't use and I can't sell," he said, "To just shove it outside the door, I can't do that."

Among the keepsakes was a framed photograph of himself, his late wife, and the little boy he hadn't seen much of since he'd grown up. It was inscribed: "To Aunt Evelyn and Uncle Earl, with love, Tommy."

23

Hot Times Inside

As impactful as it was for fans who saw and met Elvis outside Ocala's Commercial Bank and Trust, those inside were fortunate enough to have even longer and more engaging interaction with the film's leading man. What a memorable month it was for Ocala thespian Michael Hall. He went from directing one-act plays for the Marion Players to directing Elvis Presley. Besides playing a variety of extras in the film, like a bank teller and a member of the "curious crowd," Hall was enlisted to cue Presley when it was time for his character to enter the bank.

That thrill didn't take away from the fact that it was still hot as blazes, and he was standing on Silver Springs Boulevard in a dark suit, long sleeves, and a tie. In an article he wrote for his old hometown paper shortly after filming was over, Hall reflected on the nature of film work: "It's hot, tiring, repetitious and not one bit glamorous, but nonetheless exciting," Hall wrote. "I would have gladly done it for nothing. It's interesting, fascinating work."

Inside the bank was no better. Because the air-conditioning made too much noise, it had to be turned off. For employees and others inside thrilled to have a front-row seat to watch filming, spotlights turned the bank lobby into a sweltering hot box. The most run-of-the-mill scenes required dozens of takes. Photographs show Presley sweating through his long-sleeved denim shirt, something that happened again and again. Bill Layton, a seventeen-year-old local extra, recalled Presley wearing down from the heat, sweat, and monotony of doing scenes repeatedly in the oppressive environment.

Throwing in a loud expletive, Presley groused, "What's it going to take to get this scene done?" Though Layton was surprised at the salty language, he said that was atypical. "He was human," Layton said. "But that was an exception, because as soon as you were around him you knew Presley was a genuinely nice guy." After Presley sweated through yet another shirt, Layton's mother, Jean, was dispatched to go home and fetch an iron to press the many replacement shirts Presley needed that steamy July day.

Another meeting of American icons came when Presley's character inadvertently gave a nervous bank officer, played by Howard McNear, the impression that he'd come to rob the place. McNear faints, and Presley's ham-handed but good-hearted character Toby Kwimper scoops him up, cradles McNear like a baby, and calls out for help.

There, in the lobby of the Commercial Bank and Trust in Ocala, Florida, Elvis Presley stands holding the actor who went on to play one of television's most beloved characters, Floyd the Barber on the *Andy Griffith Show*. "Every time we watched Andy Griffith, we said we met him," the bank's phone operator Bonnie Benningfield said of McNear. "We were sitting in the teller's cages watching the filming." McNear appeared in a total of three Presley films.

During downtime, when crews had to readjust cameras and lighting, Presley mingled with actors, extras, and spectators. In the break room he answered all kinds of questions, signed autographs, and posed for pictures. "I was crazy with excitement," Benningfield remembered. "He was very, very attractive." For decades Benningfield carried with her the laminated photos she took with Presley that day.

Those who saw Presley barnstorming Florida witnessed all the accompanying hype and hysteria surrounding an electrifying new performer. Inside the Commercial Bank and Trust, his fans saw a much truer version of the young star; someone at ease mingling with his fans, flirting with women, playing with children. While all the security, yes-men, and fenced-off fans outside were a reminder that Presley was now a big time film star, in the walled-off confines of the bank, people at least had a chance to feel they really got to know him. And that was the predominant sentiment from so many who interacted with him.

"I wouldn't trade seeing what I did see," said Louise Sherouse. "If I saw him in concert I wouldn't have been able to get that close to him."

Sherouse introduced Presley to her four-year-old son Tony. "Here, let me hold him in my arms so you can get a picture," he said, hoisting the boy. Presley accommodated scores of autograph requests, leaving Sherouse in a mild state of panic; she didn't have one scrap of paper to her name. "All I could find was a bank deposit slip," she recalled. With Presley's signature it became an instant family heirloom. "I had it mounted for my son for Christmas," she said.

Presley's easygoing way even melted the ice with her father, security guard Tom High, one of the adults disgusted by his early headlining performance at Ocala's Southeastern Pavilion in 1955. "My Dad came to really like Elvis," Sherouse remembered. "He said Elvis was so polite and well-mannered." Presley had won over another adult who once considered him an anathema.

Follow That Dream's fifty-four-year-old director, the established filmmaker Gordon Douglas, had worked with artists as diverse as Frank Sinatra, Doris Day, Bob Hope, and Jimmy Cagney. In 1936 his short film *Bored of Education,* starring the beloved child comedy troupe Our Gang, won Douglas an Academy Award. In his expansive career he was known to take on a wide array of serious and comedic films, moving with ease between genres.

With his dark hair and pencil-thin mustache, Douglas could have passed for a leading man of a bygone Hollywood era. *Follow That Dream* was in the hands of an experienced journeyman director who knew how to keep the production moving, even if problems cropped up while filming on location. "Elvis was a good actor, and played some damned good scenes," Douglas declared in an interview about making the film. "He could do more than sing."

Anne Helm on location with Elvis Presley in Crystal River. Courtesy of Anne Helm.

Watching all the goings-on at the bank and still taking in the magnitude of her co-star's stature was Anne Helm. In keeping with the *Beverly Hillbillies* analogy, Helm's character Holly wore her shirt tied at her partially exposed midriff, evoking the country-girl sex appeal of television character Elly May Clampett. Some thought Presley's shy co-star was standoffish, as she kept her distance from fans between takes. What young woman who harbored romantic feelings for Presley wouldn't be a little resentful of so many attractive young women fixated on him?

One of them, nineteen-year-old local beauty contestant Linda Longo, scored a part as an extra in the bank. She sat staring at Presley as he propped himself in a corner and started playing guitar. "It was like a fantasy," Longo remembered. "That man was beautiful. He had an aura about him." Getting to hear him sing between takes meant his fans had the entire Elvis experience up close. No wonder it remains such a vivid memory.

Presley looked out of the window at thousands of people still camped out in the summer sun, waiting. At that moment, when it just might have been cooler outside than inside, Presley stepped out of the door near the bank entrance to try to catch a breeze. "He began to twist and shake his body as if he were singing 'Hound Dog,'" writer Anthony Violanti reported in the Ocala newspaper. "The whole thing lasted about a minute, but that's all it took to thrill the crowd. The people began screaming, yelling and waving."

When it was time for Presley and the crew to grab some lunch, Ocala policeman Martin Stephens was one of four officers assigned to the security detail. They stood watch, keeping fans and onlookers outside while Presley ate at the old Marion Hotel. Before they left, Presley ordered steaks for the officers while he ate grilled cheese. With so much downtime required during filmmaking, Presley spent a lot of time with his security detail.

"He liked cops and respected the police," Stephens said of Presley. "I had just gotten out of the Army and Elvis got out of the Army about a year before. We talked a lot about Army life and the military." Stephens also stood guard while Presley signed endless streams of autographs and swears Presley never tired of accommodating fan requests. "It's all part of doing business," said Presley. When one wise guy in the crowd chided him as a "hillbilly" and a "pretty boy," Presley ignored it and went about his business. His early days of being mocked by people like Ira Louvin for the way he dressed and performed had steeled his reserve.

As the production progressed in downtown Ocala, work crews were putting in endless hours transforming an out-of-the-way piece of wilderness down the road from Inglis into *Follow That Dream*'s main filming location.

24

Yankeetown

Florida's State Development Commission voted to spend eight thousand dollars to turn three grown-over acres of land, owned by Yankeetown realtor Ollie Lynch and located under the Bird Creek Bridge, into a tropical paradise for the film *Follow That Dream*. This serene and out-of-the-way tip of Pumpkin Island, bordering the Gulf of Mexico along State Road 40, became the main shooting locale for the film. Limousines rolled in, turning plenty of heads in the small hamlet of Yankeetown, population 425, along the banks of the Withlacoochee River. "It was big excitement," remembered local high school teacher Pat Langley.

Once the land was cleared and the blacktop resurfaced so the road would look new, tons of sand were trucked in and coconut palms were planted—which promptly died, forcing crew members to spray-paint the wilted fronds green. A thatched structure was constructed at an eyebrow-raising cost of $6,000. All this made some locals wonder what these Hollywood types were really up to.

Seventeen-year-old twin brothers Johnny and Tommy Jones were hired to turn a big pile of sand into a pristine beach for filming. "Every day they would pick us up in a white limousine to shovel dirt then the limousine would take us home," Johnny Jones remembered. "We built a beach for the beach scene and they didn't like it, so we had to

Clockwise from top left: Elvis Presley posing for photo with Louise Sherouse and son Tony while filming inside the Commercial Bank, Ocala; Presley sweating through his shirt inside the Commercial Bank; Presley with security guard Tom High, who found Presley's concert appearance in Ocala the previous year to be obscene; Presley and Red West, actor and longtime bodyguard. Courtesy of Louise Sherouse.

Bird Creek site turned into beach for location filming in Yankeetown, Florida. Courtesy of Mike Robinson.

build them another one." Johnny and Tommy were allowed to hang around and do odd jobs. They were even paid twenty dollars to be among a group of extras pretending to catch rubber fish.

Even as a teen, Jones thought it odd to see Presley constantly in the company of his circle of Memphis friends. "I tell you the honest truth, I felt sorry for him," Jones said in a retrospective article. "Anybody who brought five guys along to play had to be lonely." Tom Parker took offense to stories in the Tampa and St. Petersburg newspapers questioning the eight-thousand-dollar state expenditure to bring the film to Florida. Not a dime of the money was paid to Presley, his manager groused—"He doesn't need it." All of the funds were used to make the main location under the Bird Creek Bridge look more like a tropical paradise, he explained. And due to the fact that people dared to question what they money was used for, Parker opined that Hollywood producers from now on "would take a second look" before filming in Florida again.

One newspaper editorial board agreed with Parker. By protesting the eight-thousand-dollar incentive, which had more than been paid back in national publicity and local economic impact, editors at the *St. Petersburg Evening Independent* concluded, "Florida has been guilty of childish conduct."

In this out-of-the-way stretch, accessible only by a lone two-lane road or by boat, there was no way to control completely what reporters and photographers might see or hear; Parker and the production team banned the press. For that reason alone, two legends of South Florida journalism, reporter John Keasler and photojournalist Charles Trainor of the *Miami News* decided to make the three-hundred-mile trek to see what kind of return taxpayers were getting on their eight-thousand-dollar investment.

Five years previously Trainor had captured numerous unforgettable images surrounding Presley's Miami concerts. To say Keasler and Trainor were *not* welcomed with southern hospitality on location in Yankeetown is an understatement. An irate deputy sheriff's threat, "I will put you in jail!," shattered the morning tranquility during one day of filming. He had just caught sight of Trainor up on the Bird Creek Bridge, snapping photographs of the faux squatters' paradise

Pumpkin Island bears little evidence of having once been a film set. Courtesy of Mike Robinson.

constructed on the island below. "I have the backing of everybody from the governor on down," the deputy thundered. Trainor kept on snapping. The deputy threatened the persistent photojournalist again, but Trainor was undeterred.

"What the sheriff didn't know was that a surefire way to get Charlie to take a picture," a blogger once remarked, "was to tell him *he couldn't*." One of Florida's great muckraking journalists long before Dave Barry became a satirist or Carl Hiaasen an investigative reporter, John Keasler faithfully recounted the goings-on with a flair common to Miami's evening newspaper. As the two South Florida journalists had it out with Presley's security team, the king himself arrived. "There he is!" girls waiting along the road shrieked.

"Teen aged girls rushed screeching from the road toward the white Cadillac," Keasler reported. "They came from everywhere. They seemed to be dropping from the trees." One of the movie men barked, "No photographers!"—an order that bounced right off Trainor; he was finally getting to see the man he'd driven three hundred miles to photograph. "Charlie took some pictures of Elvis, who was then spirited away for his noon ambrosia and the crowd settled back in for its next delicious glimpse of the King," Keasler wrote.

"Have you ever heard of invasion of privacy?" asked a man Keasler described as "a short press agent in a tall pith helmet."

"Anyway," he went on, "I thought I told you not to come."

He explained that it was none other than Elvis Presley's privacy the intrepid duo had invaded that morning on Bird Creek Bridge, though one could certainly argue that the screaming girls were already doing so. Keasler later wrote that Tom Parker and his PR cronies "seemed to be under the impression that 'publicity' was something they could turn on and off with a switch." Parker's right-hand man Tom Diskin explained that if they allowed one newspaper in they would have to allow them all. "And you can see what that would cause," he said. The bottom line, Diskin explained, was that meant no interviews with Presley or Parker, who also afforded himself celebrity status.

"Is that definite?" Keasler asked.

The Bird Creek Bridge. Photo by author.

"Definite," Diskin replied. "I told you that when you called from Miami."

"The sting and the agony of this refusal," Keasler chided, "was somewhat mitigated by the fact that I had just finished talking to Elvis, by walking across the sacred precincts while the guards were busy berating Mr. Trainor." While Keasler's photojournalist partner was being threatened with jail and heaven-knows-what-else up on his Bird Creek Bridge perch, he nevertheless managed to get a photo of Keasler and Presley, walking side-by-side with shirts open, on the steamy waterside film set. Elvis even wore shorts. This was Keasler's account of his conversation with the star of *Follow That Dream*:

> "How's it going?" I said, to Elvis, who was standing around.
> "Pretty good."
> "Hot enough for you?"
> "Sure is."
> "How do you like Florida?"
> "I like it."
> "Better than Memphis?"
> "Well, Memphis is home."

Keasler mentioned that he had also attended Humes High School in Memphis, years before Presley was a student there.

"Well," Keasler said. "We're glad to have you down here."

"Glad to be here," Presley replied as he readied himself to pass through the gauntlet of girls to get to his car.

"I mean there was not much use standing there in the hot sun talking about West Berlin or something," Keasler confessed to his readers. "Everybody who has met him said they found him to be a very nice, down-to-earth lad without a trace of Hollywood, and that's the way he seemed to me."

While other reporters might have been afraid to part from the love fest narrative Tom Parker fed them, John Keasler provided some much-needed perspective when recounting the goings-on. He wrote that Florida's economic impact for one Yankeetown merchant on the tax dollars spent for the film amounted to this: "two additional cups of coffee and two rolls of film may be traced to the movie making." A filmmaker even asked to "borrow" Yankeetown innkeeper Bud Finley's woodpile.

Another reporter who managed to find her way to Presley in Yankeetown was Anne Rowe, the *St. Petersburg Times* reporter with whom Presley got up close and personal during his 1956 tour. Because of his familiarity with Rowe she was considered a "friend" and given an audience with Presley while he sought refuge from the heat in his air-conditioned Cadillac limousine.

"The car is his home away from home," Rowe observed. "A haven from peering eyes, the shrieks and sighs of flocks of fans who have flooded the Yankeetown area, scene of the filming. He eats in the car, he naps in the car, he talks in the car."

As Rowe leaned through the car window, Presley spoke of his fondness for Florida: "It's like coming home, sort of. You know I got my start in this state—going around with a hillbilly group. I really like it here." His failure to credit or mention Scotty Moore or Bill Black is telling. Presley invited another familiar Floridian from those days, Mae Axton, to come and visit him in Yankeetown, which she did.

When the cameras stopped rolling, at night Presley seemed to vanish without a trace, rarely venturing out. Keasler concluded there was simply nothing to do around Crystal River after dark. "Well," one local near the Port Paradise Lodge said, "sometimes around dusk we go down to the feed store and watch them roll up the awning."

Nighttime was no time for Presley and the crew to wind down. In the governor's suite, the largest on the property, Presley hosted card games for money and caroused with his buddies Red West and the other Memphis Mafia. Anne Helm was in on it too. "I sort of went along for the ride," she remembered. "He was a night owl. He loved to play music. He loved to play cards and be silly." Helm found it odd that while she was trying to further a romantic relationship with Presley, his all-male entourage of six or seven was always around. There was a price to be paid when the time came for the crew call early every morning. Presley solved the problem the same way he did in the army, with prescription drugs.

"We had to prop ourselves up in the morning," Helm said. "Elvis had Dexedrine. It was not called speed in those days. And we would take them if we were feeling tired." She said Presley also took Valium and other pills to get to sleep. Helm bristles at the notion either of them was an addict or even drug dependent. "There was an innocence to it," she explained. "It wasn't like we were popping drugs."

While Presley got his start with pills in the military, they became part of Helm's life as a young New York model. "We were sent to diet doctors and given Dexedrine to keep the weight down," she said. In New York Helm was introduced to speed at fourteen. She says she never developed the kind of prescription drug addiction that ravaged Presley. As he performed day in and day out in the hot sun, clear-eyed, engaged with the material and the throngs of adoring fans, Helm saw the signs of a developing dependence and a diet she described as "atrocious. He could eat a pound of bacon at one sitting." Presley remarked that he thought he looked fat in some of the scenes.

From her intimate view of Presley, Helm saw boredom as another developing issue in his career. "I can't sit back in judgment of the Colonel," Helm reflected. "He did launch Presley's career." But clearly, she said, Presley longed for more challenging material than doing a take on Li'l Abner for *Follow That Dream*. "He might have won an Academy Award," Helm believed, if he had been able to accept some of the films

Parker turned down as too risqué or beneath Presley. Among them, *The Fugitive Kind*—that went to Marlon Brando, and years later, the lead opposite Barbara Streisand in *A Star Is Born*. Parker dismissed Streisand, a superstar who by that time had already won an Academy Award, as unworthy to share the screen with Presley. The role went to relative newcomer Kris Kristofferson.

"Elvis was very loyal and naïve," said producer Steve Binder. "He felt he never could have made it without the Colonel." More than most, Binder saw the controlling, stifling effect of Parker's treatment of Presley as a moneymaking commodity, not an artist; his willingness to take Presley's career into the ditch and ignore what his client was doing to himself, if it meant Parker's enormous gambling debts got paid and his own luxurious lifestyle was supported.

One of the longest-tenured members of the Memphis Mafia, Red West, one of the few who dared to question Presley about his drug use, was fired for the transgression. Then in the minds of many fans West betrayed Presley at his lowest point by writing a tell-all book. West believed Presley became "bored with his life. . . . The songs were terrible, the scripts were terrible." Yet Parker was more than willing to keep Presley sweating it out on a treadmill of mediocre films and a breakneck schedule as a Las Vegas saloon singer.

Parker always quashed Presley's dreams of conquering new territory in Australia or Germany—so many places where his fans would have died to see Presley perform. But that would mean Parker risking his well-guarded illegal alien status finally being laid bare to the world and his own fictional legend crumbling. "I think we all have to take responsibility for our own actions," said Binder definitively. "It has to fall back on Elvis."

In the short term, many Presley fans enjoyed weeks of up-close encounters with him. In his home away from home, Presley constantly accommodated fan requests for autographs and photos. The weeks spent filming *Follow That Dream* represented the last time Florida fans could still see young Elvis walk among them.

25

Weeki Wachee and
the Mayor's Daughter

On Sunday July 30, 1961, Presley and Anne Helm went out on what she called their "first date." Sanctioned and arranged by Tom Parker, their visit to the City of Mermaids at Weeki Wachee Springs became a tour de force photo op with hundreds of fans.

For Helm, who had seen how fans reacted to her co-star in Ocala and Yankeetown, this was her first big dose of the magnitude of Presley's stardom: "I was always separated from that," she said. "I could never get a handle on how famous he was until we went out."

Parker was running interference in a jaunty white cap, chomping a Havana cigar and sweating noticeably through his shirt. The madness all around didn't appear to bother Presley, who was dressed like Mack the Knife in a dark suit and white shirt. Helm, in a summer dress with her hair up, having a chance to display her own Hollywood sex appeal, looks ill at ease in photos from that evening. "I was really overwhelmed by it because I'd never seen such madness for someone," she recalled.

Weeki Wachee is a vintage Florida attraction, a beloved tourist destination located at the intersection of State Roads 50 and 19, and a throwback to days before megaparks and combustible thrill rides. It was the brainchild of a former U.S. Navy Seal and swimming instructor named Newton Perry, who chose the spring in 1946 as the site for his new underwater business. To facilitate freedom of movement, he also perfected the method of breathing through an air hose without bulky scuba apparatus.

Newton carved out a theater six feet into the limestone, so that as many as eighteen spectators at a time could view the beauty of the springs. On October 13, 1947, he staged his first mermaid show in Weeki Wachee Springs. The swimmers breathed through air tubes hidden within the underwater scenery. Those who think synchronized swimming fifteen to twenty feet down in a free-flowing spring is easy have never tried it.

Three days before Presley showed up, newspapers all over the state reported his plan to make a rare public appearance while on location on Florida. A front page article in the July 27 *St. Petersburg Evening Independent* carried the headline, "Okay Girls—Get Set, Elvis Readies Outing." Parker told the newspaper any fan who brought a photograph would get it signed. That ensured Presley would have a lot of fans there and a tremendous amount of work to do.

"Spending the afternoon with Presley is like taking a friendly walk with a forest fire," wrote Lynn Chadux, teen reporter for the *St. Petersburg Times*. "The tall Greek God, olive skinned legend in his own time . . . and his entourage swept into [the] Springs in a miraculously white Cadillac at 4:30 p.m." Presley asked the young reporter, "Are you Miss Florida?" Then he kissed the smiling teen four times. Even on this so-called date with Anne Helm, Presley found plenty of opportunity to flirt with other young women. "That day we got along like a house on fire," Chadux recalled. "He asked me to walk with him all day and we held hands part of the time."

After an hour of taking photos and glad-handing, Presley and Helm were seated next to his father, Vernon, and new wife, Dee, to watch the show. One memorable image of the performance came when a pair of mermaids held up a sign that read: "Elvis Presley Underwater Fan Club." Presley stood at the window drinking in the view of a shapely young performer holding the sign in her right hand, a

Elvis Presley at Weeki Wachee Springs with Underwater Mermaid fan club. Reprinted by permission of Bob Moreland, *Tampa Bay Times*.

breathing tube in her left, while giving the evening's star attraction a sexy smile. After the show Presley sent his overwhelmed leading lady back to the hotel and stayed behind to make sure the crowd of an estimated two thousand did not go home disappointed.

Behind a long fence stood some of the fans who had watched him perform live back in the 1950s when they were twelve or thirteen and who were now seventeen or eighteen. "Oh Elvis, do you remember me at all?" asked one. He just smiled and made an inquisitive face. Another who got a kiss from him declared: "Elvis IS famous, he IS handsome, and he IS a legend in his own time, but he's also the sincerest guy I ever met or kissed."

Another notable photographer, Bob Moreland of the *St. Petersburg Times*, brought with him on assignment his eleven-year-old daughter Michele Marie. After a long afternoon in the swimming park, she held her place in that long autograph line, with a new brownie camera slung around her neck.

She stayed out of the way as her father snapped photos of Presley fans. When it was his daughter's turn, beaming with pride Moreland pointed out to Presley, "That's my daughter." With that, Presley bent over and gave Michele Marie an autograph and a kiss on the cheek. "It was magical!" she remembered more than a half century later. Her only regret: "I was 'all shook up.' And couldn't even snap a picture of him myself with my new little brownie camera."

In a retrospective she wrote about meeting Presley at Weeki Wachee, Lynn Chadux said the friendship she had with Presley after meeting him on assignment also turned to romance: "He would call me twice a day, between scenes or call me from his motel room."

Presley's interest during his bachelorhood in girls barely old enough to be in high school is well documented. When he met future wife Priscilla Beaulieu in Germany, she was fourteen. Such dalliances would be met with greater scrutiny today, given the prevalence of scandal-hungry gossip magazines, websites, and TV shows.

On location in Florida, after all he had done to curry favor with his adoring fans, and the populace of the area in general, Presley could do just about anything he wanted. With his coterie of deputies never far away, Presley showed a keen interest in law enforcement and they responded favorably. But that relationship was put to the test when he developed a friendship with sixteen-year-old Katie Williams, daughter of former Inverness mayor Francis "Cowboy" Williams, then serving as clerk of courts in Citrus County.

Presley befriended the girl after her father helped Katie land a role as an extra. "I bet you're a cheerleader." Presley said to the charmed high schooler.

After asking more questions and having Williams and her friend Ann Gibbs sit next to him while he signed autographs, Presley made it his mission to get to know Williams's family. That night her father told her, "I had a visitor in my office today, Elvis Presley."

"You what?" the stunned girl replied. "You gotta be kidding me."

Presley had contacted Williams's mother too, even inviting her out on location under the Bird Creek Bridge, to an area called "Red Level." After ingratiating himself and assuring the girl's parents his intentions were honorable, Presley contacted Katie again. Presley told her, "I want you to come over here to Red Level like your Mom did and you can come over and spend the day."

Less than enthused, her father "Cowboy" Williams told his daughter, "You cannot go over there unless you have a chaperone."

After a security guard nearly turned their car around at the Bird Creek Bridge, Katie Williams and her very pregnant sister-in-law chaperone Emily arrived on location. "Oh my God, is she gonna have that baby right now?" an alarmed Presley asked. They sat her down and made Emily as comfortable as she could be at that late stage of pregnancy. Williams remembers fondly the interaction between Presley and the crew: "I remember them playing games together—they had Frisbee, football, and stuff like that, and played and played."

After a fun day on the film set, Emily drove the car while Katie rode back on the rumble seat of the limo listening to Presley and his entourage lamenting the lack of things to do when they got back to Crystal River. "For them it was like falling off the earth," Williams said.

Two days later Presley called again and sent flowers to the Williams home. Emboldened by their mutual crush, Katie decided to go back by herself to Presley's motel. "Whatever possessed me to do this I have no idea," she confessed. "I wasn't going to lie to Dad. I told him I needed a new bathing suit, which I did." She didn't tell Presley she was coming.

For a high school sophomore, the atmosphere when she made her surprise visit to Presley's villa was eye-opening. His whole entourage of men was there, along with shapely blond women in bikinis. "All these guys were partying and the music was going and Elvis was acting out, you know. Then he snaps his fingers three times," Williams recalled. The finger snapping along with a hand gesture was an obvious signal for the traveling party to clear out, leaving Presley and his teen crush all alone.

"Do you want to go out in the boat?" Presley asked. When his young admirer said yes, Presley took Williams for a chauffeured spin around King's Landing. After that Presley and his special high school friend decided to go for a swim in his private pool. Williams changed into her new bathing suit, and Presley promptly threw her in the pool. Soon the entourage of men and bikini-clad women reappeared and joined in the fun.

Just then a knock on the door interrupted the good times. Burton "BR" Quinn, the imposing and no-nonsense sheriff of Citrus County, had come with a message for Katie Williams. Extending his arm to move Presley physically out of the way like a petulant teenager whose keg party was being busted, Quinn told the girl: "Little lady, I just want you to know that your daddy knows you're over here." With that Quinn stopped restraining Presley and left. Used to being a law unto himself, Presley realized he was putting law enforcement goodwill to the test by partying with the underage daughter of a county official. "I can't believe that just happened, what kind of connections does your Daddy have?" he asked.

"My Dad is Citrus County," she told him.

"Then I think the best thing for you to do is to get your things together," Presley told the girl, laughing. When she saw her father back at the house, Katie Williams claimed he wasn't angry. The sheriff's demeanor, acting on her father's behalf, had suggested the opposite.

Tom Parker's downtime at Port Paradise was far tamer and more solitary. He might walk over to Presley's villa for a game of cards, but mostly he stayed to himself in his own room tending to business. That was where *Miami News* writer John Keasler was granted an audience. When all of the Hollywood pretense and unnecessary chest-thumping he encountered at Bird Creek fell away, Keasler found Parker to be quite friendly, lonely even; happy for a visit. "Do come in and sit," offered the round-faced huckster with an ever-present cigar. Keasler asked Parker about an autobiography he claimed to be writing entitled *How much does it cost if it's free?*

"Well, every time I sell another ad in it I have to take out another chapter," Parker explained.

"Every time what?"

"I sell another ad," Parker replied, as if it were perfectly plausible to write a biography accompanied by paid advertisements. "No sense writing a book without selling ads in it." He pulled out of a giant cardboard box one of his promotional triumphs, an oversized picture of Presley standing in his now iconoclastic gold lamé Nudie Cohen suit—another definitive image of Elvis in the 1950s. "I made one million prints of this picture and sold them for a nickel apiece," Parker boasted.

"He smiled to his secret angels," Keasler said, summing up Parker, the ultimate hustler. For Presley's Svengali-esque manager, turning a buck was his all-consuming passion; losing tens of thousands of dollars at games of chance his malignant vice. "When passing time yanked the snake oil wagon, his spiritual home from beneath him, he landed on his feet and never missed a beat of the spiel," Keasler wrote about Parker. "And his product—Elvis, sells like mad."

As July turned to August, shooting continued inside the historic courthouse in Inverness, the goings-on like a shot of adrenaline to Citrus County residents.

26

Inverness Courthouse

The climactic scenes filmed at the 1912 courthouse in Inverness gave Elvis Presley a chance to make a case for his fictional family and his own dramatic acting ability. When his character Toby Kwimper spurns the advances of *Follow That Dream's* femme fatale, social worker Alicia Claypoole, played by Joanna Moore, she hatches a scheme to have the Kwimper twin boys and their baby sister, Ariadne, removed from the family. Before an audience of sympathetic townspeople, Toby and Pop Kwimper, played Arthur O'Connell, try to keep their family intact without the benefit of a lawyer to make the case for them.

The old courthouse is situated right in the middle of Inverness like a crown jewel. US 41 snakes around the historic building, which made the filming location accessible to the curious. Policemen had to blow their whistles to keep traffic flowing. While filming went on in the courtroom upstairs, the newspaper reported, "necessary business was conducted" on the lower floors. Crowds stood behind a police barricade. Linda Conner told the town newspaper she brought her daughters Cheryl and Harlyn Sanders from Teaneck, New Jersey, in hopes of getting a glimpse of Presley.

"We came all the way here just to see Elvis," Conner told the *Citrus County Chronicle*. "And we were lucky enough to be kissed."

Now a museum, the historic Inverness courthouse where Elvis Presley's 1961 filming took place is well documented and is celebrated every day. Courtesy of Mike Robinson.

The casting call had gone out for extras twenty-one and older to fill out the audience. In publicity stills from the film, the courtroom's segregated balcony, the African American section, remained empty. The bottom rows were all white faces. Though they were only sixteen, Katie Williams and Ann Gibbs plied Court Clerk Cowboy Williams's connections to be allowed as courtroom extras. "The scene, which lasts about ten minutes in the movie, took about six days of shooting," Gibbs remembered. "We did the scene so many times all of us in the courtroom knew each of the characters lines and we knew when they messed up." That led to laughter and a close bond between townspeople, cast, and crew. To preserve the film's continuity, after each day of filming, extras were expected to wash the clothes they had on and then wear them again the following day.

Every morning Presley appeared from his dressing room at the Valerie Theater across the square and made his way up to the north entrance of the courthouse. That gave the extras a chance to stand on the steps, tell him hello, and shake hands. One morning on his way upstairs he turned to Ann Gibbs unexpectedly, "Want to go out?" Then he laughed and was on his way.

Gibbs was stunned, "I didn't say anything, I was flabbergasted." For Gibbs, Presley was unlike any other adult man she'd seen in Citrus County. Young men walked around with cigarettes rolled up in their shirt sleeves, dressed for a day of farming or other blue collar work. When he wasn't in costume, Presley dressed in high style, even in the Florida low country. "His shoes were Italian leather with a lightning bolt, and everything he had and had on bore his initials on it—pants, shirt, shoes, bathing suit. Everything was custom—the most expensive fabric, custom for him," Gibbs remembered, "just as if he was stepping out on stage."

In a sense the world was indeed Presley's stage. There was nowhere he could go in public where he wouldn't become a spectacle. Yet he maintained a genuine ability to relate to his fans and show them gratitude for putting him where he was; just six years earlier he had been making fifty dollars a night performing up the road in Ocala. One day fans were delighted to see Presley passing the time, feasting on watermelon one of his fans brought, tossing a football with some local boys. The *St. Petersburg Times* reported one "wayward football allegedly thrown by the King himself" broke a window of the Valerie Theater. Not only Presley's dressing area, the quaint 1925 one-screen movie theater was also where the crew watched daily footage shot in the courthouse. Other accounts suggest the football broke the theater marquee. Presley sent a check to cover the damages.

Another photo shot on location shows members of the cast including Presley, Helm, O'Connell, and others taking a break in the jury room, one of the few cool places in the building. A man is bouncing one of the twin boys on his knee, Helm adjusts her makeup, Presley is drinking a Coke. Bill Bram, a dedicated researcher into all facets of Presley's film career, caught up with a particularly opinionated extra from the courthouse scenes, Miss Mary Brent. "One day Elvis started playing his God-awful guitar which I cannot bear, and without thinking I said, 'Do we have to have that dreadful noise?'"

Knowing full well Presley could have fired her on the spot, she was relieved when instead he stopped and apologized like a chastised school boy: "Sorry Miss B." Brent was all too happy to share

The courtroom where Elvis Presley filmed the climactic scene of *Follow That Dream*. Stills from the film were used as a guide to re-create the courtroom for historic preservation. Courtesy of Mike Robinson.

her opinions with and about Presley, his co-stars, even his personal business. "Elvis and I had many discussions," she told Bram. "He complained very little." When Vernon Presley showed up with his new wife, Dee, Presley was obviously icy toward them both, failing to acknowledge their presence.

"I had a long talk with him stressing that Vernon was not being disloyal to his mother by remarrying," Brent explained. "After that he did a complete reversal and they worked out their differences." Miss Mary did not mince words about one Presley co-star whom she labeled "a letch, always chasing broads." Another she called a "BIG NO TALENT, who cost the company untold amounts by being totally inadequate." Of Presley and his co-star Anne Helm, Miss Mary was equally honest: "Elvis was very good at remembering his lines, not so good at interpretation. . . . Anne Helm was a really lovely girl, smart enough to listen and learn."

Some of Helm's fondest memories of Presley derive from the days spent on location in Inverness—the publicity shots showing the two so young and vibrant outside the courthouse—and remembering his acting in the film's climactic scene. His plea to the judge not to break up the Kwimper family came across as genuine and heartfelt. To Helm, it was proof of the deep well of dramatic talent Presley possessed, if only his domineering manager had allowed him to spread his wings creatively.

"I think he really identified with the character," Helm said. "He had a lot of them in tears when he did his monologue in the courtroom. They believed him and they were crying." On film it was more than enough to convince the grandfatherly judge, played by journeyman actor Roland Winters, to side with Toby and Pa Kwimper.

Presley left another important legacy in Inverness; when the courthouse was renovated in 1994, noted historic preservationist John Parks used scenes from *Follow That Dream* as key reference points during the seven-year, $2.5 million restoration. Today the Old Courthouse Heritage Museum is a daily celebration of Citrus County history and a reminder of Presley's time there. In 2011, on the fiftieth anniversary of the making of the film, a musical entitled *When Elvis Came to Town* was staged in Inverness. Standing in that same courtroom today, the history is palpable.

It could be argued that other important architectural treasures throughout Florida, like the Polk Theater in Lakeland, were saved and still stand today at least in part because of Presley's history within their walls. With the final, climactic courtroom scenes now in the can, Presley's days in Florida were almost over.

27

Bye Bye Bird Creek

During the final days on location Tom Parker made yet another shrewd decision. To smooth over any bad public relations remaining from the eight thousand dollars in tax money paid to producers to transform Pumpkin Island into a squatters' paradise, Parker arranged for the thatched building used as the Kwimper family cottage to be donated to the Florida Sheriffs Boys Ranch in Live Oak.

On August 8, 1961, with other cast members surrounding him, Presley handed over the keys to the building to Sheriff James Turner. The entire structure had to be hoisted up on a trailer and hauled slowly across the Bird Creek Bridge to the boys ranch in north Florida, where it remained for decades. Miami journalist John Keasler was still around digging for the real story beneath all of Colonel Parker's public relations. He found it in Giles Gete, who ran the Pure Oil station in Crystal River and handled all the film crew's fuel needs. "The first week, they paid me right on time," Gete said. "Second week I had to go after it." Finally, Gete took his $587 fuel bill and receipts to the film crew offices. Despite every cent being accounted for, the company bean counters balked.

Gete recalled, "Messed around, fooled around, arguing, wouldn't honor 'em they said." With that he went back to the Pure Oil station and waited. He opened up the next day, fueled up a Cadillac, kept servicing trucks, and waited until the big camera rig with all the equipment pulled in. Giles Gete proceeded to impound it for nonpayment of monies owed.

"You could hear the screams to Bird Creek Bridge," said Gete. "The drivers shouted, 'You can't do this!' Already done. Bring my money you can have your truck." The film honchos came huffing and puffing to the Pure Oil station ready to see to it that the suspected hijacker be thrown in jail. But that never happened. "In addition to running the Pure Oil station," Keasler reported, "he is a special deputy sheriff. He got his money."

That evening Gete changed his shirt and reported to his night job as a member of Elvis Presley's security team. "Fine boy, everybody likes him. Nothing put on. Nothing phony," Gete assessed. "More than I can say for a lot of other. . . ." Those "other" folks couldn't very well have someone on their own payroll thrown in jail.

Back at the Port Paradise, Anne Helm insisted on writing Presley a personal check for ten dollars to cover her cumulative card game losses. "I didn't want to owe him in another life," Helm said. As she expected, her relationship with Presley fizzled soon after they finished shooting the final interior scenes back in Hollywood. Some shots inside the Crystal River High School gymnasium, deemed unsatisfactory, were scrapped.

Long after Helm had forgotten about it, the canceled check came back in the mail. It appeared Presley had endorsed it and cashed it at a liquor store. For years she doubted the authenticity of Presley's signature. To satisfy her own curiosity, she consulted an expert, who assured her it was indeed his. Generations later Helm retained the quirky souvenir of her days working with Elvis Presley and being his on-location girlfriend.

To commemorate Presley's time there, town leaders in Inglis and Yankeetown entertained a motion to rename Levy County Road 40 "Follow That Dream Parkway." In Inglis, where the earliest scenes were shot, the measure passed, and now that one-mile stretch bears the name of the film. "If it'll bring people into our little town that's a good thing," said Inglis mayor Carolyn Risher in 1996. Next door in Yankeetown, where the bulk of filming had gone on around Bird Creek, the measure was voted down. "Elvis Presley does not personify Yankeetown," said Mayor Jimmie Wall in a veiled reference to the drug use that contributed to Presley's death in 1977. "He only came to this area to make a movie for his own benefit."

As a result of that decision, for fifteen more years, only the Inglis mile of State Road 40, so imbued in Presley lore, commemorated his time there. Follow That Dream Parkway ran out miles before reaching the site of the main film location. Thick plant growth and litter thrown from the roadway make it hard to fathom that Pumpkin Island was ever a film set. The Bird Creek Bridge is unremarkable except for the occasional folks fishing there. Few know that the guardrail along the bridge is where Presley sat for many of the film's publicity photographs.

"Elvis boarded a plane at Tampa, his cigar tilted jauntily," Keasler wrote of Presley's departure from Florida's west coast. There were more films to be made, the next all the way across the country in Seattle. "Colonel Tom Parker, who evidently went back by flying carpet, left a wake of secret laughter," Keasler concluded. Something about covering Elvis brought out the best in Miami journalist John Keasler, who could just as deftly elicit smiles or tears. Sixteen years to the week after his adventures with Elvis in Yankeetown were published, Keasler was with him one more time at Graceland: "Elvis had been a skinny country kid who lived in a tiny frame house and made river rafts and dreamed of being a truck driver. Now they came—wearing overalls, business suits, high fashion, rags—to see him in his copper casket, in his plush and fabled palace. . . . I took a last look down at Elvis and left."

With apologies to Yankeetown's former mayor, he could not have been more wrong. The reason innumerable people were able to come into contact with Elvis Presley in the summer of 1961 and cherish those memories was his willingness to interact with them; to do something for *their* benefit. Besides those who appeared in the film with Presley, many others showed up on his doorstep for a photo or autograph at the Port Paradise Hotel and out on location.

The girls on a road trip, the young boy who dreamed of being a musician and got an autograph and a ride on Presley's boat, the grandmother who baked him a pie, fans who came from thousands of miles away just to get a glimpse of Presley, the young men who became security guards, the stand-ins, the extras, the bank president, the girls who formed a club consisting of those who'd gotten a kiss from Presley—to a remarkable degree he accommodated them all.

Jeanette Dundas convinced her hard-working single mom to drive her to Crystal River to try to see Elvis Presley. "I was on the verge of tears from the pure joy of it," she recalled. "Then I started to panic. What if he wasn't as nice as I thought he'd be? What if he rejected me?" Like many thirteen-year-old girls, she struggled with a negative self-image that tugged at her to run and hide from the audacious notion of meeting the one and only Elvis Presley. "I was clumsy, awkward, plain and scrawny," said Dundas. "I felt so ugly with my Lilt permed hair flying in every direction."

Yet she resisted the urge to withdraw from her one chance to meet Elvis. So there outside the Port Paradise Hotel she waited alongside her mom and best friend. Dundas tried to remember all the details: the exact date and time, August 8, 1961, 6:45 p.m. When a white Cadillac pulled up, she stood frozen in her spot while other fans rushed up to it.

Presley moved along until eventually he was right beside the shy teen. Not knowing what to do, Dundas asked him to say the word "bare," like only he had said it in the spoken-word interlude from "Are You Lonesome Tonight?" He didn't respond. Only after agonizing silence and his signing more autographs did Dundas finally get the interaction she was waiting for. He wheeled around and said the word. "Now are you happy little girl?" Not exactly; it all happened so fast that Dundas didn't have a chance to reply.

Just then someone in the crowd pushed forward, very nearly causing Dundas to fall. Presley reacted, took hold, and tucked the starstruck teen under his right arm: "Little girl you better stick close to me so you don't get hurt." The ugly, scrawny girl who couldn't stand

In 2011 Yankeetown leaders finally approved a proposal to rename State Road 40 "Follow That Dream Parkway." Photo by author.

the way she looked spent the rest of the autograph session under Elvis Presley's arm like the junior prom queen of the world.

"I was so happy my insecurities flew out the window," she recalled. And when Presley finally finished the last of his day's work signing autographs and posing for photos, he started off for his room. For a few fleeting moments, he had made Jeanette Dundas feel special like no one ever had. She blurted after him, "Elvis, I love you. I really love you."

He looked at her, nodded and smiled, "I know you do and I love you too." Perhaps some of the details have grown a bit more melodramatic with the passing decades, but that's how Dundas recalled the special time with her childhood idol. Presley gave fans moments like that again and again at the end of long days spent working in the hottest time of the year in Florida. Had he just been in it for himself, he could easily have waved them all off or left it to members of his security team who were all adept at being the bad guys.

How does that not personify Yankeetown?

In the countless articles generated, and among people interviewed during Presley's time in Crystal River, few recall him uttering a harsh word. And when he did, it wasn't directed at someone personally. Even Tom Parker, the manager many revile as a money-grubbing manipulator, brought Elvis to *Pioneer Go Home* as an honest homage to those like himself who came to Florida to begin anew; to stake their claims in the sunshine gold rush. Presley was one of them.

Finally, in September 2011, Yankeetown mayor Dawn Marie Clary went before the Levy County Board of Commissioners with a request to approve Resolution 2011-57, the motion that designated State Road 40 from Yankeetown to the Gulf of Mexico as Follow That Dream Parkway. Fifty years after principal filming wrapped under the Bird Creek Bridge, fifteen years after Inglis town leaders saw fit to rename State Road 40 passing through their part of town, Yankeetown followed suit.

Generally speaking, *Follow That Dream* is regarded by his fans as one of Presley's better films; a chance to show comedic as well as dramatic range. Critics like Bosley Crowther of the *New York Times* were dismissive: "Judging by this laboriously homespun and simple-minded exercise about just plain folks, somebody must have decided that the Presley films have been getting a little too glossy lately." The film premiered in April 1962 at the Marion Theater in Ocala. The evening's star attraction did not attend. By then Presley was back in Hawaii filming *Girls, Girls, Girls*.

No more would Presley's Florida fans have a chance to see and interact with him up close. Most of them were resigned to the fact that Elvis Presley the young rocker had morphed into a B-movie actor-singer for good, and that was that. They moved on to other artists and music, until Presley finally made a move to get out of his artistic rut and reignite his cultural relevance.

28

Coming Back

In a darkened sound studio illuminated only by the small red lights of amplifying equipment, television producer Steve Binder witnessed Elvis Presley recording a brand new song. So new that it had been written for him only hours earlier by composers Billy Goldenberg and Earl Brown. Presley asked for all the lights to be turned off and to have a hand-held microphone rather than the overhead boom type more commonly used in recording. It was June 1968.

Binder and co-producer Bones Howe commissioned the new song, "If I Can Dream," in hopes of providing an appropriate commentary on America's emotionally charged political climate during filming of Presley's 1968 television special. It had been eight years since Presley appeared on television, seven since he finished filming *Follow That Dream* in Florida, and six years since he topped the Billboard charts. In the meantime, singer songwriters like Bob Dylan, and groups who wrote and recorded their own material like the Beatles and the Byrds, marginalized Presley and his cavalcade of profitable but forgettable B-movie fluff. Only his heartfelt and soulful gospel recordings had brought Presley recent critical acclaim, but in a genre far away from the pop culture mainstream.

The first time they met to discuss doing a variety special for NBC, Binder was blunt: "Your career is in the toilet." A dejected Presley told

Binder, "I'm scared of television. Berle made fun of me. Allen made me sing to a hound dog." And despite stellar ratings, many thought his special with Sinatra in Miami to be contrived and boring. Still, Binder assured him, a successful television special would put him back on top overnight as no other medium could.

The night Bobby Kennedy was assassinated, the two sat up for hours talking about America's political and racial tumult. Kennedy's assassination, and the murder of Dr. Martin Luther King two months beforehand, left Presley shaken, wanting to say something relevant in front of a national television audience. Presley had come to trust and respect Binder, a man younger than he, who refused to sacrifice his creative vision in the face of Tom Parker's usual bullying and bombast. His resolve emboldened Presley for once in his life to tune out Parker and listen to someone in touch with young America; the violence and inner strife was widening its generational divide like never before.

Binder and Howe wanted "If I Can Dream" to give Presley something hopeful to say. Parker had been pushing for a benign Christmas song to end the special, or a monologue following the formula of establishment performers like Andy Williams. Hearing the lyrics to the new song Binder wanted Presley to sing, "If I can dream of a better land, where all my brothers walk hand in hand," Parker said Presley would record it "over my dead body." Presley was moved and asked the songwriting team to play it for him over and over, then finally declared, "I'll do it."

Parker pulled Presley into his office like a shamed little boy. While his manager lectured Binder, whom Parker derisively called "Bindle," Presley stood at his side mute, head bowed and hands crossed in front of his crotch. When they left Parker's office, Presley nudged Binder in the ribs and said, "Fuck him."

In the dark at United Western studios, Presley began recording "If I Can Dream." "He started to feel it, and went to the floor and curled up," said Binder, who was witnessing the remarkable scene made barely visible by the light of amplifiers, the fetal imagery not lost on him. This was an artist bursting from a straightjacket of years

Steve Binder with Elvis Presley, 1968. Courtesy of Steve Binder.

of unfulfilling creative pursuits, rediscovering his true essence. The passion Presley poured into the song is evident.

When the time came to perform "If I Can Dream" with Presley's live vocals over a backing track to close the television special, he was filmed performing it in multiple settings. The version chosen to close the TV show was unforgettable. Fronting a giant wall of magenta lights that spelled out "Elvis," Presley stood dressed all in white. He performed the song with the look and all-consuming passion of a Sunday preacher, complete with dramatic arm gestures. Then, out of breath, he wished viewers a simple, "Good night." It was a defining Presley performance.

"I was so happy for him, that was the true Elvis," said his former *Follow That Dream* co-star Anne Helm. "I think everyone was stunned by that performance." Fans who'd gotten close to Presley back in Florida, including Linda Moscato, who said seeing Presley in Miami in 1956 is burned in her brain, was thrilled to see the televised improv scenes between Presley and his surviving bandmates from the early days: Scotty Moore and D. J. Fontana. "He was fabulous, I loved him in the black leather jacket," Moscato raved. "You could tell he was happy. That was excellent."

Doris Tharp-Gurley, who had skipped school and ridden the bus from Daytona Beach to Orlando in 1955 to see the new singing sensation on whom she was fixated, picked up on the notion that Presley was returning to his roots as a performer: "He was more like what I think he wanted to be, rather than what the Colonel wanted him to be."

After the special aired to wide acclaim on December 3, 1968, *New York Times* critic John Landau wrote, "There is something magical about a man who has lost himself find[ing] his way back home. . . . He sang with the kind of power people no longer expect from rock 'n' roll singers." Presley had gotten his wish; the special sparked a career renaissance. At that moment in time, once again anything seemed possible for Presley as a singer and entertainer.

With his newfound independence, Presley asked Scotty Moore if at long last he would be interested in embarking on a European tour. "A part of me wanted to be excited about the European tour Elvis discussed," Moore recounted. "A part of me was afraid to be excited about it. At thirty-six, I didn't want to be disappointed yet again."

Anyone who thought Tom Parker would back off from his control of Presley's career, or thought Presley himself would be able to forget about the ball-and-chain pledge he had made to let Parker handle the business, was dreaming.

Despite Moore's repeated attempts to get back in touch with Presley, the call back never came. Moore never worked with Presley again. Binder too, after successfully marginalizing Parker's power over Presley, became persona non grata. Parker closed ranks around his star. Despite Presley's assurances that the special was only the beginning, Binder had made a prescient prediction: "I hear you Elvis, but I don't think you're going to be strong enough."

The following year Presley did make another move contrary to Parker's wishes, recording the album *Elvis in Memphis*, a clutch of personally and socially relevant songs. Mac Davis's "In the Ghetto" lamented the circle of violence and the lack of care for impoverished children and gave Presley a top-five smash. Later that year his cover of Mark James's song mourning a crumbling relationship, "Suspicious Minds," became Presley's final number 1 hit in America during his lifetime.

Between 1970 and 1977 Presley performed twenty-five more live shows in Florida; the early '70s performances reflected the glitzy flair of Presley's Las Vegas shows. Tom Parker had won again, squelching Presley's overseas ambitions and confining him to a golden cage in Vegas with a breakneck schedule of shows to fuel Parker's penchant for gambling—and losing—and Presley's own free-spending binges.

The later years showcased a legend in decline from years of prescription drug abuse, chronic physical ailments, and weight gain caused by poor eating habits. Still, loyal fans always turned out, and Presley never lost the deep, resonant, and soulful voice that made him such an iconic figure. Ardys Bell saw Presley in Jacksonville four times, including on May 30, 1977, less than three months before his death. Bell, who happened upon Presley the first time crazed fans tore the shirt off his back in Jacksonville twenty-two years earlier, was shocked by his appearance that last time she saw him: "It made me sick," Bell lamented. "I remember thinking how sad it was."

St. Petersburg journalist Anne Rowe also attended the last Jacksonville show and came away similarly saddened. "I remembered him young and full of fun and life. I could hardly look at him now," she recounted. "The sparkle was gone." Scotty Moore never spoke to Presley again after the 1968 comeback special. All his attempts to penetrate Presley's Howard Hughes–like retreat from the world were thwarted. Moore was spared seeing the spectacle of Presley late in his career. "When I think of Elvis, I think of the man I knew in the early years," Moore wrote in his memoir, "when he was young and vibrant, and ready to set the world on fire."

What performer twenty years past an era indelibly emblazoned in his fans' hearts and minds could possibly live up to that early standard? The ruminations about what could have been if Presley had been allowed to grow as a singer and entertainer and bypass his B-movie period, the endless angst about Tom Parker's lust for money over any career considerations for his star—the raft of misgivings makes those fleeting early barnstorming days all the more important. He didn't just entertain and inspire young fans; Elvis Presley set them free. He gave them a reason to sing, shout, scream, cry, dance, and laugh. For a performer to elicit such an array of emotions and such everlasting loyalty and love is a rare and wondrous thing.

In an interview marking what would have been Presley's eightieth birthday, James Burton, the Rock and Roll Hall of Fame inductee and Presley's lead guitarist the final decade of recording and performing, was asked if he could imagine Presley at eighty. "I can," Burton said. "And I'll tell you how I picture him: An incredible gospel singer, and I would say a great gift to the young folks today to bring them to Jesus, to encourage them towards the Christian way. That's what I think."

The indelible marks Elvis Presley left behind in Florida are all around us. We sense them in great theaters like the Olympia in Miami, the Polk in Lakeland, and the Florida Theater in Jacksonville where the threat of jail and Presley's final utterance of the August 1956 tour were so memorable. In the century-old Inverness courthouse, Presley's time there is remembered and celebrated day in and day out. We feel them in Tampa's formerly forgotten Hesterly Armory, where a local photographer captured the defining image of those electric early shows, and in a small suburban home in Jacksonville where a part-time teacher and her journeyman musician partner composed Presley's first million-selling single, "Heartbreak Hotel," and convinced Glenn Reeves to record a demo version.

In St. Cloud a local developer tells the tale of getting a phone call from Elvis Presley's people in the mid-1970s about a house he had built at 606 Sequoia Circle in the Pine Lake Estates. As the story goes, Presley hoped to buy the house, build a theater there, and use it as a Florida touring base. The zoning couldn't be worked out, and Presley's hopes of having a home near Walt Disney World fell through. Many locals familiar with the tale still talk about what could have

A wall is all that remains of the Copacabana Motel, destroyed in a hurricane. Photo by author.

been. It's a plausible story, given that Presley toured Florida in 1975 and spent two days in Lakeland, just sixty miles away.

After the nightmare of imprisonment in Pensacola in 1932, Tom Parker built a fictionalized persona in Tampa, caught on in carnivals, and built a career at the local humane society and then as a promoter and manager. Parker struck show-business gold in the person of young Elvis Aaron Presley and introduced him to Florida crowds again and again. He brought Presley back to the area to film *Follow That Dream* as an homage to his own journey. His influence on and over Presley remains a topic of endless debate.

Residents of Ocala and Crystal River cherish memories of seeing young Presley in concert and being part of his film career. Finally, Follow That Dream Parkway stretches all the way past the Bird Creek Bridge and ends where brilliant sunsets paint the Gulf of Mexico in a Technicolor sky. In Daytona Beach, girls chanting "We want Elvis, we want Elvis" outside his dressing room window live on in a remarkable radio interview, and the Peabody Auditorium still basks in the glow as the first Florida venue Presley played.

His early years in Florida could not have been preserved in such detail without the dedicated efforts of Mae Axton and journalists like Anne Rowe, Elvalee Donaldson, Jean Yothers, John Keasler, and Charles Trainor, who would not let the uninformed, preconceived notions of others jaundice their own memorable reportage.

On pre-interstate roadways like the old Tamiami Trail, US 1 and 441, State Roads 40, 19, 50, and 17-92, and a tapestry of others, there's an old Florida spirit that lingers like early morning fog, damp and brooding, like an apparition just out of reach. In this back country, there's something palpable about the spirit of young Elvis traveling these ghost roads day and night: blazing along in a pink Cadillac with Bill Black and Scotty Moore, in a lavender Lincoln with his spitfire Mississippi girlfriend June Juanico, or in a sparkling white limo with his awestruck co-star Anne Helm.

It's worth it to take a trip through time just to see what history might be waiting at the end of a two-lane Florida road less traveled. At Daytona Beach where Presley's Florida barnstorming days began, down a long beach approach past parked cars where the concrete ends, stands a retaining wall at the edge of a rolling stretch of vacant land reclaimed by low-slung weed growth and small yellow flowers. At its highest point, facing the ocean, the wall still bears the name Copacabana: the only remaining piece of the oceanfront swimming pool that scores of yesteryear tourists enjoyed, Elvis Presley among them.

Like a verse from the Marc Cohn song "Walking in Memphis," the ghost of twenty-one-year-old Elvis lounges by the Copacabana Motel's pool on a sultry August day in 1956, his pink Lincoln in the parking lot nearby. Like any other kid his age he flirts with pretty girls in bathing suits and cuts up with the ducktailed guys in white tee-shirts. This wasn't just another stop on that historic tour; here at the Copacabana, Presley finally managed some real relaxation before facing the possibility of jail in Jacksonville the very next night. Already the tsunami of fame was overtaking him.

Thanks to his words and deeds, songs and shows, young Elvis will never die. On stamps and photographs, in YouTube videos dressed in gold lamé, in Google searches, and in endless Twitter, Facebook, and Instagram feeds, classrooms, and concert halls, he remains an American icon for the ages; a beckoning candle, a defining cultural reference point, and those who cherish his legacy are moths to an eternal flame. Just ask those lucky enough to have been in the vapor trails during Presley's ignition and launch to superstardom; to a kind of immortality like no other.

THE EARLY FLORIDA TOURS
AND VENUES

1955

THE HANK SNOW ALL-STAR JAMBOREE

May 7	Peabody Auditorium, Daytona Beach
May 8	Homer Hesterly Armory, Tampa
May 9	City Auditorium, Fort Myers
May 10	Southeastern Pavilion, Ocala
May 11	Municipal Auditorium, Orlando
May 12	Wolfson Park, Jacksonville

WITH "DEACON" ANDY GRIFFITH

July 25	City Auditorium, Fort Myers
July 26–27	Municipal Auditorium, Orlando
July 28–29	Wolfson Park, Jacksonville (two shows daily)
July 30	Peabody Auditorium, Daytona Beach (two shows)
July 31	Homer Hesterly Armory, Tampa (two shows)

1956

HEADLINING

February 19	Homer Hesterly Armory, Tampa (three shows)
February 20	Palms Theater, West Palm Beach (four shows)

February 21	Florida Theater, Sarasota
February 22	City Auditorium, Waycross, Georgia (two shows)
February 23–24	Jacksonville, Wolfson Park
February 25	*Louisiana Hayride*, Shreveport
February 26	City Auditorium, Pensacola (three shows)

PRESLEYMANIA

August 3–4	Olympia Theater, Miami (seven shows)
August 5	Homer Hesterly Armory, Tampa (two shows)
August 6	Polk Theater, Lakeland (three shows)
August 8	Municipal Auditorium, Orlando (two shows)
August 9	Peabody Auditorium, Daytona Beach (two shows)
August 10–11	Florida Theater, Jacksonville (six shows)

ON SOURCES

Considering how long ago Elvis Presley burst into America's consciousness, it came as a pleasant and most welcome surprise to find so many people willing to share their stories of seeing him live, coming into contact with him even.

One day I received a phone call from the 305 area code: "Mr. Kealing? Bob Graham. Tell me about Elvis." That was my first interaction with Florida's former governor and United States senator. I replied, "Well, hello Governor, I was hoping you would tell me." Indeed, Graham was kind enough to share his memories and impressions of seeing Presley at the Olympia Theater in Miami when Graham was a nineteen-year-old freshman at the University of Florida.

Anne Helm, who co-starred with Presley in the film *Follow That Dream*, shot on location in Florida, provided a unique take on being romantically involved with a superstar who was still, in many respects, just a big kid. Helm also gave me an important insight on how innocently Presley started to use prescription medications. That aspect of her time with him is not a primary focus in this book exploring Presley's early days as a performer, but it cannot be ignored.

Steve Binder, the producer-director of Presley's 1968 television comeback special, did not come into contact with him until long after Presley's early years in Florida. Binder nonetheless gave me important perspective on Presley's domineering manager, Tom Parker. I'm indebted to him for the hours Binder spent with me. The late Jim Kirk, a beloved radio man and political figure in Ocala, also gave me some wonderful stories of dealing with Tom Parker and giving Presley his first headlining opportunity in Florida. I'm glad to have his first person insights in this book.

I want to thank the myriad teens of yesteryear, among them Ardys Bell, Doris Tharp-Gurley, Holmes Davis, and Linda Moscato. Through their eyes we see a talented diamond in the rough emerge as a star for the ages. I am deeply in their debt. Also, thanks to the many people in Ocala, Crystal River, and Inverness who shared their stories and photographs of coming into contact with Elvis Presley during the filming of *Follow That Dream*. When possible, I relied on these first person interviews.

I was fortunate to find the reportage of Anne Rowe, Jean Yothers, and Elvalee Donaldson in the archives of their respective newspapers. Donaldson's daughter was kind enough to share her mother's souvenirs of covering Presley in Lakeland. I also culled the archive of the *Miami News* for John Keasler and Charles Trainor's memorable coverage of Presley while filming *Follow That Dream*. Thanks go as well to Tom Petty's biographer, Paul Zollo.

To reconstruct the events surrounding Mae Boren Axton and Tommy Durden's composition of Presley's first national number 1 hit, "Heartbreak Hotel," I relied on interviews with Axton and quotes from her memoir *Country Singers as I Know 'Em*. I was fortunate to find an interview with Durden on YouTube from a Michigan television station. It was a revelation to find out the song was not only written but also recorded for the first time in Axton's home in Jacksonville, the very same day. I confirmed Axton's home address in 1955–56 through the St. John's County Historical Society. Glenn Reeves's original demo of the song is available on YouTube. Also on YouTube you can hear what is arguably Presley's most candid and combative early interview, which he gave at the Polk Theater in Lakeland in August 1956.

There are excellent memoirs from Scotty Moore and June Juanico that I used along with their quotes from period newspaper and magazine articles. Scottymoore.net is a fine resource on early Presley tours and the indispensable role Moore played in Presley's rise to fame. I relied on Alanna Nash's biography of Tom Parker for some of the details on his imprisonment, diagnosis, and discharge from the army. Anyone searching for the definitive Presley biography need go no further than Peter Guralnick's two-volume set, *Last Train to Memphis: The Rise of Elvis Presley* and *Careless Love: The Unmaking of Elvis Presley*. For historical perspective I also consulted Guralnick's biography of Sam Phillips.

Dedicated chroniclers of Presley history run many websites on the topic. Thanks to the remarkable database at Elvisconcerts.com, I was able to conclude that Presley played more live shows in Florida than in any other state during his most important and transformative year, 1956. The site 706unionavenue.nl is an excellent clearinghouse of Presley ephemera and well-researched information, as is Graceland.com. The Florida Memory Project provided historical materials, as did Elvis-history-blog.com. That is only a sampling of worthy websites dedicated to various aspects of Presley's personal life, career, and legacy.

There was no substitute for taking to Florida's roadways to absorb the vibrations of history remaining from Presley's early barnstorming days. Just traveling Florida's pre-interstate roadways evoked the spartan life of touring musicians of the mid-1950s. I spent time in the front room of Mae Axton's old house in Jacksonville; my son Will and I ate at the Waffle Stop in Sarasota; I lingered in Presley's small dressing room and stood center stage at the Polk Theater in Lakeland. I walked the grounds of the Hesterly Armory in Tampa; I interviewed Charlie Louvin inside City Auditorium in Waycross, where he and his brother Ira opened for Presley in February 1956. My children and I sat in the judge's chair in the old courtroom of the historic courthouse in Inverness. In Yankeetown we tried to position ourselves along the Bird Creek Bridge guardrail at the very spot where Presley posed for *Follow That Dream* publicity photos. I walked through the bank building on Silver Springs Boulevard where interior scenes were filmed.

And this final note: one of the most memorable experiences was not only interviewing Jim Kirk but doing so at the Southeastern Pavilion in Ocala, where he haltingly moved Presley to headlining status in May 1955 at the behest of an insistent Tom Parker. Being with Mr. Kirk in that historic spot made the interview all the more meaningful and memorable.

NOTES

Chapter 1. In Waves

"The rest of the session": Peter Guralnick, *Sam Phillips: The Man Who Invented Rock 'n' Roll* (New York: Little, Brown and Company, 2015), 212.

"Hillbilly Cat": Presley's nickname in myriad programs from his 1955 tours.

"Ambition is a dream": www.elvis.net.

"The man who invented Rock and Roll": Guralnick used this phrase in the title of his 2015 biography.

"To say Elvis Presley": Richard J. Parfitt, "The Quasi-Religious Significance of Elvis, King of Rock 'n' Roll," theconversation.com, December 11, 2014.

"I wanted to see the powerful": Douglas Brinkley interviews Bob Dylan, Rollingstone.com, May 14, 2009.

"Before Elvis there was nothing": John Lennon, Graceland.com.

"Miz Axton look at the ocean": Peter Guralnick, *Last Train to Memphis: The Rise of Elvis Presley* (New York, Little, Brown and Company), 186.

"That just went through my heart": ibid.

"Nervous Ned Needham": Curt Synness, *Goodrich Had Fascinating Musical Career*, www.helenair.com, September 2, 2004.

"I don't think there was a better time": author's interview with former Florida governor and United States senator Bob Graham, October 22, 2015 (hereafter cited as Graham).

"I knew he wanted to go out": author's interview with Steve Binder, producer and director of Presley's 1968 NBC-TV show that has come to be known as his comeback special, April 20, 2013 (hereafter cited as Binder).

"The Colonel got him where he was": Red West interview with Todd Slaughter (interview for EIN by UK official Elvis Presley Fan Club), 1999.

Chapter 2. May 7–9: Daytona Beach, Tampa, Fort Myers

"Biggest Jamboree of the year": concert advertisement from *Daytona Beach Morning Journal*, May 7, 1955.

"Special Added Attractions": ibid.

"Grand Ole Opry stars": ibid.

"The way he sort of bounced around": author's interview with Holmes Davis, an usher at Presley's first-ever Florida concert, 2013 (hereafter cited as Davis).

"I was there to see him": author's interview with Doris Tharp-Gurley, 2013 (hereafter cited as Gurley).

"Everybody there was speechless": ibid.

"How do you think things are going": Davis.

"Things seem to be going pretty good": ibid.

"He was kind of innocent": Marsha Connelly, quoted in Gary Corsair, *The Boy Who Would be King*, from a series by senior writer in the *Villages Daily Sun*, June 2008 (hereafter cited as Corsair).

"I didn't pack the car": Scotty Moore, *Scotty and Elvis: Aboard the Mystery Train* (Jackson: University Press of Mississippi), 83 (hereafter cited as Moore).

"I was amazed at the reaction of the crowd": Corsair.

"I used to tell him": ibid.

"Well it's goin' over": ibid.

"He did steal the show": ibid.

"I said I don't": ibid.

Chapter 3. May 10–13: Ocala, Orlando, Jacksonville

"World's smallest pony": Fred Goodman, "Without You I'm Nothing," *New York Times*, August 24, 2003.

"Doctor": Alanna Nash, *The Colonel: The Extraordinary Story of Colonel Tom Parker and Elvis Presley* (New York: Simon and Schuster, 2003), 88 (hereafter cited as Nash).

"The kid": ibid. 117.

"He was a ball of fire": ibid., 103.

"He was one of the rarest": author's interview with Jim Kirk, legendary Ocala radio pioneer and civic leader, February 17, 2014 (hereafter cited as Kirk).

"Just sit there": ibid.

"This pink Cadillac": ibid.

"I told him": ibid.

"He choreographed": ibid.

"I want it to center": ibid.

"He's not exactly country music": ibid.

"I guarantee": ibid.

"*This kid is going somewhere*": Corsair.

"*A mournful soul*": Curt Synness, Synness, *Goodrich Had Fascinating Musical Career*, www.helenair.com.

"*Ned was a marvel*": ibid.

"*I was worried*": ibid.

"*Were cussing*": ibid.

"*He was unbelievable*": ibid.

"*It was quiet for a minute*": Kirk.

"*He was jumping*": Corsair.

"*We were impressed*": ibid.

"*We just lost control*": Kirk.

"*The man should be ashamed*": author's interview with Louise Sherouse, High's daughter, February 12, 2014.

"*The fella who managed*": Kirk.

"*He was the damnedest*": ibid.

"*Muni-Aud*": an oft-used nickname for Orlando's Municipal Auditorium.

"*I didn't really know*": author's correspondence with Larry Grimes, August 2013.

"*Could you teach me*": ibid.

"*He seemed to enjoy it*": ibid.

"*Awkward*": ibid.

"*To me, he was just*": ibid.

"*Janet and I stayed up*": ibid.

"*Could we get a picture*": ibid.

"*Sure, but you're gonna*": ibid.

"*I never had the nerve*": ibid.

"*To be part of that audience*": Rowland Stiteler, "Gamble's Winning Bet," *Orlando Sentinel*, August 2, 1987.

"*What really stole the show*": Jean Yothers, "On the Town," *Orlando Sentinel-Star*, May 14, 1955.

"*They ate it up*": ibid.

"*What Hillbilly music does*": ibid.

"*His clothes were a little freaky*": Mae Boren Axton, *Country Singers as I Know 'Em* (Self-Published, 1972), 245 (hereafter cited as Axton).

"*We felt Elvis was on the wrong show*": www.706unionavenue.nl (hereafter cited as Union Avenue).

"*I was just getting acquainted with life*": author's interview with Ardys Bell, August 2013 (hereafter cited as Bell).

"*He was watching the entertainers*": Union Avenue.

"*The crowd came over*": ibid.

"*Thanks you ladies and gentlemen*": Axton.

"It was like a sudden": ibid.

"Ripped to pieces": ibid.

"Well, he's just a great big": ibid.

"When we saw him": Bell.

"Dollar marks": Axton.

Chapter 4. July 25–27: Fort Myers, Orlando

"Elvis Presley continues to gather speed": Cecil Holifield, *Billboard*, June 4, 1955.

"A little cocky": Union Avenue.

"He'll never make it": ibid.

"I only know seven songs": ibid.

"Where are you going?": Nash, "Interview with June Juanico," www.elvis.com.au, August 22, 2015.

"Blue-eyed": ibid.

"The first thing I said": ibid.

"What do you mean": ibid.

"Moonglow with Martin": Arjan Deelan, "Interview with Scotty Moore," Scotty-moore.net, March 28, 1998 (hereafter cited as Deelan).

"Hi to you big doc": www.old-time.com.

"If you let Elvis drive": Deelan.

"Mom and Dad won a Jitterbug contest": author's interview with Diane Maddox, December 15, 2013 (hereafter cited as Maddox).

"funny lookin' little punkin": Deacon Andy Griffith, *What It Was Was Football* (New York: Capitol Records, 1953).

"And I know friends": ibid.

"The town was so small": Maddox.

"I don't remember": ibid.

"Cmon' they're playing music": ibid.

"Come on let's dance": ibid.

"He could have been": ibid.

"That Presley boy": Jean Yothers, "On the Town," *Orlando Sentinel-Star*, July 31, 1955.

"The little mother's club": ibid.

"Andy's preacher act": ibid.

"I'll give it to you": ibid.

"I'm still waiting": ibid.

"I fully realize": ibid.

"Now, it's none of my business": ibid.

Chapter 5. July 28–29: Jacksonville

"*Don't worry, work hard*": Marshall Rowland, *Fertilizer 'Tween My Toes* (IUniverse, 2013), 42 (hereafter cited as Rowland).

"*You're more of a bebop artist*": Mae Axton, Presley radio interview, July 29, 1955, youtube.com.

"*Well I never have*": ibid.

"*We musn't forget*": ibid.

"*They sure do*": ibid.

"*What I don't understand*": ibid.

"*It just automatically*": ibid.

"*We were the only band in the world*": Moore, 97.

"*The damndest freak storm*": Bill Foley, *Jacksonville.com*, August 8, 1997.

"*I just stood there laughing*": ibid.

"*Elvis Presley was recently presented*": *Cash Box* magazine, August 1955.

"*Roses are red*": Moore, 98.

"*I was holding my breath*": Rowland, 45.

"*When we got to his room*": ibid. 45–46.

"*Inherent sense of rightness*": Axton, 248.

"*I'll write your*": ibid., 252.

Chapter 6. July 30–31: Daytona Beach, Tampa

"*I never looked at him as a son*": Nash, *The Colonel*, 337.

"*Parker is nothing short*": Fred Goodman, "Without You I'm Nothing" (review of Nash, *The Colonel*), *New York Times*, August 24, 2003.

"*Oh how proud they were*": Axton, 249.

"*Elvis was sold*": ibid.

"*His rise to fame*": *Tampa Tribune*, July 29, 1955.

"*This will be*": ibid.

"*Tonsil photo*": elvispresleymusic.com.

"*Elvis you have to stand up*": Moore, 93.

Chapter 7. A New Place to Dwell

"*I walk a lonely street*": Durden video interview for *Michigan Magazine*, 1991 (hereafter cited as Durden).

"*That just struck me*": ibid.

"*There is something*": ibid.

"*It worries me*": ibid.

"*Think of the heartbreak*": William McKeen, *Rock and Roll Is Here to Stay* (New York: W. W. Norton and Company, 2000), 247.

"*She sat down at the piano*": Durden.

"*I'll be back in about thirty minutes*": Axton, 253.

"*Elvis was even breathing*": Durden.

"*Morbid mess*": Lydia Hutchinson, "The Story Behind Heartbreak Hotel," www. performingsongwriter.com.

"*Hot darn Mae*": Axton, 253.

"*Sole and exclusive Advisor*": Nash, 115.

"*I'll have about*": Union Avenue.

"*At the time I couldn't*": Moore, 78.

"*As bad are things*": ibid, 94.

"*I thought hey*": Nash, 188.

"*I feel Elvis*": Robert Johnson, *Memphis Press-Scimitar*, November 21, 1955.

"*My biggest thrill*": Jerry Osborne, *Elvis Word for Word: What He Said, Exactly As He Said It* (New York: Harmony Publishers, 2000), 10 (hereafter cited as Osborne).

"*Semi-skilled*": Elvis Presley's Employment History, www.elvispresley.com.au.

"*In January, 1956*": William McKeen, "What We Talk About, When We Talk About Elvis," in Other Writing, www.williammckeen.com.

Chapter 8. February 19–21: Tampa, West Palm Beach, Sarasota

"*The most talked about*": February 1956, Presley concert advertisement, www.elvisrecords.com.

"*Blue Moon Boys*": ibid.

"*We think tonight*": Guralnick, *Last Train to Memphis*, 245.

"*When I'm back here*": author's interview with Charlie Louvin, September 2009 (hereafter cited as Louvin).

"*We went by her house*": ibid.

"*That cost our catalogue*": ibid.

"*All we knew was drive*": Moore, 251.

"*Booking him in to all*": Nash, 136.

"*All the girls were hooting and hollering*": West Palm Beach Memories, www.elvis-collectors.com.

"*Where can someone get a beer?*": author's interview with Jim Ponce (hereafter cited as Ponce), August 19, 2013.

"*Can I go with you*": ibid.

"*Don't you know who this is?*": ibid.

"*He came on*": ibid.

"*Two block walk*": ibid.

"*I'm ninety-seven*": ibid.

"*I thought my God*": ibid.

"*When I turned that young man down*": ibid.

"The biggest commotion Elvis created": Mark D. Smith, "Elvis Barely Rocks Sarasota," www.sarasostahistoryalive.com.

"There are naturally an abundance": editorial, *Sarasota Journal*, February 23, 1956.

"If you give me": Billy Cox, "Waffle Stops Queen Served the King," *Sarasota Herald-Tribune*, August 13, 2007.

"Your skirt should be shorter": ibid.

"If you remember what I ordered": ibid.

"Queen of the Waffle Stop": ibid.

"I thought he was conceited": ibid.

Chapter 9. The Florida-Georgia Line, February 22–26: Waycross, Jacksonville, Pensacola

"He prowled the stage like a big jungle cat": Jim Dickinson, "The Search for Blind Lemon," *Oxford American Magazine*, April 20, 2015.

"I talked about the show for months": ibid.

"He was my first bass hero": Norbert Putnam, "We Had It All," *Oxford American Magazine*, December 8, 2013.

"Scotty Moore was my icon": Keith Richards and James Fox, *Life* (Boston: Back Bay Books, 2010), 72.

"From that day on": author's correspondence with Billy Ray Herrin, March 23, 2014.

"To say Gram Parsons was impressed": author's correspondence with Dave Griffin, March 26, 2014.

"I always thought Elvis was a fad": Louvin.

Chapter 10. The Promoter and Deserter: February 26, 1956

"Emotional instability": Nash, image from Parker medical records dated August 19, 1933.

"Heartbreak Hotel *zoomed Elvis' star*": Axton, 255.

Chapter 11. A Tsunami Storms Ashore: August 3–4, Miami

Photos in this chapter are from http://www.miamibeach411.com/news/index.php?/news/comments/elvis-presley/.

"Who wasn't aware of Elvis in 1956?": Graham.

"Just being alive, breathing": ibid.

"He's already told me": June Juanico, *Elvis in the Twilight of Memory* (New York: Arcade Publishing, 1997), 140 (hereafter cited as Juanico).

"He'll shit a brick if he sees you": ibid.

"I'm the first one to say": Binder.

"Bully is a good word": ibid.

"*Miami bustles under a golden sun*": Jack Kofeod, *Moon Over Miami* excerpt, www.cuban-exile.com.

"*His kind of music is deplorable*": Alan Hanson, "Did Sinatra Really Bad Mouth Elvis and His Music in '57?" www.elvis-history-blog.com.

"*Sinatra was on his way out*": author's interview with Linda Moscato, August 30, 2013 (hereafter cited as Moscato).

"*Elvis was a breaking out*": ibid.

"*Every delinquent kid in town*": Herb Rau, quoted in Bill Cooke, "Elvis Presley's Miami Connection," www.miamibeach411.com.

"*To prevent the kind*": ibid.

"*The Pelvis is due to arrive in Miami*": ibid.

"*We've had the biggest advance sale of tickets*": Herb Rau, "Protection for the Pelvis," *Miami Herald*, August 1, 1956.

"*Don't expect him for a rehearsal*": www.randompixels.blogspot.com.

"*He'll never last*": Moscato.

"*Just don't end up in the newspaper*": ibid.

"*The Pelvis*": www.miamibeach411.com.

"*For one hell of a favor*": Ponce.

"*It was an exciting night*": Graham.

"*I don't wear 'em*": www.miamibeach411.com.

"*Except for his gold and brown sideburns*": ibid.

"*He knew he was being heckled*": Gwen Harrison, "It's the Same Old Hysteria," www.brian56.dk.com.

"*Golly Presley doesn't know anything about the news*": ibid.

"*Velvet curtains*": Moscato.

"*But it did add an element*": ibid.

"*Like a drunken Brando*": Denne Petitclerk, taken from www.scottymoore.net.

"*Believe me, I wasn't ready*": Ponce.

"*I knew the effect it had on me*": Juanico, 167.

"*It's imprinted on my mind*": Moscato.

"*His legs were like rubber*": ibid.

"*Had seen me on television*": Moore, 115.

"*I and other band members were not sharing*": ibid.

"*We went outside and the crowd was in a frenzy*": Moscato.

"*Lots of times if I'm in a crowd*": Osborne, 8.

"*Held my hand in a death grip*": Juanico, 168.

"*It was hot in Miami, Elvis was hot*": Graham.

"*I don't know if I'm No. 1*": "June Juanico . . . The Day Elvis's Girlfriend Talked Too Much," www.elvis-history-blog.com.

"*In stormed the Colonel*": Juanico, 169.

"*Son we can't have this kind of publicity*": ibid.

"*His relationship with his manager*": ibid., 140.

"*I've got about 25 girls*": Alan Hanson, "Parade of 'Elvis Girls' in the 50s Boosted Presley's Sex Appeal," www.elvis-history-blog.com.

"*When he's in Biloxi*": Nash, "Interview with June Juanico," www.elvis.com.au, August 22, 2015.

"*If only your mother hadn't talked to that damn reporter*": Juanico, 169.

"*Idol of the infantile*": Damon Runyon Jr., "They Rock-n-Riot for Elvis," *Miami News*, August 4, 1956.

"*His pelvis performance is clearly contrived*": ibid.

"*It was apparent the teen agers present*": Bob Posnak, "Letters to the Editor," *Miami News*, August 1956.

"*Elvis can't sing, can't play guitar*": Alan Hanson, "Some Elvis Critics in the Fifties Urged Parents to React Violently," www.elvis-history-blog-com.

"*A gift, A SOLID SLAP ACROSS THE MOUTH*": ibid.

"*It was a totally unforgettable experience*": Moscato.

Chapter 12. Home Away from Home: August 5, Tampa

"*She's not good for you son*": Juanico, 177.

"*And what do you think*": ibid.

"*He was a prisoner of his own career*": Red West Interview, May 2008, www.elvisinfo.net.

"*What'd you kids do, rob a bank?*": Juanico, 180.

"*Yes maam*": ibid.

"*That aint the only thing*": ibid.

"*Reputation*": Anne Rowe, "Broom-Sweeping Elvis a Regular Guy," *St. Petersburg Times*, August 6, 1956.

"*The king of rock 'n' roll*": ibid.

"*One minute he's out on the make*": Ger Rijff and Jan Van Gestle, *Elvis the Cool King* (Wilmington, DE: Atomium Books, 1990).

"*Like a regular guy*": Rowe, "Broom-Sweeping Elvis."

"*It has the most meaning*": ibid.

"*All I thought about that suit*": ibid.

"*I'll probably sit back*": ibid.

"*I won't give up singing for acting*": ibid.

"*Those people have a job to do*": ibid.

"*Elvis displayed his terrific showmanship*": ibid.

"*America's only male hootchy-kootch dancer*": Paul Wilder and Harry Roberts, "Shouting, Pushing Mass of Youngsters Stampedes Elvis Presley Show Here," *Tampa Tribune*, August 6, 1956.

"*Ordinary, suburban-type*": ibid.

"*The weird pulsating rock and roll song*": ibid.

"*With a masculine version*": ibid.

"*Stupid*": ibid.

"*A mad rush of hundreds*": ibid.

"*Attractive*": ibid.

"*That drew stares*": ibid.

"*I can take him or leave him*": ibid.

"*A dozen jumping, frenzied teenagers*": ibid.

"*The negro section*": ibid.

"*Only twelve negroes attended*": ibid.

Chapter 13. They're Somebody's Kids: August 6, Lakeland

"*Finally, Elvis and his entourage drove up*": Elvalee Donaldson, "Real Gone: Presley Is Really Gone but the Aroma of His Day Lingers," *Lakeland Ledger*, August 7, 1956.

"*Honey, you'll have to come inside*": ibid.

"*I'm a reporter for the* Lakeland Ledger": ibid.

"*Oh, I just thought*": ibid.

"*His girlfriend of the moment*": ibid.

"*Four Cadillacs*": Elvalee Donaldson, "The Cool Cat in the Cadillac," *Lakeland Ledger*, August 6, 1956.

"*We were parked*": ibid.

"*His latest is lamps*": ibid.

"*He aint nothin' but an idiot*": Paul Wilder, interview of Elvis Presley, www.youtube.com, August 6, 1956.

"*Do you shake your pelvis*": ibid.

"*He should know*": ibid.

"*I just don't see that he should call*": ibid.

"*My pelvis had nothing to do*": ibid.

"*There is also gossip*": Elvis Presley de-classified FBI File, www.fbi.gov.

"*Rivals for the attention*": ibid.

"*The bureau has no specific information*": ibid.

"*Elvis Presley, Memphis Tennessee*": ibid.

"*Crank*": ibid.

"*He doesn't drink, he doesn't smoke*": Elvalee Donaldson, "How Different Is Elvis?" *Lakeland Ledger*, August 1, 1956 (hereafter cited as Donaldson).

"*Overly polite, extremely self-conscious*": ibid.

"*Actually this guy is just sorta different you know?*": ibid.

"*The first male burlesque dancer*": "Three Unbiased Males Give Views of Elvis," *Lakeland Ledger*, August 7, 1956.

"*Well worth*": ibid.

"*As the tumult rages*": "Presley and the Frenzy," *Lakeland Ledger*, August 6, 1956.

"*Presley is a fad*": ibid.

"*Not because he is an important figure*": ibid.

"*The thought of him*": "Elvis Played to Swooning Fans in Lakeland 40 Years Ago," *Lakeland Ledger*, August 4, 1996.

"*He lumbered from behind the curtain*": Donaldson.

"*It was just absolutely fascinating*": Steve Turner, "The Day Elvis Played the Polk Theater," *Lakeland Ledger*, February 21, 1982.

"*He was such an egotist*": ibid.

"*He went out with the mike*": ibid.

"*Is June just one of your 25 regulars?*": Donaldson.

"*She means more to me*": ibid.

"*Surely Elvis*": ibid.

"*Part of it is put on*": ibid.

"*I don't know if they tore them apart*": ibid.

"*It's hard to make a clear cut statement*": ibid.

"*Who never took a guitar lesson*": ibid.

"*To set a new all-time high*": ibid.

"*To Elvy, from Elvis the Pelvis*": Presley autograph information provided by El-valee Donaldson family.

"*What's it like being loved*": Juanico, 196.

"*It's almost like*": ibid.

"*Point of no return*": Juanico, 197.

Chapter 14. A Real Test: August 7, St. Petersburg

"*Today's the day!*": "The Town Rocks Today," *St. Petersburg Times*, August 7, 1956.

"*I look back now*": Billy Watkins, "Arthritis Silences Notes, but Scotty Moore, Elvis Presley's First Guitarist, as Sharp as Ever." www.clarionledger.com, July 20, 2013.

"*Dressing him up*": Anne Rowe, "Hey Cats! Elvis the Pelvis Presley Rockin to Town," *St. Petersburg Times*, August 7, 1956.

"*We were the first in line*": Anne Rowe, "Elvis Came, He Sang and He Conquered," *St. Petersburg Times*, August 8, 1956.

"*Champion Presley pursuers*": ibid.

"*We want Elvis!*": ibid.

"*Is that your wife*": Elvis Interview, August 7, 1956, www.youtube.com.

"*That's my wife yes*": ibid.

"*Now Joanne will be the envy*": ibid.

"*We do three, four shows a day sometimes*": ibid.

"*Pat Boone is one of the nicest guys I know*": ibid.

"I believe that I won": ibid.

"Non-Southerners don't understand": Moore, 106.

"I never was a lady killer": Paul Wilder, interview of Elvis Presley, www.youtube. com, August 6, 1956.

"The startling impact": Alan Hanson, "Record 100,000 Paid Tribute to Elvis in 1956 Florida Tour," www.elvis-history-blog.com.

"He was the most beautiful": Juanico, 198.

"I can't stand still": Rowe, "Elvis Came."

"Had he been travelling with black entertainers": Jerry Blizin, "Elvis Concerts Showed 1956 Racial Divide," www.tampabay.com, September 7, 2010.

"Integrated music just didn't happen": ibid.

"I can't stand it": Rowe, "Elvis Came."

"I hope we never": Alan Hanson, "Profile of an Elvis Crowd," www.elvis-history-blog.com.

"These men have faced": ibid.

Chapter 15. Just for You: August 8, Orlando

"He takes his banjo": Jack Kerouac to Helen Weaver, *Selected Letters: 1957–69* (New York: Viking, Penguin, 1999).

"We had a certain little game": Elvis Australia, interview with Red West, www. elvis.com.au, May 29, 2008.

"Take his shoes off": ibid.

"One of the craziest guys": ibid.

"How long do you think you'll stay": Jean Yothers, "Elvis Makes 'Em Shriek, Yell, Jump," *Orlando Sentinel-Star*, August 9, 1956 (hereafter cited as Yothers).

"I wish I knew ma'am": ibid.

"He's going into movies": George Miller, "I Hear ya Knockin'," *Orlando Evening Star*, August 9, 1956 (hereafter cited as Miller).

"He can spend": ibid.

"Elvis, in a bright red sport coat": ibid.

"Style of singing and his flashy clothes": Yothers.

"My mother was there": Randi Russi, correspondence with the author, August 2014.

"The rubber busted": Moore, 81.

"Elvis was certainly an original thinker": Moore, 82.

"Half and Half": Miller.

"His large eyes": ibid.

"We want Elvie": ibid.

"He's really wound up tight": ibid.

"Play one": ibid.

"Ladies and gentlemen": ibid.

"A delighted squeal": Yothers.

"Real nice kid": ibid.

"I egged him on": ibid.

"I've been working on something new": Juanico, 198.

"He sang beautifully": ibid., 199.

"That special afternoon": ibid.

"The service station": author's interview with Roy Brand, September 2014.

"My God that's Elvis": ibid.

"What do you boys do?": ibid.

"A little good ol' boy talk": ibid.

"That's great, that's great": ibid.

"So here he is": ibid.

"He was free": ibid.

Chapter 16. Boiling Over: August 9, Daytona Beach

"Everyone in the show was on edge": Moore, 116.

"It was one of those God awful": ibid.

"All I remember": ibid.

"It was a pretty good fight": ibid.

"We drove for miles": Juanico, 199.

"The colonel's been on my ass": ibid., 200.

"We had a nice picture of Elvis": Joy Keener-Borreson, feedback to www.scotty-moore.net.

"I remember sitting by a woman": Marsha Connelly, quoted in www.scottymoore.net.

"We cried so hard": ibid.

"Touch me Elvis": Drew Murphy, "Summer of '56, The Pelvis Packs Peabody—Twice," *Daytona Beach Morning Journal*, August 10, 1956.

"Is there some special girl somewhere?": ibid.

"It's pretty busy here in the dressing room": Ed Ripley, *interview with Elvis Presley*, www.youtube.com.

"Peggy": ibid.

"Uh, do you like the girls": ibid.

"I have another one": ibid.

"That's neat": ibid.

"Uh, someone just broke a window": ibid.

"A couple months yet": ibid.

"Actually, the Tennessee Troubadour": Dotti Einhorn, "Yes, Elvis Did it Again," *Daytona Beach Morning Journal*, August 10, 1956.

"There were three cops": ibid.

"Elvis Presley, whose tortured moans": Max Norris, "Waiting, Waiting, for Their Elvis," *Daytona Morning News*, August 10, 1956.

"A nice boy": ibid.

"Marsha!": Gary Corsair series, *Villages Daily Sun*, June 2008.

Chapter 17. The Morals of Minors: August 10–11, Jacksonville

"American Cool": Ann Greer, "American Cool at the National Portrait Gallery," *Washington Post*, June 6, 2014.

"Elvis had the ability": ibid.

"Achieved a new low": "Elvis Presley Jacksonville, FL," quoting Robert Gray in *Life*, www.elvispresleymusic.com.au, August 10, 2011.

"An obscene burlesque dance": Ron Wolfe, "Nation's Only Atomic Powered Singer," www.elvis-collectors.com.

"To put him straight": ibid.

"Gooding used the threat": Moore, 116.

"I would say he was certainly": Graham.

"He was kind of on the leading edge": ibid.

"The fans were screaming": ibid.

"That was my belief": ibid.

"I knew when we went": interview with Ardys Bell, August 2013.

"Our parents thought he was going": ibid.

"I don't know what I'm doing": Eddie Deezen, "Elvis Presley's Strangest Concert," www.mentalfloss.com.

"Wait a minute, I can't do this": ibid.

"Everybody got the biggest charge": ibid.

"They had me convinced": ibid.

"Fuck you very much": ibid.

"I showed them sons of bitches": Juanico, 201.

Chapter 18. Presley and Sinatra TV Special: March 1960, Miami

"Memphis Mafia": around 1960 this nickname was given to Presley's group of yes-men due to the fact that they often wore black suits.

"Except members of his entourage": Moore, 132.

"Tom Parker had us": ibid.

"It was like Elvis was kidnapped": Moore, 133.

"He was so full of energy": Peter Guralnick, *Careless Love: The Unmaking of Elvis Presley* (Boston: Little Brown and Company, 1999), 21.

"I made it just like everybody": Osborne, 110.

"Everybody would just get in his car": Guralnick, *Careless Love*, 61.

"Here, these'll keep you awake": ibid.

"*I'm not exactly worried*": Osborne, 122.

"*It was all about power*": Binder.

"*The kid's been away two years*": Guralnick, *Careless Love*, 62.

"*You'd never know Elvis*": "Elvis in Miami," Flashback Miami, *Miami Herald*, March 26, 2014.

"*I loved him for the early years*": Moscato.

"*A cookie-cutter thing*": Gurley.

"*Some were just silly*": ibid.

"*I didn't like 'em*": Bell.

"*It was fun going to Miami*": Moore, 150.

"*It was just one of the many*": Axton, 266.

"*Sammy took over*": ibid.

"*I reassured him*": ibid., 267.

"*Two years in the Army*": "Television: One of the Worst," *Time*, May 23, 1960.

"*A Vaseline halo*": ibid.

"*Pretentious and dull*": ibid.

Chapter 19. Follow That Dream: July–August 1961

"*I believe that there is as much*": www.elvisinfo.net.

"*Many friends I know*": ibid.

"*I think that this is a great story*": ibid.

"*Maybe they'll have a screen credit*": Erskine Johnson, column, *Hollywood Today*, August 21, 1961.

Chapter 20. Crystal River

"*I remember when I tested*": author's interview with Anne Helm, Presley's *Follow That Dream* co-star, December 2014 (hereafter cited as Helm).

"*Southern enough*": ibid.

"*When I found out I did get the role*": ibid.

"*Boy this is really a beautiful place*": "Elvis Arrives—So Do Crowds," *Suncoast Sentinel*, August 13, 1961.

"*Presley's villa at Port Paradise*": ibid.

"*Somebody's over there*": Helm.

"*You know he's checking*": ibid.

"*There he was*": ibid.

"*I didn't know*": ibid.

"*He was so sweet*": ibid

"*There was something very surreal*": ibid.

"*He was caged*": ibid.

"*Elvis has been dating*": Louella Parsons in Hollywood (column), "Elvis a Spender," July 25, 1961.

"Don't worry": Anthony Violanti, "Ocala Residents Remember the Day Elvis Came to Town," Ocala.com, August 12, 2007. (hereafter cited as Violanti).

Chapter 21. Weall House, Inglis, and Commercial Bank and Trust, Ocala

"Finally someone yelled": "Elvis Comes to Yankeetown," *Tampa Tribune*, July 16, 1961.
"Elvis' interest in leading lady": ibid.
"I've got someone you have to meet": author's interview with Betty Larson, September 2013.
"It was very hard to believe": ibid.
"They started to leave": ibid.
"The Colonel made him a star": Debbie Shafer, "Local Folks Remember When Elvis Was Here in '61," *Ocala Star-Banner*, August 17, 1977.
"I got my name on": Michael Hall, "Life Among the Stars Is Surprisingly Hard Work," *Edinboro Independent*, August 10, 1961 (hereafter cited as Hall).
"I thought he was pulling my leg": author's interview with George Langdon, September 2013.
"I was blessed": author's interview with Louise Sherouse, High's daughter, February 12, 2014 (hereafter cited as Sherouse).
"We arrived at the bank": Hall.

Chapter 22. A Fella Who Wiggled

"I was eleven years old": Bill Dean, "Tom Petty's Life Changed When He Met Elvis," www.gainesville.com, August 16, 2007 (hereafter cited as Dean).
"I could feel so clearly": author's correspondence with Paul Zollo (hereafter cited as Zollo).
"My Aunt pulls in the drive": Dean.
"I've always thought": Tom Petty as told to Paul Zollo, in Zollo, *Conversations with Tom Petty* (London: Omnibus Press, 2005, hereafter cited as Petty to Zollo).
"He was known to me": Petty to Zollo.
"There was a huge crowd": ibid.
"And suddenly I go": ibid.
"These are my nieces and nephews": "When the King Came to Ocala," www.williammckeen.com.
"It was like a religious feeling": Zollo.
"He had on a pair of jeans": author's correspondence with Jeremiah Wesley.
"I just enjoyed the music": ibid.
"That is one hell of a job to have": Petty to Zollo.
"Ya'll will sell them": Bill DeYoung, "Lights, Camera, Action," *Gainesville Sun*, September 22, 1992 (hereafter cited as DeYoung).

"I just loved music": Petty to Zollo.

"A little abused child": Andy Greene, "Tom Petty's True Confessions," *Rolling Stone*, October 22, 2015.

"I have stuff here": DeYoung.

"To Aunt Evelyn": ibid.

Chapter 23. Hot Times Inside

"Curious crowd": Hall.

"It's hot, tiring": ibid.

"What's it going to take": Violanti.

"He was human": ibid.

"Every time we watched Andy Griffith": author's correspondence with Bonnie Benningfield.

"I was crazy": ibid.

"I wouldn't trade": Sherouse.

"Here, let me hold him": ibid.

"All I could find": ibid.

"My Dad came to really like Elvis": ibid.

"Elvis was a good actor": Gordon Douglas, quoted in Ronald L. Davis, *Just Making Movies* (Jackson: University Press of Mississippi, 2005).

"It was a fantasy": author's correspondence with Linda Longo.

"He began to twist and shake": Violanti.

"He liked cops": ibid.

"It's all part of doing business": ibid.

"Hillbilly": ibid.

Chapter 24. Yankeetown

"It was big excitement": Jeff Kunerth, "When Elvis Came to Yankeetown," *Orlando Sentinel*, August 14, 1987.

"Every day they would pick us up": ibid.

"I tell you the honest truth": John McKinnon, "The King," *St. Petersburg Times*, January 8, 1985.

"He doesn't need it": John Keasler, "My Man Elvis Don't Need Yo Money," *Miami News*, August 4, 1961.

"Would take a second look": Martin Waldron, "Made Us Look Cheap," *St. Petersburg Times*, August 2, 1961.

"Florida has been guilty": ibid.

"I will put you in jail": John Keasler, "The Saga of Bird Creek Bridge," *Miami News*, August 13, 1961 (hereafter cited as Keasler).

"I have the backing": ibid.

"What the sheriff didn't know": Random Pixels (blog), "For Elvis Fans Only," randompixels.blogspot.com/2011/03/for-elvis-fans-only.html, March 21, 2011.

"There he is": Keasler.

"Teen aged girls rushed": ibid.

"Have you ever heard": ibid.

"Anyway": ibid.

"Seemed to be under the impression": ibid.

"And you can see": ibid.

"Is that definite": ibid.

"The sting and the agony": ibid.

"How's it going": ibid.

"Glad to be here": ibid.

"I mean there was not much use": ibid.

"two additional cups of coffee": ibid.

"Friend": Anne Rowe, "Elvis Wants to Be Alone," *St. Petersburg Times*, July 14, 1961.

"The car is his home": ibid.

"It's like coming home": ibid.

"Sometimes around dusk": Keasler.

"I sort of went along": Helm.

"We had to prop ourselves up": ibid.

"There was an innocence": ibid.

"We were sent to diet doctors": ibid.

"Atrocious": ibid.

"I can't sit back": ibid.

"He might have won": ibid.

"Elvis was very loyal and naïve": Binder.

"Bored with his life": interview with Red West, www.elvisaustralia.au, May 29, 2008.

"I think we have to take responsibility": Binder.

Chapter 25. Weeki Wachee and the Mayor's Daughter

"First date": Helm.

"I was always separated": ibid.

"I was really overwhelmed": ibid.

"Okay Girls—Get Set": "Elvis Coming Out Sunday," *St. Petersburg Evening Independent*, July 27, 1961.

"Spending the afternoon with Presley": Lynn Chadux, "Elvis Presley Kissed Me Four Times," *St. Petersburg Times*, July 31, 1961 (hereafter cited as Chadux).

"Are you Miss Florida": ibid.

"*That day we got along*": ibid.

"*Elvis Presley Underwater*": Bob Moreland photograph.

"*Oh Elvis do you remember me*": Chadux.

"*Elvis IS famous*": ibid.

"*That's my daughter*": Michele Marie Moreland Self, in Elvis Presley, *Summer of '61*, (FTD Books, 2013), 176 (hereafter cited as *Summer of '61*).

"*It was magical*": ibid.

"*I was 'all shook up'*": ibid.

"'*He would call me*'": Chadux.

"*I bet you're a cheerleader*": *Summer of '61*, 292.

"*I had a visitor*": ibid.

"*You what?*": ibid.

"*Red Level*": ibid.

"*I want you to come over*": ibid.

"*Oh my God*": ibid.

"*I remember them playing*": ibid.

"*For them it was like*": ibid.

"*Whatever possessed me to do this*": ibid.

"*All these guys were partying*": ibid.

"*Do you want to go out*": ibid.

"*Little lady*": ibid.

"*I can't believe that just happened*": ibid.

"*My Dad is Citrus County*": ibid.

"*Then I think the best thing*": ibid.

"*Do come in and sit*": John Keasler, "The Saga of Bird Creek Bridge (part 2)," *Miami News*, August 14, 1961.

"*How much does it cost*": ibid.

"*Well, every time*": ibid.

"*Every time what?*": ibid.

"*I sell another ad*": ibid.

"*No sense writing a book*": ibid.

"*I made one million prints*": ibid.

"*He smiled to his secret angels*": ibid.

"*When passing time*": ibid.

Chapter 26. Inverness Courthouse

"*Necessary business was conducted*": "Movie News," *Citrus County Chronicle*, August 10, 1961.

"*We came all the way*": ibid.

"*The scene, which lasts*": *Summer of '61*.

"Want to go out?": ibid.

"I didn't say anything": ibid.

"His shoes": ibid.

"Wayward football allegedly thrown": *St. Petersburg Times*, November 19, 2000.

"One day Elvis started playing": Bill Bram, interview with Miss Mary Brent, cited in *Summer of '61*.

"Sorry Miss B.": ibid.

"I had a long talk": ibid.

"Big no talent": ibid.

"Elvis was very good": ibid.

I think he really identified": Helm.

Chapter 27. Bye Bye Bird Creek

"The first week": Keasler, "The Saga of Bird Creek Bridge (Part 3)," *Miami News*, August 15, 1961.

"The second week": ibid.

"Messed around": ibid.

"You could hear the screams": ibid.

"In addition to running": ibid.

"Fine boy": ibid.

"I didn't want to owe him": Helm.

"If it'll bring people": "Yankeetown Denies Elvis a Road," *Ocala Star-Banner*, July 2, 1996.

"Elvis Presley does not personify": ibid.

"Elvis boarded a plane": Keasler, "Bird Creek (Part 3)."

"Elvis had been a skinny country kid": ibid.

"I was on the verge of tears": *Summer of '61*, 321.

"I was clumsy": ibid.

"Now are you happy": ibid.

"Little girl you better stick close to me": ibid.

"I was so happy": ibid.

"I know you do": ibid.

"Judging by this": Bosley Crowther, "Follow that Dream," *New York Times*, August 9, 1962.

Chapter 28. Coming Back

"Your career is in the toilet": Binder.

"I'm scared of television": ibid.

"If I can dream of a better land": lyrics by Walter Earl Brown.

"Over my dead body": Nash, 240.

"*I'll do it*": Binder.

"*Bindle*": ibid.

"*Fuck him*": ibid.

"*He started to feel it*": ibid.

"*I was so happy for him*": Helm.

"*He was fabulous*": Moscato.

"*He was more like*": Gurley.

"*There is something magical*": John Landau, "Review of Elvis," www.Graceland. com.

"*A part of me wanted to be excited*": Moore, 183.

"*I hear you Elvis*": Binder.

"*It made me sick*": Bell.

"*I remembered him young*": Craig Basse, "Anne Goldman, Former Times Features Editor," *St. Petersburg Times*, February 6, 2003.

"*When I think of Elvis*": Moore, 201.

"*I can*": "Guitar Legend Burton on Elvis at 80," www.clarionledger.com, August 25, 2015.

"*We want Elvis*": Elvis Interview: August 9, 1956—Daytona Beach Florida, www. youtube.com.

INDEX

Sinatra, Frank, 15, 101, 165, 171, 174, 226
"Sixteen Tons" (Ford), 46–47
Slavonian Lodge (Biloxi), 46
Slayton, Mildred, 131
Smiling Jack Herring and his Swingbillies, 63–64
Smith, Billy, 181
Smith, Mark D., 82
Snow, Hank, 17–18, 29–31, 38–40, 67, 69
Songs (Presley): "Are You Lonesome Tonight?" 222; "Blue Moon of Kentucky," 9, 19, 51; "Don't Be Cruel," 116, 132; *Elvis in Memphis* (album), 228; "Fame and Fortune," 174; "In the Ghetto," 228; "Heartbreak Hotel," 64–66, 69, 72, 76, 78, 82, 85–86, 89–90, 95–96, 102, 144; "Hound Dog," 99, 118, 120, 133, 144, 152, 160; "If I Can Dream," 225–27; "I Forgot to Remember to Forget," 47, 82; "I've Got a Woman," 52; "I Want You, I Need You, I Love You," 99; "Jailhouse Rock," 167; "Known Only to Him," 174; "Long Tall Sally," 144; "Love Me Tender," 174; "Mystery Train," 47, 82; "Never Been to Spain," 72; number 1 hits, 96, 99, 229; "Rock Around the Clock," 52; "Shake, Rattle and Roll," 37, 52, 76; "Stuck on You," 167, 174; "Suspicious Minds," 229; "That's All Right Mama," 7, 19, 21, 30, 48, 51; "Unchained Melody," 145; "Witchcraft," 174
Songwriting: Beatles and, 225; Bob Dylan and, 225; Byrds and, 225; Hoyt Axton and, 55; Mae Axton and, 57, 63–66, 69, 71–72, 76, 89, 95–96; Tommy Durden and, 64–65, 72
Southeastern Pavilion (Ocala), 28–32, 28
Southern venues, 2; Arkansas, 45; Mississippi, 46; Texas, 45, 166; Waycross (Ga.), 86, 88. *See also* Florida
South Street Casino (Orlando), 37
Stage manner: gyrating and, 15, 21, 30–31, 79, 108, 127, 132, 160; negative impressions of, 31, 157–60
Stage Show, 76, 78
Stanley, Dee, 168
Stardom: headlining, 75, 77–78; press coverage and, 89–90; television appearances and, 76–77; Tom Parker and, 58–60
Stefaniak, Elisabeth, 169
Stephens, Connie, 180
Stephens, Martin, 197
Steve Allen Show, 99, 116, 136
St. Petersburg (Fla.): performances in, 135–40; segregation and, 139–40
St. Petersburg Evening Independent, 201, 208
St. Petersburg Times, 115, 135, 208–9, 216
"Stuck on You," 167, 174
Sullivan, Ed, 76, 79, 135
Summers, Dale, 30
Sun Records, 1, 6; contract with, 69–70, 70; limited distribution by, 15, 20, 55, 67; promotion by, 11–12, 14; recording sessions, 7, 47–48, 76
"Suspicious Minds," 229
Swift, Bob, 130

Tampa (Fla.), performances in, 20–21, 59–61, 75, 114–20
Tampa Bay Times, 125
Tampa Tribune, 118, 126, 139, 185
Taylor, Dub, 185
TCB Band, 87
Teenagers: in audience, 40–41; impressions on, 12; rebellion and, 10, 36, 112, 141–42; spending power of, 99–100
Television: appearances on, 76–77, 116, 225–28; appearance with Sinatra, 171–74, 226; *Ed Sullivan Show*, 2, 13, 48, 51, 99, 135; *Steve Allen Show*, 99, 116, 135, 173
Texas: Lubbock performances, 45; Midland performances, 45

BOB KEALING is an Edward R. Murrow and four-time Emmy award-winning broadcast journalist who has appeared on *Dateline NBC*, C-Span, the *Today* show, CNN, MSNBC, and CBS *This Morning*. Kealing is the author of four books, including *Life of the Party* from Crown Archetype, in development as a major motion picture. Kealing's research has led to the establishment of the Jack Kerouac House in Orlando and Gram Parsons Derry Down in Winter Haven, both historic landmarks. Kealing lives north of Orlando with his wife and two children.